Susan Blanchard

Save yourself hours
of painstaking data entry ...

Order the
MIDI Sequencing in C
disk today.

All of the programs in this book are provided in both source code and executable form on disk with full C source code (MS-DOS format) and are compatible with Microsoft C 5.1 and Turbo C 2.0.

This optional disk is highly recommended. For the non-programmer, there is a ready-to-use eight-track MIDI sequencer with editing features. For the developing programmer, the source code for the multi-track sequencer follows the programming examples in *C Programming for MIDI* and expands them into a full application. This can serve as a starting point for experiments and additions to the basic multi-track program. And for the experienced programmer, the source code provides functions that can be applied to a wide range of MIDI projects. Utilities for converting to and from the Standard MIDI Files 1.0 format are also provided for those wishing to exchange data with other sequencers. The multi-track program will run on IBM PCs, ATs, or equivalent computers using the Roland MPU-401 MIDI interface (or equivalent).

To order, simply return this postage-paid self mailer with your payment of $20, plus sales tax if you are a California resident, to: M&T Books, 501 Galveston Drive, Redwood City, CA 94063. Or, call toll-free 800-533-4372 (In CA 800-356-2002) between 8 a.m. and 5 p.m., Monday through Friday, Pacific Standard Time. Ask for **Item #047-8**.

YES! Please send me the *MIDI Sequencing in C* Disk for $20 _____

California residents add applicable sales tax ____ % _____

TOTAL _____

Check enclosed. Make payable to **M&T Books**.

Charge my ____ VISA ____ MasterCard ____ American Express

Card # _____ Exp. date _____

Name _____

Address _____

City _____ State _____ Zip _____

MIDI Sequencing in C

M&T BOOKS

MIDI Sequencing in C

Jim Conger

M&T BOOKS

M&T Publishing, Inc.
Redwood City, California

M&T Books
A Division of M&T Publishing, Inc.
501 Galveston Drive
Redwood City, CA 94063

M&T Books
General Manager, Ellen Ablow
Editorial Project Manager, Michelle Hudun
Project Editor, David Rosenthal
Editorial Assistant, Kurt Rosenthal
Cover Art Director, Michael Hollister
Cover Designer, Cynthia Engler

Library of Congress Cataloging in Publication Data

Conger, Jim
    MIDI Sequencing in C / Jim Conger. -- 1st ed.
        p.   cm.
    Bibliography: p. 459
    Includes index.
        1. MIDI (Standard) 2. C (Computer program language)
3. Sequential processing (Computer science) I. Title.
MT724.C65   1989
786.7'6--dc20   89-32620
                                                            CIP
                                                            M N

ISBN 1-55851-045-1   (book) $24.95
ISBN 1-55851-046-X   (set) $39.95
ISBN 1-55851-047-8   (disk) $20.00

93 92 91 90   5   4   3   2

Limits of Liability and
Disclaimer of Warranty

How to Order
the Accompanying Disk

All of the programs in this book are provided in both source code and executable form on disk with full C source code (MS-DOS format) and are compatible with Microsoft C 5.1 and Turbo C 2.0.

This option disk is highly recommended. For the nonprogrammer, there is a ready-to-use eight-track MIDI sequencer with editing features. For the developing programmer, the source code for the multi-track sequencer follows the programming examples in *C Programming for MIDI* and expands them into a full application. This can serve as a starting point for experiments and additions to the basic multi-track program. And for the experienced programmer, the source code provides functions that can be applied to a wide range of MIDI projects. Utilities for converting to and from the Standard MIDI Files 1.0 format are also provided for those wishing to exchange data with other sequencers. The multi-track program will run on IBM PCs, ATs, or equivalent computers using the Roland MPU-401 MIDI interface (or equivalent).

The disk price is $20.00. California residents must add the appropriate sales tax. Order by sending a check, or credit card number and expiration date, to:

MIDI Sequencing in C Disk
M&T Books
501 Galveston Drive
Redwood City, CA 94063

Or, call our toll-free number between 8 A.M. and 5:00 P.M. Pacific Standard Time: 800/533-4372 (800/356-2002 in California). Ask for **Item #047-8**

Contents

Part 2
Sequencer Design

Part 3
Documentation of the MT Sequencer

Part 4
Source Code Listings

Preface

Eliminating program bugs is not easy, but finding them is even more difficult. Although we probably did not find every one, the MT sequencer was greatly improved from the help and criticism offered by five volunteers. Bob Tolz, Dave Goodwin, Frank Reed, Matt Donnelly, and Fred Bunn all contributed greatly to the quality of the final product. Thanks.

Foreword

When will the first number one hit be written by a computer? Now that the touch of a button can set hundreds of musical voices into motion, the question arises: has music technology reached the artistic equivalent of the nuclear age? Many feel that technology may ultimately usurp the identity of the musician.

A few years ago, computer-controlled sound generators were a laboratory curiosity—affordable only by large research institutions, and far too big to consider for live performance. Though some of these early synthesizers were capable even by today's standards, they weren't a threat to performing musicians.

When MIDI synthesizers were introduced, they were sometimes viewed as "puppets on a cable" for computers, but time has proven that MIDI will change the face of music. New hardware can duplicate virtually any natural sound, and powerful software systems are getting more precise about being imprecise—in other words, they are starting to sound human.

It is no wonder that some musicians feel threatened. The sounds of instruments which previously took years to master can now be played by simply typing in pitches. With artificial intelligence techniques, programs can write music "in the spirit of" the great classical composers, or they can make up completely new styles.

Computers are able to "watch" video tapes of Olympic athletes and to follow body motion in order to analyze and correct flaws in technique. Why not use this system to analyze Leonard Bernstein conducting the Philharmonic? The resulting data could certainly help to derive tempo and dynamics for piloting a bank of synthesizers through the score.

How about encoding the motion of Jimi Hendrix's fingers? As Stravinsky's piano rolls are the true archives of his music, old video tapes may actually be the ideal way to archive a musician's "touch." Whether you call it timing, rubato, or soul, it is this that distinguishes great music and musicians from a printed score.

In essence, the "musical personality" of any musician can now be "sampled" by a computer. A disturbing thought perhaps, yet an interesting one. Though some may not appreciate the origin of Beethoven's tenth symphony (pieced together from fragments by a computer) they may still want to hear it.

Far from capturing souls in a bottle, the computer has definite limitations when competing with humans. It is this simple: people want to see human performers somewhere in the chain. Like tape decks and record players which have been able to mimic the sounds of human performers for years, computers are just no fun to watch—especially in the mind's eye. Jimi or Ludwig wouldn't seem quite the same if they were ultimately made of software. It is the personal vision of a brilliant performer or composer which is inspiring: the product of their life as a human.

As it turns out, the computer's real worth will be proven in helping humans achieve greater mastery of technique and compositional skill. Far from being demoted to button-pushing drones, modern composers can instantly modify and test their work—the same way software engineers polish the rough edges of a program. This interactive concept is very important. By constantly monitoring sensors or MIDI data, the computer can even provide instant feedback about a player's performance. The next generation of musicians may learn on instruments that play and score like video games.

In creating music software you become part of the creative chain. You will influence the music as surely as if you were playing the instruments—because, in a sense, you are. Whether you are a musical visionary or a vindictive musician who plans to write programs to replace MIDI programmers, I hope this book will help you.

As a musician and software engineer, I want to see what the future has to offer. I want to hear the music of the year 3000. Who knows, maybe it will be possible to see a robotic performance of the Philharmonic.

Mark Garvin
Technical Editor

Introduction

Sequencing is a term describing the process of recording, editing, and playing back sequences of musical notes. All major manufacturers of musical instruments and equipment now support the MIDI (Musical Instrument Digital Interface) standard for sending and receiving musical data. This allows one program to act as a sequencer for any group of MIDI instruments.

This book approaches MIDI sequencing on the IBM PC on several levels.

- For the non-programmer, the MT sequencer provided on the program disk is a ready-to-use, 8-track MIDI sequencer with editing features. The program will run on IBM PCs, ATs, or compatible computers, using the Roland MPU-401 MIDI interface (or equivalent). MT adapts to the CGA, EGA, and VGA video standards; displaying more data on screen with the higher-resolution modes.

- For the developing programmer, the source code for the MT sequencer follows the programming examples in *C Programming for MIDI*, and expands them into a full application. This can serve as a starting point for experiments and additions to the basic MT program.

- For the experienced programmer, the source code provides functions that can be applied to a wide range of MIDI projects. The simple disk file format used by MT to store MIDI data allows you to create separate programs for computer composition experiments which write to a file, and then let MT do the work of playing and editing the results. Utilities for converting to and from the Standard MIDI Files 1.0 format are also provided for people wishing to exchange data with other sequencers.

The first three chapters provide a tutorial, describing MT from the user's point of view. The remainder of the book describes how the MT program works. Each C function is described individually. Many of the functions can be used without modification in any MIDI project you are working on.

Readers who have read *C Programming for MIDI* will find the approach to programming used in this book very familiar. In a few places I have repeated discussions of topics covered in *C Programming for MIDI*. Most of this book assumes that the programming reader has already experimented with MIDI and the C language. If you buy the book primarily to use MT, but later get interested in MIDI programming, I suggest working through *C Programming for MIDI* before attacking chapters 5 to 11. Once you have a grasp of MIDI interfacing and general programming techniques used in sequencers (pointers, structures, and linked lists) from the first book, the application of these tools in the MT program will be much easier to understand.

Some highlights of the programming techniques covered are:

- Both Microsoft and Turbo C compilers are supported by the coding examples.

- The compiler libraries available today include functions for controlling the video display. These were not available when *C Programming for MIDI* was written.

- Color monitors and graphics displays are supported. The INSTALL program and related functions provide a general approach for programmers who have to deal with the several display formats available today.

- The use of a mouse as a pointing device is supported through a simple mouse menu.

- Test programs for trying out individual portions of the code have been omitted. I am assuming that the reader can create these if needed.

- More advanced programming techniques were used where appropriate. Discussion of managing global variables, pointer operations, etc., is included.

- Recent additions to the C language, such as function prototyping and the void data type, are used. The more recent evolution of C into the C++ language is not supported by the programming examples, primarily due to the rarity of C++ compilers and C++ programmers at the time of writing.

In the creation of the book I was faced with a number of compromises between extending the MT example program's usefulness, and keeping the C code simple enough to follow. In every case I chose the route of simplicity. I hope that readers will feel comfortable adding to MT for the functions they want in their applications. Some suggestions for extensions to MT are discussed in the last chapter.

Good luck with your programming projects.

Jim Conger
San Ramon, California
February, 1989

PART 1

User's Guide to MT 8-Track MIDI Sequencer/Editor

1

User's Guide to MT 8-Track MIDI Sequencer/Editor

Installation and Record Functions

This chapter begins the tutorial on using the MT (Multi-Track) sequencer/editor. First-time installation and operation of the RECORD and HELP menus are explained.

1.1 MIDI Setup

Your computer will need a Roland MPU-401 or compatible interface installed to use the MT program. The interface will hold the MIDI IN and OUT ports. With older Roland MPU-401 interfaces, the computer holds a simple communications board in a slot (Roland's is called the MIF-PC board). The communications board is connected to an external box (the MPU-401) which has the MIDI ports. Most of the newer MIDI interfaces are one piece units, with all of the components on the board that goes into the computer's slot. The MIDI ports are located at the rear, exposed part of the interface.

Throughout the book, I will be assuming that you are using a synthesizer with a keyboard as your input device, and possibly other synthesizers as extra sound sources. Any MIDI input device, such as a wind controller or MIDI drum pads, will work fine in place of the master MIDI keyboard. A typical setup with a keyboard would look like:

Figure 1.1 Typical MIDI Cable Hookups

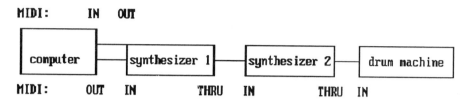

Synthesizer 1 is the master keyboard, and the only device that is hooked up to transmit MIDI data to the computer's MPU-401 MIDI IN port. The other two instruments act as slave units, responding to the MIDI data transmitted from the computer. Typically synth 1 is set to MIDI channel 1. Synth 2 would be set to another channel from that synth's front panel, and so on. Only synth 1 needs to have a keyboard or other input device. The other instruments can be sound generators such as the Yamaha FB-01, TX-81Z, or Roland MT-32.

In more complex setups you can have more than one synth connected to the computer. Typically a MIDI "patch bay" device is used to allow control to be switched from one keyboard or controller to the next. This avoids having to reconnect all of the MIDI cables each time a change is made.

1.2 Program Files

The files on the MT sequencer disk needed to run MT are:

MT	EXE	The ready-to-run program.
INSTALL	EXE	The installation program (described in Section 1.3).
SIMPMOUS	MNU	The Microsoft Mouse menu—only needed
SIMPMOUS	DEF	if a mouse will be used.
MT1	SCR	Screen files used by the program.

```
MT2      SCR
MT3      SCR
MT4      SCR
MT5      SCR
MT6      SCR
INSTALL  SCR

MTHELP1  SCR          Help files.
MTHELP2  SCR
MTHELP3  SCR
MTHELP4  SCR
MTHELP5  SCR
MTHELP6  SCR
MTHELP7  SCR
MTHELP8  SCR

DRUMDICT SNG          Example song files.  Put these on a separate
EXAMPLE  SNG          disk or hard disk subdirectory.
DABACO   SNG
FANTASY  SNG
```

The second disk contains program source code files. If you have pur-
chased the disks, make backup copies, or copy the entire disks to new
subdirectories on your hard disk.

1.3 Installation

Before you can run MT, you must run the INSTALL program to select
the type of video equipment and colors you will be using. To do this,
type INSTALL at the DOS prompt. You will see the INSTALL menu:

Figure 1.2 INSTALL Menu

INSTALLATION MENU

Use the arrow keys to select an item, then hit return to enter a value.

Text Mode	2) 80 X 25, 2 color 3) 80 X 25, 16 color (default) 7) 80 X 25 for monochrome monitors.
Graphics Mode	6) Color Graphics Adapter mode (CGA) (default). 14) 16) Enhanced Graphics Adapter mode (EGA). 15) Hercules Monochrome Graphics mode. 17) VGA hi resolution 2 color. 18) VGA hi res. color.
Attribute Number **Color** **Background**	0 1 2 3 4 5 6 7 8 9 10 11 12 13 14 15 0 1 2 3 4 5 6 7 8 9 10 11 12 13 14 15 0 1 2 3 4 5 6 7 8 9 10 11 12 13 14 15
Normal Letters **Background**	**Cursor Highlighted Lets.** | **Other Highlighted Lets.** **Background For Cursor** | **Background For Highlight**
Save Choices **Quit Install**	**Normal** letters will look like: These letters. **Cursor** letters will look like: These letters. **Emphasized** letters will look like: These letters.

Use the arrow keys to move the cursor block to the Text Mode option. Then hit Return. The program will ask you to enter the Text Mode number. The video card and monitor you are using will determine your input:

Text Modes For INSTALL	Mode
CGA Card/Monitor (Most common)	3
EGA Card/Monitor	3
VGA Card/Monitor	3
Monochrome or Hercules Card	7

Mode 2 is a color suppressed mode that shows black and white characters on a color monitor. This is not of much use.

Now move the cursor to the Graphics Mode option and hit Return. Again you will want to select a mode corresponding to the equipment you are using. The higher mode numbers allow you to see more on the screen. This will be important to MT in the Note Editor mode as the screen resolution limits the number of octaves that will be displayed. More on this later.

Graphics Modes For INSTALL.	Mode	MT Displayed Octaves
CGA Card/Monitor (Most common)	6	2
EGA Card/Monitor	14	4
VGA Card/Monitor	18	6
Monochrome (Hercules Card)[1]	15	5

The last thing you should do before leaving INSTALL is to pick the colors you would like to see on the screen for Normal, Emphasized, and Cursor selections. As you change the numbers for the letters and backgrounds, you can see the results in the lower right side of the IN-STALL menu screen. The type of video equipment you have hooked up will determine the colors you see.

Most configurations leave the background for the normal and empha-sized letters as black (color number 0). Be sure that the letter and background colors are not the same. Otherwise, the letters will not be visible.

---

[1] The compiled programs distributed on the program disk use the Microsoft C graphics functions which do not support the Hercules monochrome graphics mode. If you want to use MT with a Hercules card, you can compile the pro-grams on the source code disk with Turbo C. The Turbo C file HERC.BGI will need to be on your program drive/directory for the program to find the graphics driver. This subject is discussed in Appendix 4.

The default colors INSTALL starts up with are ideal for a monochrome system. For color systems, I use the following colors for attractive screens:

Character Type	Letter color	Background color
Normal characters	3 (light blue)	0 (black)
Cursor characters	3 (light blue)	1 (dark blue)
Emphasized characters	4 (red)	0 (black)

Once you have the modes and colors selected, move the cursor to the SAVE option and hit Return. This writes your selections to a file called INSTALL.DAT. You can run INSTALL again any time you wish to change options. INSTALL reads INSTALL.DAT before starting, so you do not have to start from scratch each time you want a new installation.

1.4 Using a Mouse

MT was designed to use a mouse. You do not have to use a mouse to run MT. However, MT (and a lot of other software) is easier to use if you have one. I will give the commands assuming you have a Microsoft mouse. The Logitech mouse supports the same commands. Most other mice have similar software.

Microsoft or Logitech Mouse:

You will need two files that come with the mouse:

MOUSE.COM   Loads the mouse driver software into memory.
MENU.COM   Allows you to load a custom mouse menu.

Before running MT, type

```
C:>MOUSE
```

from the DOS prompt. Assuming the software detects a mouse, the mouse driver software will be loaded into memory. It will stay there until you reboot or type `MOUSE OFF` from DOS.

The file SIMPMOUS.MNU contains the mouse movement commands. To load them, type

```
C:>MENU SIMPMOUS
```

at the DOS prompt. If you are running a floppy-based system, you will probably want to copy both MOUSE.COM and MENU.COM to your MT disk. On a hard disk system, you can issue a PATH command so that DOS can find these two commands in another subdirectory.

The end result of running MOUSE and MENU is that the mouse will emulate pressing cursor keys. The key mapping is:

Left mouse button:	Return (Enter) key
Right mouse button:	ESC (Escape) key
Mouse movement:	Arrow keys

While running MT, any time you need to hit Return, you can either hit the left mouse button or the Return key on the keyboard. Likewise for the ESC and the arrow keys.

Other Mice:

Some inexpensive mice, such as those offered by Radio Shack, do not come with mouse driver software and cannot be used with MT. Most mice are compatible at a low level with the Microsoft mouse, but come with different software to produce mouse menus. The default mouse menu software is almost always acceptable for use with MT, as it will map mouse movement to the arrow keys, and the left mouse button to the Return key. Some, like the Genius mouse GMENU, default to having the right mouse button mapped to the ESC key—ideal for MT. Try the default mouse menu and see how you like it.

1.5 Starting MT—The Primary Menu

MT is started by typing

`C:>MT`

at the DOS prompt. MT checks for the existence of the INSTALL.DAT file containing your video configuration data, and for all of the MT_.SCR files listed in Section 1.2. If any of these are missing MT will put a message on the screen and quit to DOS. MT will run without the HELP files, but you will not be able to get online help.

If the files are found, MT will display a header with ordering information, and then ask you to hit Return. Hitting Return puts you in the primary menu.

Figure 1.3 MT's Primary Menu

```
┌─────────────────────────────────┐
│  M T - MIDI SEQUENCER/EDITOR     │
└─────────────────────────────────┘
```

Commands:	Function:	Current Settings:
DRIVE	Select a drive or directory.	C:\
LOAD	Load song file from disk.	NO_NAME.SCR
EDIT	Edit MIDI data.	
RECORD	Multi-track recorder screen. Record and play up to 8 tracks.	
TITLE	Give the song a title - up to 50 characters long.	
SAVE	Save all MIDI data to disk.	
CLEAR	Erase all sequencer data (does not affect disk files).	
IMPORT	Insert a track from another song file into current song.	
HELP	Help on all aspects of MT.	
QUIT	Title:	

Like the INSTALL program, moving the cursor block to a command and hitting Return causes the selection to be executed. You can select an item by:

1)   Using the arrow keys to move the cursor block.

2) Typing the first letter of the command. If there is more than one command with the same first letter, the cursor will go to the first one in the order left to right, top to bottom.

3) Using the mouse to move the cursor (if you have a mouse).

Hitting the Return key or the left mouse button executes the function. Hitting the ESC key or the right mouse button escapes from a menu or option. We will try this in a moment.

1.6 The HELP Option

Move the cursor down to the HELP command and hit Return. You will see the HELP menu:

Figure 1.4 MT's HELP Menu

```
┌─────────────────────────────────┐
│          HELP MENU              │
│  M T - 8 TRACK MIDI SEQUENCER   │
└─────────────────────────────────┘
```

Commands:	Move the cursor a HELP item and hit Return.
GENERAL	How MT is organized and how the menu structure works.
MOUSE	Using a Microsoft Mouse with MT.
FILES	Help with the DRIVE, LOAD and SAVE commands.
EDITING	Measure level and Note level Edit fuctions in MT.
RECORDING	The 8 track Record/Playback fuctions.
TITLES	How to save a Title along with your MIDI data.
CLEAR	How to clear the song Memory and start fresh.
IMPORT	How to insert a track from a song file into the current song.
QUIT	Return to MT's primary menu

You can get a quick overview of the program by selecting each of the subjects in sequence and hitting Return.

With this option, and all others in MT, you can abort the input by just
hitting the ESC key. This will take you back to the menu you were last
in. Repeatedly hitting the ESC key will take you to the primary menu's
QUIT option (to exit MT).

1.7 Loading a Song File

It is best to keep the song files on separate disks, or separate hard disk
directories from the MT program files. Several .SNG (song) files are
provided on the program disk. Copy these to a new formatted floppy
or a new subdirectory.

For MT to be able to find the .SNG files, you will need to input the
drive or directory you are using. On a two-drive system, you will have
the MT program disk in drive A: and the song files in B:. Select the
DRIVE (top) option on the MT primary menu and hit Return. MT will
prompt you for the drive/directory to use. Enter B:<Return>. You
should see the drive change in the upper right-hand corner of the
menu.

On hard disk systems, select DRIVE and enter the full path name to the
directory you are using for your songs. For example, if you have set up
directories like:

Figure 1.5 C:\SONG Directory

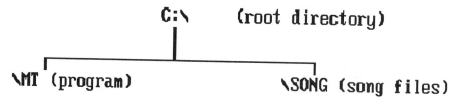

you would enter C:\SONG<Return> as the drive/directory. MT will
check for the existence of the directory before proceeding. If it does not
exist, MT will print a message and return to the primary menu with
the directory left set to the default value.

Once you have the drive/directory set to the right value, you can load a song file. Pick the LOAD option on the primary menu and press Return. Assuming that you have the drive/directory set to where you copied the example .SNG files, you will see a screen that looks like Figure 1.6.

Figure 1.6

```
Files matching *.sng on your selected drive (C:\C\RECORD):

 EXAMPLE.SNG      ABACO.SNG       DRUMDICT.SNG       FANTASY.SNG








Select a song file to load.  ESC to escape without loading.
```

If you do not see any files on the screen display, hit ESC and make sure that you have the drive/directory set to where you placed copies of the .SNG files.

You can move the cursor to highlight any of the songs on the screen. Note that you can also move the cursor to a number of empty spaces below the four songs. These are places reserved for other song files you create.

Move the cursor to ABACO.SNG and hit Return. After loading the song file, MT will return you to the primary menu. The song's file name will be shown in the upper-left corner of the screen, and the title will show at the bottom. The song file is now in the computer's memory.

1.8 The RECORD Menu

From the primary menu, select the RECORD option and hit Return. You will see a screen like Figure 1.7.

Figure 1.7 MT's RECORD Menu

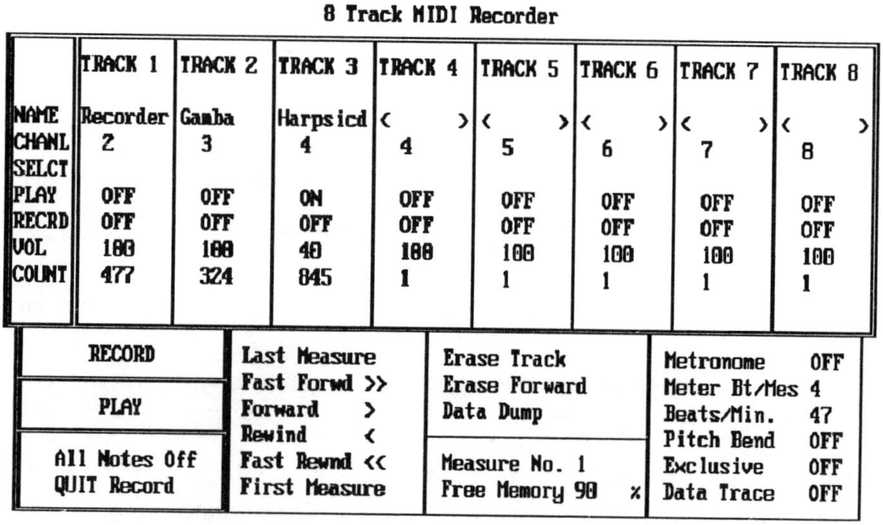

8 Track MIDI Recorder

	TRACK 1	TRACK 2	TRACK 3	TRACK 4	TRACK 5	TRACK 6	TRACK 7	TRACK 8
NAME	Recorder	Gamba	Harpsicd	< >	< >	< >	< >	< >
CHANL	2	3	4	4	5	6	7	8
SELCT								
PLAY	OFF	OFF	ON	OFF	OFF	OFF	OFF	OFF
RECRD	OFF	OFF	OFF	OFF	OFF	OFF	OFF	OFF
VOL	100	100	40	100	100	100	100	100
COUNT	477	324	845	1	1	1	1	1

RECORD	Last Measure	Erase Track	Metronome	OFF
	Fast Forwd >>	Erase Forward	Meter Bt/Mes	4
PLAY	Forward >	Data Dump	Beats/Min.	47
	Rewind <		Pitch Bend	OFF
All Notes Off	Fast Rewnd <<	Measure No. 1	Exclusive	OFF
QUIT Record	First Measure	Free Memory 90 %	Data Trace	OFF

This is the RECORD menu of MT. It simulates an eight-track tape recorder with a few added features. The top box on the screen contains the track status information. Each of the track numbers is listed at the top. Below that are the status rows. Here is a brief description of each one:

Track Name:

You can change the name of a track by moving the cursor to the NAME row and hitting Return. MT will prompt you for a new name, with an eight letter maximum width. In ABACO.SNG the first three tracks have names reflecting the type of instrument controlled on that track.

Track MIDI Channel:

Each track is assigned to one MIDI channel. These can have any value from 1 to 16. If you have only one synthesizer, you will probably use channel 1 for all channels. If you have more than one synth, or a multi-timbral synthesizer (Roland MT-32, Yamaha TX-81Z, etc.), you can use the different channels to sound different types of instruments simultaneously. I use channel 1 for my main keyboard, and the upper channels for other MIDI instruments. You can use the same channel number on more than one track.

Track Selected:

Only one track can be set to record new MIDI data at any time. If a track is set to record, the word *ACTIVE* will show in the track's SELECT row. To set a track to record, move the cursor to the track's SELECT row and hit Return. Repeating this will turn the track off. Selecting another track will shut off the previously SELECTed track, preserving the maximum of one track set to record.

Track Play:

Any number of tracks can be set to Play. To turn the play status on, move the cursor to the track's PLAY row and hit Return. The word ON will show. Hitting Return again on this spot will convert the ON to an OFF, shutting the track down. All tracks with ON showing will be played when either the RECORD or PLAY commands are started.

Track Record:

The record status (abbreviated RECRD) works the same as the Track Select option. In both cases *ACTIVE* will show on the one track set to record. Also, ON will show on that track's RECRD row.

Track Volume:

Each track's MIDI volume can be adjusted by selecting the VOL row. MT prompts for a volume number between 1 and 100. Normally, all tracks are left at 100, meaning that all MIDI key velocity values are transmitted untouched. Values less than 100 will cause MT to reduce the MIDI velocities transmitted by the ratio of the velocity to 100. For example, a value of 50 will cut all note velocities transmitted for that track in half.

(Note that the calculation is skipped completely if all note velocities are set to 100. This saves a little computer time, which might be a factor if the sequence has a lot of MIDI data playing rapidly. Normally, the calculation delay does not have any impact on note timing.)

MIDI Data Count:

The last row in the top section of the RECORD menu is the MIDI data count. This is the number of MIDI events stored on the track. A blank track contains one event. This value gives you an idea how much data is in each track. Using pitch benders or controllers during recording will quickly add a lot of data to a track.

The bottom box of the RECORD menu contains the commands. Let's go through them quickly before we try playing the song:

RECORD:

This turns on the recorder. All of the tracks with PLAY marked ON will start sending MIDI data on their assigned channels out via the MPU-401 MIDI OUT port. Any data received will be stored on the *ACTIVE* track. If the metronome option is on, the MPU-401 metronome will sound (see below). Pressing the ESC or SPACEBAR keys on the computer's keyboard will stop the RECORD process.

PLAY:

This plays all tracks marked with PLAY ON. Each track's MIDI data is sent out of the MPU-401's MIDI OUT port. Pressing the ESC or SPACEBAR keys on the computer's keyboard will stop the PLAY process.

All Notes Off:

Selecting this option sends MIDI All Notes Off commands out the MPU-401's MIDI OUT port on all sixteen channels. This is handy in complex MIDI setups where things can get "stuck" once in a while. Consider it a panic button. Unfortunately, not all synths respond to this command.

QUIT Record:

QUIT exits the RECORD menu and returns you to MT's primary menu. This is the same as hitting the ESC key or right mouse button.

Last Measure:

Moves current measure to the last measure of the longest track in memory. The Current Measure is displayed at the bottom center of the RECORD menu. This is the point any PLAY or RECORD activity will start from. It also controls the start of the Erase Forward command (discussed below).

Note that PLAY and RECORD always start from the beginning of a measure. It is not possible to start in the middle of a measure.

Fast Forward >>:

Moves the current measure forward ten measures. Stops at the end of the longest measure.

Forward >:

Moves the current measure forward one measure. Stops at the end of the longest measure.

Rewind <:

Moves the current measure backward one measure until the beginning of the song is reached.

Fast Rewind <<:

Moves the current measure backward ten measures until the beginning of the song is reached.

First Measure:

Moves to the start of the song.

Erase Track:

Selecting this option allows you to erase all of the data in one track. After hitting Return, MT will ask which track number you wish to erase. You enter a number from 1 to 8. Just to make sure you really want to wipe out the track, the program asks:

Erase track # (Y/N)->

The track will not be erased unless you type the Y key on the computer.

Like all commands in MT, hitting the ESC key (right mouse button) allows you to exit the command without doing anything.

Erase Forward:

This is just like Erase Track, except that only the data after the current measure is erased. Use Forward, Rewind, etc., to get the current measure where you want it before using Erase Forward.

MT will double check that you want to delete the MIDI data before it proceeds.

Data Dump:

Selecting this option displays the MIDI data for all eight tracks in hexadecimal on the screen starting from the current measure. This is for debugging and educational uses. More on this in Chapter 3.

Measure Number:

This is where the current measure number is displayed. During RECORD and PLAY the measure number shown will advance as the song progresses.

Free Memory %:

As data is loaded and recorded, the RAM memory in your computer gradually fills up. MT checks the amount left after every operation that uses or frees memory. MT takes about 110K bytes by itself. All of the rest of RAM is available for song files. Loading memory resident programs (Sidekick, etc.) will reduce the amount of memory available. The mouse driver also eats a few K.

MIDI data is fairly compact until you start using a lot of pitch bend and controller outputs. Some controllers also output *aftertouch data* if keys are held down. This causes MIDI data to be spit out at a rapid rate, so keep an eye on the amount of memory left.

Metronome:

This command toggles the MPU-401's internal metronome on and off. You will want it on when recording the first track or two to stay in sync. After that you can use the drum or bass tracks as a reference. The MPU-401 accents the first beat of the measure with a higher pitch sound.

Some MPU-401 compatible interfaces do not have an internal speaker. A track with just one note each beat can be used to provide the metronome.

Meter Beats/Measure:

This allows you to set the number of beats per measure. The default is four. The meter can only be changed if all of the tracks are empty. MT will not change the meter of an existing song.

Beats/Min:

Sets the metronome rate in beats per minute. Higher values give a faster rate of playback. All tracks will be sped up by the same amount. You can "cheat" by recording at slow tempo and then speeding it up for playback.

Pitch Bend On/Off:

Toggles the Pitch Bend option on and off. In the default (start up) mode the MPU-401 will screen any pitch bend data out before it gets to the computer. If you set this switch on, pitch bender data will be allowed through and will be recorded. During playback the recorded data will bend the pitch just as it was played.

Exclusive On/Off:

The MPU-401 defaults (starts up) screening all MIDI Exclusive messages out. These are things like patch settings and data dumps. Choose this option if you want this type of data recorded along with your song data. You can even make a track with nothing but MIDI exclusive data and play it back to accomplish some task. This is explained in Chapter 3.

Data Trace On/Off:

This option allows you to see the MIDI data being exchanged between the computer and the MPU-401 interface. Each byte of data is shown on the screen in hexadecimal notation as it is sent.

The process of displaying the bytes is slow, and slows down playback. Expect the note timing of any complex track to be distorted if Trace is on. This option is for debugging and educational uses. Chapter 3 gives some examples.

That covers all of the commands on the RECORD menu.

1.9 Playing a Song File

Let's go ahead and play some MIDI data. Load the ABACO.SNG file and go to the RECORD menu. To play the song you need to:

1) Set the MIDI channel on each track.

If you have a one-synth system, you will probably want to transmit just on channel 1. Set each track to MIDI channel 1 on the RECORD menu.

If you have several synthesizers or a multi-timbral synth, you will be transmitting on several channels. For example, the Roland MT-32 receives on channels 2 – 10, with 10 being the drum tracks.

2) Adjust your synthesizer to play the right sound(s).

The ABACO.SNG song is a piece of baroque music, so it sounds best with a recorder (flute), gamba (cello), and harpsichord patch on your synthesizer.

On a one-synth system, you can play each track separately. Set the synth to a recorder or flute sound.

On a multi-timbral setup, set the synth sounds to match the channels you are using for each track. For example, using the MT-32 you might have channel 2 set to the recorder, channel 3 for the gamba (cello), and channel 4 for the harpsichord. Make these settings on your synthesizer.

3) Set the desired patches to PLAY ON.

Move the cursor to the upper PLAY row and press Return on every track that you want to transmit. Hitting Return a second time toggles the PLAY status back to OFF.

4) Select PLAY.

Move the cursor to the PLAY command box at the lower left of the RECORD menu and hit Return. The message:

```
Hit ESC or SPACEBAR to stop playback.
```

will appear at the bottom of the screen. MIDI data from every track marked with Play status ON will be transmitted out the MPU-401's MIDI OUT port. The measure number will advance as the file is played. This continues until the song ends or a key is pressed.

To replay a song, select the First Measure command and hit Return. The measure number counter will return to 1. You can start the PLAY process from any measure by moving to the desired measure number and hitting PLAY. Use Forward, Rewind, etc., to move to the right spot in the song.

Experiment with playing one, two, and then three tracks. Try different sounds on your synthesizer. Try playing your synth keyboard during playback. It should send out additional notes that will sound, but are not recorded in the PLAY option. This is a great way to practice "playing along" once you get drum and bass parts in a song file.

1.10 Possible Problems with PLAY

If you did not get the song to play back from your synth when you hit PLAY, look at the following possible causes:

1) MIDI cable problems.

Make sure that your cables are set correctly. If you have a complex setup, reduce the number of variables by taking just one synthesizer and hooking it up directly the the MPU-401. Just connect cables from the MIDI OUT of the MPU-401 to the MIDI IN on your synth, and the MIDI IN on the MPU-401 to the synth's MIDI OUT. Once you get one working, add the other devices one at a time.

2) Wrong MIDI channels.

You may be transmitting the song data on a channel that your synthesizer is not receiving. Always start using the lowest channel on the synth. This is almost always channel 1 (the MT-32 is an exception. It starts up with channel 2 being the lowest channel recognized). Check the MIDI channel number on your synth. If you are not sure which channel your synth is responding to, try the OMNI mode. OMNI causes the synth to respond to all channels.

3) MPU-401 problems.

Unlikely, but you can check by setting the Metronome to ON and then playing the track. You should hear the metronome beep. If not, you are not communicating with the interface. Check that the board inside your computer is all the way in, and that the cables are fully inserted. More complex problems can be:

- Lack of power to the computer's boards. Other boards inserted in the bus may be taking up most of the power supplies output, robbing the MPU-401.

- Conflicts with other boards that use the same ports or interrupts as the MPU-401.

- Too fast a bus speed. Some of the faster PC "clones" do not keep the bus speed constant as the CPU speed is increased. Try slowing down the computer's CPU speed if this is an option.

1.11 Recording a Track

We will want to clear all of the tracks before starting our record session. There are two ways to do this (three if you count turning the computer's power off). From the RECORD menu you can erase each track using the Erase Track command. This has to be done once for each track with data. Erasing the tracks individually does not erase the track name, song title, or the song file name. To erase everything and start fresh, return to the MT primary menu. You can get there by hitting the ESC key (right mouse button) or by selecting the QUIT command on the RECORD menu.

Once in the MT primary menu, select the CLEAR command and hit Return. MT will ask to make sure that you want to purge memory. Hitting the Y key will cause all tracks and names to be cleared from memory. Hitting any other key will cause the CLEAR command to be skipped.

Note that CLEAR does not affect disk files. Only the data in memory is erased.

With the song file cleared from memory, go back to the RECORD menu. Let's practice by recording some MIDI data to track 1. Move the cursor to track 1's RECRD row and hit Return. The RECORD status row will show ON and *ACTIVE* will be displayed on the SELCT row. Your screen should look like Figure 1.8.

Figure 1.8 MT RECORD Menu

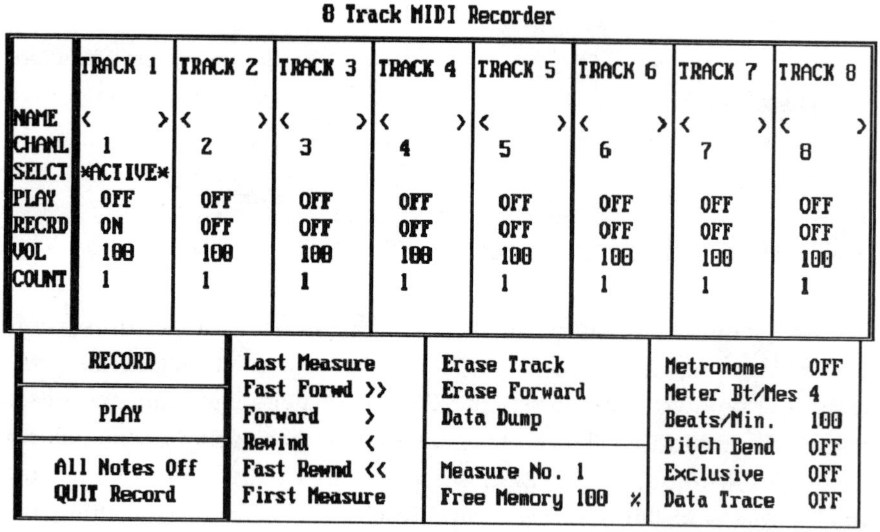

8 Track MIDI Recorder

	TRACK 1	TRACK 2	TRACK 3	TRACK 4	TRACK 5	TRACK 6	TRACK 7	TRACK 8
NAME	‹ ›	‹ ›	‹ ›	‹ ›	‹ ›	‹ ›	‹ ›	‹ ›
CHANL	1	2	3	4	5	6	7	8
SELCT	*ACTIVE*							
PLAY	OFF	OFF	OFF	OFF	OFF	OFF	OFF	OFF
RECRD	ON	OFF	OFF	OFF	OFF	OFF	OFF	OFF
VOL	100	100	100	100	100	100	100	100
COUNT	1	1	1	1	1	1	1	1

RECORD	Last Measure	Erase Track	Metronome	OFF
	Fast Forwd ››	Erase Forward	Meter Bt/Mes	4
PLAY	Forward ›	Data Dump	Beats/Min.	100
	Rewind ‹		Pitch Bend	OFF
All Notes Off	Fast Rewnd ‹‹	Measure No. 1	Exclusive	OFF
QUIT Record	First Measure	Free Memory 100 %	Data Trace	OFF

Move the cursor over to the Metronome command and hit Return. The Metronome status will change to ON. Now move the cursor over to the RECORD box and hit Return. The message:

```
Hit ESC or SPACEBAR to stop recording.
```

will show up at the bottom of the screen. You will also hear the MPU-401 metronome start beeping. The Measure Number will advance after each four beeps. Move over to your synthesizer and play a few notes. These will be recorded into the current measure's data. When you are done, hit ESC or SPACEBAR to stop the RECORD process.

Before you can play back your notes you need to:

1) Move back to the beginning of the track data, or at least back a few measures. Use the Rewind, Fast Rewind, and/or First Measure commands.

2) Make sure that track 1's MIDI channel is set to match your synthesizer's MIDI channel. In most cases both should be set to channel 1. MT adjusts all of the data on a track to match the track's MIDI channel. Even if your synth transmitted on channel 8, if the track is set to channel 1, all data will be transmitted on channel 1. Changing the channel number on the RECORD screen changes all of the track's data to the new channel.

3) Change track 1's status from RECORD to PLAY. You can turn off the *ACTIVE* status by moving the cursor up to the RECRD row and hitting Return. Select the PLAY row on track 1. Track 1 should show ON on the PLAY row. (A shortcut here is to just select the PLAY status. As a track can either PLAY or RECORD, but not both, selecting PLAY shuts off RECORD, and vice versa.)

With track 1 set to play, select the PLAY command. You should hear the MIDI data play your instrument on track 1's channel just like you played it a moment ago. If it took you a few measures to get around to playing the notes, you will have to wait the same length of time before anything sounds.

1.12 Time to Experiment

At this point you will probably want to experiment a little with recording and playing back a few pieces you have been working on. If it sounds really good, ESCape back up to the primary menu and use the SAVE command to save the song on disk.

In the next chapter we will look at editing features that will allow you to change track data, enter note data from the computer keyboard, and fix mistakes.

2

Editing Functions in MT

2.1 Entering Measure Level Edit

In the last chapter you experimented with recording and playing back MIDI data. If this was all you could do, sequencers would be somewhat less useful than a multi-track tape recorder. The real advantages of MIDI come in when you start manipulating the data in the computer's memory.

Start MT and load the song file called EXAMPLE.SNG (supplied on the program disk). This file contains just two tracks: a bass guitar part and a percussion track. The percussion track is set up for a drum machine, or for the percussion on a Roland MT-32 synthesizer. Table A-1 in Appendix 1 shows the percussion note assignments. This is not critical at this point, as we plan to use EXAMPLE.SNG as a disposable song (no great loss to the music world if you trash this example file).

With EXAMPLE.SNG loaded, select the EDIT option from MT's primary menu. You should see a display similar to Figure 2.1.

Figure 2.1 Measure Level Edit (MLE) Display

```
       MIDI Data Editor - Measure Level Edit Display

Measure:          1   2   3   4   5   6   7   8   9   10  11  12  13  14  15

    Track    MIDI   Select a measure and hit Return to start Note Editor.
1 <       >   2    [ ][ ][ ][ ][ ][ ][ ][ ][ ][ ][ ][ ][ ][ ][ ]
2 bassguit    2    [•][♫][♫][♫][♫][♫][♫][♫][♫][♫][♫][♫][♫][♫][♫]
3 <       >   3    [ ][ ][ ][ ][ ][ ][ ][ ][ ][ ][ ][ ][ ][ ][ ]
4 <       >   4    [ ][ ][ ][ ][ ][ ][ ][ ][ ][ ][ ][ ][ ][ ][ ]
5 <       >   5    [ ][ ][ ][ ][ ][ ][ ][ ][ ][ ][ ][ ][ ][ ][ ]
6 <       >   6    [ ][ ][ ][ ][ ][ ][ ][ ][ ][ ][ ][ ][ ][ ][ ]
7 <       >   7    [ ][ ][ ][ ][ ][ ][ ][ ][ ][ ][ ][ ][ ][ ][ ]
8 drums      10    [♫][♫][♫][♫][♫][♫][♫][♫][♫][♫][♫][♫][♫][♫][♫]


   Start Block      Last Measure      Curnt Measure 1
   End Block        Fast Forwd >>     Erase Track
   Block Paste      Forward    >      Erase Forward
   Block Empty      Rewind     <      Data Dump
   Block Repeat     Fast Rewnd <<     Free Memory 95   %
   Block Transp.    First Measure     QUIT Edit

                                               mt3.scr
```

This is the Measure Level Edit (MLE) display. This screen controls editing functions that work on whole sections of a song. The Note Level Editor (NLE) will be discussed later.

2.2 Moving Around in Measure Level Edit

If you press the arrow keys (move the mouse) you will find that most of the spaces on the MLE screen can be accessed. Each area has a special purpose. The large upper box contains spaces marked off with [ ] brackets that show the status of fifteen measures worth of MIDI data for all eight tracks. If the measure contains MIDI note data for the start of one or more notes, the measure block will contain a ♩ symbol. If the track has measure timing data, but does not contain MIDI Note Ons, the measure block will contain a ↔ symbol. This is called the "empty measure" symbol. If the measure does not contain any MIDI data, the block will be blank. In EXAMPLE.SNG only tracks 2 and 8 contain MIDI data. The rest are blank.

The top line has the measure numbers. Move the cursor to one of these numbers and hit Return. The measure you selected becomes the new Current Measure, and now appears as the left-most measure. Note that the Current Measure number shown in the bottom box also changes. This is the same Current Measure used on the RECORD screen. In fact, if you hit ESC and go to RECORD, you will find that the current measure is set to the same number you picked on the MLE top line. The PLAY and RECORD commands would start from this measure.

Use the First Measure command to make measure 1 the current measure.

The upper-left columns show the track names and MIDI channel assignments. You can change either set of values by moving the cursor to a spot and hitting Return. Try changing a channel assignment and adding a name. Again, these changes will be reflected on the RECORD menu the next time you enter it.

In the middle of the bottom box you will find the familiar Forward, Rewind, Fast Rewind, etc., commands. These are the same as the RECORD menu items and are in the same order. Try moving to Last Measure. All but the last two measures of MIDI data will be off of the screen. The Rewind and Forward commands move one measure at a time. Fast Forward and Fast Rewind move ten measures at a time.

The last way to change current measures in MLE is to move the cursor to the Current Measure command and hit Return. MT will prompt you to enter a measure number. This becomes the Current Measure and the display adjusts accordingly.

2.3 Block Editing Commands

The most common editing needs are to repeat, copy, and transpose parts of a song. To do this efficiently, MLE uses the concept of a "block." This is one or more measures that have been marked off in a track. We will practice by marking off a block on track 2. You should be in the MLE menu with the current measure set to 1.
To mark a block:

Start   Block

Select the Start Block command. A cursor will be highlighted in the upper left corner of the measure display. Use the arrow keys or mouse to move to measure 4 on the second track and hit Return. A ⊢symbol will appear on the measure you marked. Hitting ESC before you hit Return quits the Start Block command. Selecting Start Block again removes the block marker.

End   Block

Select the End Block command. Again the cursor appears in the upper left corner. Move the cursor to measure 8 on the second track. A ⊣ will appear, marking the end of the block. If you were to mark the same measure for both the start and stop of a block, you will see a ‖ . This is called a "one measure block."

At this point your display should look like Figure 2.2.

Figure 2.2

MIDI Data Editor – Measure Level Edit Display

Measure:	1	2	3	4	5	6	7	8	9	10	11	12	13	14	15

	Track		MIDI															

```
Measure:         1   2   3   4   5   6   7   8   9   10  11  12  13  14  15

    Track   │MIDI      Select a measure and hit Return to start Note Editor.
1  <      > │ 2     [ ][ ][ ][ ][ ][ ][ ][ ][ ][ ][ ][ ][ ][ ][ ]
2  bassguit │ 2     [*][♪][♪][ ][♪][♪][♪][ ][♪][♪][♪][♪][♪][♪][♪]
3  <      > │ 3     [ ][ ][ ][ ][ ][ ][ ][ ][ ][ ][ ][ ][ ][ ][ ]
4  <      > │ 4     [ ][ ][ ][ ][ ][ ][ ][ ][ ][ ][ ][ ][ ][ ][ ]
5  <      > │ 5     [ ][ ][ ][ ][ ][ ][ ][ ][ ][ ][ ][ ][ ][ ][ ]
6  <      > │ 6     [ ][ ][ ][ ][ ][ ][ ][ ][ ][ ][ ][ ][ ][ ][ ]
7  <      > │ 7     [ ][ ][ ][ ][ ][ ][ ][ ][ ][ ][ ][ ][ ][ ][ ]
8  drums    │ 10    [♪][♪][♪][♪][♪][♪][♪][♪][♪][♪][♪][♪][♪][♪][♪]
```

Start Block	Last Measure	Curnt Measure 1
End Block	Fast Forwd >>	Erase Track
Block Paste	Forward >	Erase Forward
Block Empty	Rewind <	Data Dump
Block Repeat	Fast Rewnd <<	Free Memory 95 %
Block Transp.	First Measure	QUIT Edit

mt3.scr

With the block of five measures marked off, we can use the Block Paste, Block Empty, Block Repeat, and Block Transpose commands. Let's copy these five measures onto an empty track.

Block Paste

Move the cursor down to the Block Paste command and hit Return. Again a cursor will appear in the upper left-hand corner of the measure display. Move this cursor to measure 4 of track 4 (which has no data now) and hit Return. The contents of the marked block will be copied into track 4, starting at measure 4. Your display should look like Figure 2.3.

Figure 2.3

MIDI Data Editor - Measure Level Edit Display

Measure:		1	2	3	4	5	6	7	8	9	10	11	12	13	14	15

	Track	MIDI	Select a measure and hit Return to start Note Editor.
1	< >	2	[ ] [ ] [ ] [ ] [ ] [ ] [ ] [ ] [ ] [ ] [ ] [ ] [ ] [ ] [ ]
2	bassguit	2	[•] [♫] [♫] [♩] [♫] [♫] [♫] [♩] [♫] [♫] [♫] [♫] [♫] [♫] [♫]
3	< >	3	[ ] [ ] [ ] [ ] [ ] [ ] [ ] [ ] [ ] [ ] [ ] [ ] [ ] [ ] [ ]
4	< >	4	[•] [•] [•] [♫] [♫] [♫] [♫] [♫] [ ] [ ] [ ] [ ] [ ] [ ] [ ]
5	< >	5	[ ] [ ] [ ] [ ] [ ] [ ] [ ] [ ] [ ] [ ] [ ] [ ] [ ] [ ] [ ]
6	< >	6	[ ] [ ] [ ] [ ] [ ] [ ] [ ] [ ] [ ] [ ] [ ] [ ] [ ] [ ] [ ]
7	< >	7	[ ] [ ] [ ] [ ] [ ] [ ] [ ] [ ] [ ] [ ] [ ] [ ] [ ] [ ] [ ]
8	drums	10	[♫] [♫] [♫] [♫] [♫] [♫] [♫] [♫] [♫] [♫] [♫] [♫] [♫] [♫] [♫]

Start Block	Last Measure	Curnt Measure 1
End Block	Fast Forwd >>	Erase Track
Block Paste	Forward >	Erase Forward
Block Empty	Rewind <	Data Dump
Block Repeat	Fast Rewnd <<	Free Memory 94 %
Block Transp.	First Measure	QUIT Edit

mt3.scr

Notice that three empty measures were automatically added to track 4 at the beginning of the track. This is because the Paste destination was after the beginning of the track. If you ESCape to the RECORD menu and PLAY only track 4, you will have to wait through three measures of silence before the notes begin.

A few comments on the Paste command:

If a block is "pasted" into a track with no data, or after the last data in a track, Paste will add empty measures up to the added block of data.

If the block is pasted into a track which contains MIDI data, the pasted block will be merged into the existing notes. Both the original notes and the notes from the pasted block will sound when the track is played. All of the added data will be adjusted to match the destination track's MIDI channel number.

If the start or end of the block cuts through the duration of notes in the source track, only part of the note data will be copied. Notes that begin before the block start, but end within or after the block, are not copied. Notes that start inside the block, but end outside of the block are copied, but stop sounding at the end of the block when copied to the destination track.

Since the source block remains marked after you use the Block Paste command, you can keep pasting over and over. Repeating a block is such a common task that MT provides an automated method called Block Repeat.

Let's put two copies of the marked block onto track 5.

Block Repeat

Move the cursor down to Block Repeat and hit Return. Now move the block cursor to measure 2 on track 5 and hit Return. MT will ask you to:

```
Enter the number of times to repeat the marked block ->
```

Enter the number 2 and hit Return.

Two copies of the marked block are added to the track. Note that the Free Memory % is reduced a little as the data is added. Also note the empty measure at the end of the block. This just means that the end-of-track marker fell in the measure outside of the marked block. No note data exists in the measure.

Block Repeat is ideal for repeating drum patterns. However, for bass tracks you will want to repeat the rhythm, but transpose the notes up and down various intervals. This is where Block Transpose comes in handy.

Block Transpose

Let's mark a new block and transpose the notes up an octave:

1) Move the cursor to the Start Block command and hit Return. The previously marked block will disappear. This is the normal way to "unmark" a block.

2) Hit Return on the Start Block command and move down to measure 2 on track 5. End the block on measure 5.

3) With the block marked, move the cursor to the Block Transpose command and hit Return. MT will prompt you with:

`Enter the number of MIDI note numbers to add/subtract to the data->`

4) Each MIDI note number is one musical half-step from the next. An octave is twelve half-steps, so up an octave is a +12. Enter the number 12 and hit Return. MT transposes all of the notes in the block up an octave.

The most common musical intervals to transpose are fourths, fifths, and octaves. Here are the number of MIDI note numbers to add or subtract for the perfect intervals:

Interval	Up	Down
Octave	+12	-12
Perfect fourth	+5	-5
Perfect Fifth	+7	-7

Right now the only way you have to make sure the notes were transposed is to PLAY the track from the RECORD menu before and after the transposition. We will get to the Note Level Editor soon.

2.4 Deleting MIDI Data

The MLE screen provides three separate ways of deleting MIDI data:

Block Empty:	Removes MIDI data in a marked block.
Erase Track:	Erases the entire track's data.
Erase Forward:	Erases data after the current measure from the track.

There is a subtle difference here between emptying and erasing track data. Block Empty removes the MIDI note data, but leaves behind empty measures (measure rests). This means that the position of measures before and after the block are not affected by the Block Empty command.

In contrast, Erase Track and Erase Forward remove all traces of the track data that they cover. Not even empty measures remain after these two are used.

Block Empty

If you still have the block marked off on track 5, go ahead and try the Block Empty command. Otherwise, you will have to mark off a few measures on track 5 as a block and then try Block Empty. Try measures 3 to 5. Get rid of the block markers by using the Start Block command again. You will see a screen like Figure 2.4.

Figure 2.4

MIDI Data Editor – Measure Level Edit Display

Measure:		1	2	3	4	5	6	7	8	9	10	11	12	13	14	15

	Track	MIDI	Select a measure and hit Return to start Note Editor.
1	< >	2	[ ] [ ] [ ] [ ] [ ] [ ] [ ] [ ] [ ] [ ] [ ] [ ] [ ] [ ] [ ]
2	bassguit	2	[•] [♫] [♫] [♫] [♫] [♫] [♫] [♫] [♫] [♫] [♫] [♫] [♫] [♫] [♫]
3	< >	3	[ ] [ ] [ ] [ ] [ ] [ ] [ ] [ ] [ ] [ ] [ ] [ ] [ ] [ ] [ ]
4	< >	4	[•] [•] [•] [♫] [♫] [♫] [♫] [♫] [ ] [ ] [ ] [ ] [ ] [ ] [ ]
5	< >	5	[•] [♫] [•] [•] [•] [♫] [♫] [♫] [♫] [♫] [♫] [•] [ ] [ ] [ ]
6	< >	6	[ ] [ ] [ ] [ ] [ ] [ ] [ ] [ ] [ ] [ ] [ ] [ ] [ ] [ ] [ ]
7	< >	7	[ ] [ ] [ ] [ ] [ ] [ ] [ ] [ ] [ ] [ ] [ ] [ ] [ ] [ ] [ ]
8	drums	10	[♫] [♫] [♫] [♫] [♫] [♫] [♫] [♫] [♫] [♫] [♫] [♫] [♫] [♫] [♫]

Start Block	Last Measure	Curnt Measure 1
End Block	Fast Forwd >>	Erase Track
Block Paste	Forward >	Erase Forward
Block Empty	Rewind <	Data Dump
Block Repeat	Fast Rewnd <<	Free Memory 92 %
Block Transp.	First Measure	QUIT Edit

mt3.scr

Note that the measures before and after the block were left alone. All of the measures within the block are now empty. Notes starting within the block removed. Also, notes that started before the block but terminated inside have been shut off right before the start of the block.

Erase Track

We can use track 4 to test out the Erase Track option. Move the cursor to Erase Track and hit Return. MT prompts you with:

Which track number do you wish to erase? ->

Enter number 4 and hit Return. Note that all MIDI data is removed from the track. The track name (if it had one) and MIDI channel are not affected.

Erase Forward

Erase Forward is similar to Erase Track, except that Erase Forward starts at the current measure. To erase track 5 forward of measure 8, you must make measure 8 the current measure. Move the cursor up to the top line, on top of the number 8 and hit Return. The display will adjust with measure 8 on the left-most column. Now move the cursor to Erase Forward and hit return. MT will respond with:

Enter the track number to clear forward ->

Enter a 5 and hit Return. To see the full effects, use the First Measure to move the display back to the beginning. Note that all the data from measure 8 forward is removed from track 5.

Erase Track and Erase Forward are available from both the MLE and RECORD menus. Operation is identical in either case, but it is a little easier to see what is going on from the MLE screen.

2.5 Note Level Editing

The MLE editor is handy for working with chunks of MIDI data. For adding, deleting, and adjusting individual MIDI notes MT provides a Note Level Editor (NLE).

To enter NLE, move the cursor to measure 2 of track 2—right on the 𝅘𝅥𝅮 —and hit Return. The screen will clear and you will be presented with a picture like Figure 2.5.

Figure 2.5

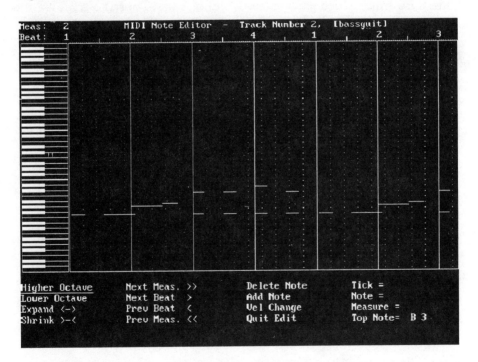

(If you do not see this screen, you probably have the graphics mode set to a value your video board does not understand. Quit MT by hitting ESC a couple of times, QUIT, and then run INSTALL again.)

As mentioned in the discussion of INSTALL, the number of octaves MT displays is limited by the resolution of your video equipment. This picture is from a VGA equipped computer which allows a maximum of six octaves to be shown.

The keyboard on the left is a reference so that you can tell which notes are active. There is an M on the central note. This marks middle C. This index moves up and down depending on what part of the MIDI scale you are looking at.

In the upper left corner of the screen is the measure number of the measure from which you entered NLE. This is not the same as the Current Measure used by RECORD and MLE. The Current Measure will be unchanged if you escape from NLE (by hitting the ESC key).

The top row of numbers displays the beat number for each measure. Depending on the meter the song was recorded with, this will show numbers from 1 to 2, or 1 to 8. A vertical line from each beat serves as a reference during editing. The rows of horizontal dots are also included as a reference. Each row is centered on a "white key" on the keyboard. I put "white key" in quotes, as although piano keyboards make the whole notes white and accidentals black, you may have chosen other colors for this display in INSTALL.

Notes are displayed in NLE as horizontal lines. The duration of the note is proportional to the length of the line. This is usually called a "piano roll" display because of the similarity to the paper rolls used to control player pianos.

At the bottom of the screen are the commands available from NLE. The three columns starting from the left contain the commands you can use. The right-most column contains status information. These values are updated during several of the commands. The bottom right value always displays the name of the highest note displayed on the screen (always a B). This is handy if the middle C marker is off of the displayed area.

As usual, commands are accessed by moving the cursor to the command and hitting Return. On this screen the cursor is marked by underlining the command. The ESC key exits from all commands without doing anything. ESC will also exit from the NLE back to the MLE screen we just left. You can think of this as the third level of menus within MT:

Figure 2.6

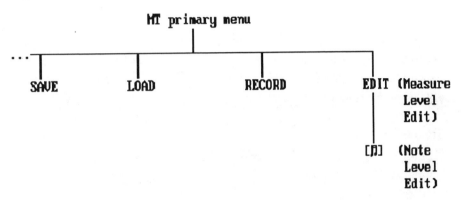

The ESC key always moves you up the menu structure. The Return key (selecting an item) always moves you down into deeper levels.

Let's take a look at each of the NLE commands in sequence.

Figure 2.7

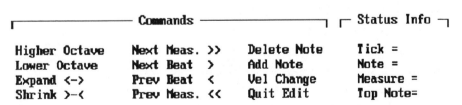

Higher Octave

Adjusts the portion of the MIDI note range displayed on the screen upward by one octave. You will see the M marking middle C move down a full octave. The Top Note indicator at the bottom right of the screen will also go down by one octave. The screen will updated so that note values are displayed opposite the correct piano key.

Lower Octave

Adjusts the portion of the MIDI note range displayed on the screen downward by one octave.

Expand <->

Expands the horizontal scale on the NLE screen. This allows you to see more detail of MIDI note timing, but fewer beats of the measure. At maximum expansion each movement of the arrow keys will advance the cursor by one tick (1/120 of a quarter note).

Shrink >-<

Shrinks the horizontal scale on the NLE screen. This allows you to see more of the song on the screen, but with less resolution.

Next Measure >>

Advances the portion of the song viewed on the NLE screen by one measure. When you quit NLE (hit ESC or select the Quit Edit command) you will be returned to the MLE (Measure Level Edit) screen. If you changed measures in NLE, the cursor will reflect the new measure when you return to NLE.

Next Beat >

Advances the portion of the song viewed on the NLE screen by one beat. This is handy if you have used the Expand command, and cannot see an entire measure on the screen.

Previous Beat <

Rewinds the part of the song viewed on the NLE screen by one beat.

Previous Measure <<

Rewinds the portion of the song viewed on the NLE screen by one measure.

Delete Note

Selecting this command makes the NLE cursor appear on the screen. Move the cursor to the note you want to delete and hit Return. The note line will disappear. Hitting ESC before you hit Return will abort the Delete Note command.

During the Delete Note, Add Note, and Vel Change commands, the right-most status information of Tick =, Note =, and Measure = become active. This will allow you to make sure you have the right timing and note values for the spot you have marked with the cursor. Appendix 1 has a table of timing values (tick =) for various musical note values.

Add Note

Selecting Add Note makes the NLE cursor to appear on the screen. Move the cursor to where you want to start the note and hit Return. This spot will be marked by a stationary cursor and another cursor will appear to the right of it. Move the second cursor to where you want the note to end and hit Return.

MT will then prompt you to enter the key velocity value for the note (1 – 127). You can enter a number or just hit Return for the default value of 64. After this the note will appear on the screen.

Vel Change

Selecting this command again puts the NLE cursor on the screen. MT will respond with:

Move the cross hair to a NOTE, then hit return (ESC to exit)

Once you put the cursor center over any part of a note and hit Return, MT will say:

```
Note vel = XX, Enter new value (1-127), RET to exit ->
```

where XX will be the current velocity value. If you enter a number and hit Return, that value will be substituted for the marked note's velocity. Hitting ESC, or just Return will exit this command without changing the velocity value.

You can take advantage of the easy exit from Velocity Change to find out what the velocity value is for a note. Use Velocity Change to mark the note and hit Return. The current value will be displayed when the command prompts you for the new value (XX above). Just hit Return or ESC key to continue without changing the value.

Quit Edit

This is equivalent to hitting the ESC key from the NLE menu. You will be returned to the Measure Level Edit (MLE) menu. If you changed measures within NLE, this will be reflected by the measure marked highlighted on the MLE screen.

Note Level Editing gives you the ability to enter music directly from the computer screen. With a mouse, this can be done rapidly, particularly if you just hit Return for the default key velocity value on each note. This is how the ABACO.SNG file was created.

A warning about direct computer input: If you just enter the music exactly as written, it will tend to sound mechanical. You can get away with this with some musical styles, but it never sounds quite right. To get some "feel" into the music takes some practice. First, vary the note velocity values to "shade" expression within measures and in larger units of music. Let the Note Off timing drag a little on some notes to get a lagato feel.

The opposite happens when you play a piece on your MIDI instrument and use RECORD to capture the data. When you look at what you played under the microscope of the NLE screen, you will probably be appalled at how far off of the notation you actually play. THIS IS OK!

Musical notation is only a means of communicating roughly what the composer had in mind. Our musical background and culture has a lot of influence on what sounds "right." Do not get caught up in the perfectionist trap of feeling you have to "fix" something that sounded just fine until you looked at it in the sequencer.

2.6 Saving Your Song File

After editing you will probably want to save your efforts to a disk file. Go back up to the MT primary menu using the ESC key. If this is going to be a new file you will probably want to put a title on it. Select the TITLE option and hit Return. You can enter anything you want, up to fifty characters. The title will be saved along with your MIDI data.

After using TITLE, select the SAVE option. SAVE will display all of the .SNG files on your directory. If you are starting fresh, SAVE will ask you to enter a new file name. Enter a name with one to eight characters. File names must start with a letter, and consist of letters, numbers, and the ^ ! # $ % ( ) - _ characters. Lower case letters are converted to upper case.

If you started by loading an existing song file, SAVE will ask you if you want to keep this file name. Answering Y will automatically save the file without your having to type in the file name. This is the most common situation; where you load an old file, edit or add to it, and then want to save it. If you answer N, MT will ask you to type in the new file name.

2.7 The CLEAR Command

Sometimes what you have in memory just is not worth keeping. Rather than having to erase each of the tracks individually, MT provides a CLEAR command from the primary menu. It gives you a fresh sequencer to start with, including:

- Clearing the song title.
- Changing all track names to <   >.
- Changing all MIDI channels back to the default values.
- Changing the song file back to the NO_NAME.SNG default.
- Deleting all MIDI data in memory on all tracks.

CLEAR does not change the drive/directory for your song files. Accidental use of CLEAR would be a disaster, so MT asks you:

`Are you sure you want to erase all track data in memory (Y/N)?`

before it starts. Hitting any key except Y will stop CLEAR from working.

3

Advanced Use of MT

In this chapter we will look at the IMPORT command, and go through typical steps used to create a new song. Also, the Data Dump and Data Trace commands will be tested.

3.1 The IMPORT Command

For pop/rock songs it is usually best to build the song from the ground up. This means first percussion, then bass, and finally solo parts.

Building a good percussion track is more difficult than it looks. If you have little background in this area, I suggest buying the book *Drum Machine Rhythm Dictionary* by Sandy Feldstein. It contains hundreds of patterns shown in both conventional notation and in drum machine layout. Eight examples from this book are in the song file DRUMDICT.SNG on the sequencer disk. The Roland MT-32 note assignments were used to map the percussion sounds to MIDI note numbers (see Appendix 1). If you are using a different drum machine, you will either want to map your drum sounds to these note assignments, or edit the drum tracks to match your machine's default assignments.

Let's go ahead and get a rhythm track from the DRUMDICT.SNG file. To do this, we will use the IMPORT command on MT's primary menu. Be sure that all tracks are empty by using the CLEAR command before following this example.

IMPORT first shows you all of the files in the drive/directory you selected using the DRIVE command. Pick DRUMDICT.SNG.

Next, you will get the IMPORT menu. The top half of the screen shows the tracks in the source file you selected. Note that the song title, track names, and track size (COUNT) are all visible. The four IMPORT commands are all on the bottom row. The sequence of commands is:

1) Select the Pick Source command and hit Return. A new cursor will appear on the SOURC row of the source track display. Move this over to the second track labeled "backbeat" and hit Return. This track will be marked with the word *Source*.

2) Select the Pick Dest. command and hit Return. Again a new cursor will appear, this time on the DEST row. Move the cursor over to track 8 and hit Return. At this point you have both the source and destination tracks selected. No data is transferred until the next step.

Figure 3.1 MT IMPORT Menu

MT Import Menu

	TRACK 1	TRACK 2	TRACK 3	TRACK 4	TRACK 5	TRACK 6	TRACK 7	TRACK 8
NAME	In Disk File:	Drum Patterns – Note Assignments for MT-32						
NAME CHANL COUNT	bass4bt 10 92	backbeat 10 312	slowblue 10 452	afrocuba 10 592	nanigo 10 592	dixielnd 10 252	conga 10 398	samba 10 590
SOURC		*Source*						
NAME	In Memory Now:							
NAME CHANL COUNT	< > 1 1	< > 2 1	< > 3 1	< > 4 1	< > 5 1	< > 6 1	< > 7 1	< > 8 1
DEST								**Dest**
	Pick Source		Pick Dest.		Import Track		Quit	

mt5.scr

3) Select the Import Track command and hit Return. The selected track is read off of your disk file and added to the tracks in memory.

If there is already data in the destination track, MT will warn you with the message:

```
Existing data in Dest track will be written over. OK?
```

Hitting the Y key will allow IMPORT to proceed. Hitting any other key will stop the command.

IMPORT also checks that the *meter* (beats/measure) of the imported track matches that of the current meter setting on the RECORD menu. If not, you will get the message:

```
Note: Song in memory has meter = X, Source meter = Y
```

where X and Y are the current meter values. MT will let you import unmatched tracks. This leads to a lot of confusion on measure numbers. In most cases, it is best to quit IMPORT, go to the RECORD menu, and set the meter value to match (before any data is imported, recorded, or added via EDIT).

4) Quit the IMPORT menu either by selecting QUIT, or by hitting the ESC key.

You will probably want to PLAY the imported track from the RECORD menu before doing anything else.

3.2 Building up Tracks

With a drum track imported, let's go to the EDIT menu and see what we have. Selecting EDIT from the primary menu puts you in the MLE screen. You will see:

Figure 3.2

MIDI Data Editor - Measure Level Edit Display

Measure:			1	2	3	4	5	6	7	8	9	10	11	12	13	14	15

	Track	MIDI	Select a measure and hit Return to start Note Editor.
1	< >	1	[ ] [ ] [ ] [ ] [ ] [ ] [ ] [ ] [ ] [ ] [ ] [ ] [ ] [ ] [ ]
2	< >	2	[ ] [ ] [ ] [ ] [ ] [ ] [ ] [ ] [ ] [ ] [ ] [ ] [ ] [ ] [ ]
3	< >	3	[ ] [ ] [ ] [ ] [ ] [ ] [ ] [ ] [ ] [ ] [ ] [ ] [ ] [ ] [ ]
4	< >	4	[ ] [ ] [ ] [ ] [ ] [ ] [ ] [ ] [ ] [ ] [ ] [ ] [ ] [ ] [ ]
5	< >	5	[ ] [ ] [ ] [ ] [ ] [ ] [ ] [ ] [ ] [ ] [ ] [ ] [ ] [ ] [ ]
6	< >	6	[ ] [ ] [ ] [ ] [ ] [ ] [ ] [ ] [ ] [ ] [ ] [ ] [ ] [ ] [ ]
7	< >	7	[ ] [ ] [ ] [ ] [ ] [ ] [ ] [ ] [ ] [ ] [ ] [ ] [ ] [ ] [ ]
8	< >	8	[♫] [♫] [♫] [♫] [♫] [♫] [♫] [♫] [♫] [♫] [ ] [ ] [ ] [ ] [ ]

Start Block	Last Measure	Curnt Measure 1
End Block	Fast Forwd >>	Erase Track
Block Paste	Forward >	Erase Forward
Block Empty	Rewind <	Data Dump
Block Repeat	Fast Rewnd <<	Free Memory 98 %
Block Transp.	First Measure	QUIT Edit

mt3.scr

Move the cursor to the track name for track 8 and put in "drums." Also, set the MIDI channel to the drum machine channel.

From the MLE display you can see that only ten measures worth of drum track were imported from the DRUMDICT.SNG file (that is the length of the tracks on this file). We will need more than that for any reasonable length song, so we will use the Block Repeat command to duplicate the ten measures we have to make fifty measures.

Mark the first and last measure of track 8 as the start and end of the block. Then pick the Block Repeat command. Move the cursor to measure 11 on track 8 and hit Return. MT will ask you to:

Enter the number of times to repeat the marked block->

Enter a 4 and hit Return. After a moment the screen will refresh with track 8 showing notes across the screen. You can check that it goes out to measure 50 by using the Last Measure or Fast Forward commands. Move back to the start with First Measure.

You now have fifty measures of percussion to play with. You can go to the RECORD menu and set track 8 to play while recording the other tracks in sequence. I'll assume that you want to add a bass pattern track next.

3.3 Adding the Bass Part

The majority of pop music uses simple chord relationships to provide the bass foundation for the song. Let's use the most common grouping based on the key of C.

Chord Changes

Measure:	1	2	3	4	5	6	7	8	9	10	11	12
Chord:	C	C	F	F	C	C	G	G	F	F	C	C

We will use the same bass pattern for each measure, but change the key in which the chord is played based on this table. The bass pattern is:

Figure 3.3

You can enter this single measure of notes either by recording it (playing it at the synthesizer keyboard), or by entering each note from the NLE screen. Call the track "bassguit" and assign it to the correct MIDI channel (I will use channel 2).

If you create the measure by recording your playing, turn the drum track on for PLAY and record to track 2. Let the first measure go by as just percussion. That will give you a feel for the beat. You can get rid of this blank measure later using the Block Move command. If you enter the notes from the NLE screen, start your input in measure 2. In either case, the measure will look about like Figure 3.4 viewed from NLE.

Figure 3.4

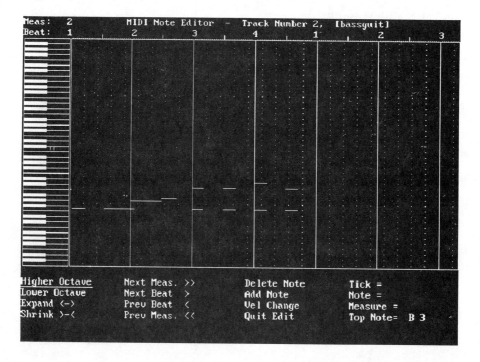

The measure we created is in the key of C. We can use this single measure to build up the entire bass track. Mark the measure containing your bass notes as the beginning and end of the block (one-measure-wide block). Paste this block onto the next measure to create two measures of notes. Select Start Block again to see what you have. The track should look like Figure 3.5.

Figure 3.5

2 bassguit| 2 | [•] ⍰ ⍰ [ ] [ ] [ ] [ ] [ ] [ ] [ ] [ ] [ ] [ ] [ ]

Do not worry if you have an empty measure at the end of your track. This just means one of the Note Offs fell a little after the beat.

Now we want the next two measures to have the same chord pattern, but to be in the key of F. That is up a perfect fourth interval from C. First, mark off the two measures you have created as a block. Paste them onto the following two measures. You now have four measures in the key of C.

To get the last two measures into the key of F, we need to transpose them five half-steps (five MIDI note numbers) upwards. Mark off the two measures containing note data as a block and hit Block Transpose. Respond to the prompt:

`Enter the number of MIDI note numbers to add/subtract ->`

with 5 and hit Return. (You would enter a negative number, like -5, to go down that many half-steps). Now you have the first four measures, two in C and two in F.

Continue the process of adding blocks and then transposing until you have the bass line for your song. You can save some time by making a bunch of measures in the key of C using the Block Repeat command, and then just moving forward through the song doing transpositions.

Now that you have the bass and drum parts laid down, it is a good idea to give your efforts a title and SAVE the two tracks to a file. Once you have done this, you are ready to add more tracks, either by playing your synth, or from the NLE screen.

I usually do not bother recording my first efforts at a solo line. I set the bass and percussion to PLAY, hit the PLAY command, and then listen to the mix as the computer plays the background and I work on the solo

solo lines. When it starts getting close I will set one track to record. If it does not sound right on the first take, it is a simple matter to erase the recorded track and try again.

If you make a mistake in the middle of a track, you can start recording from that "current" measure forward. MT leaves all of the measures before the current one untouched, but erases the measures forward from the current measure when you hit Record. It is best to start these "punch in" takes on a new track. You can Block Paste the new measures into the old track after recording. Using a separate track to record the portion you want to insert also allows you to start the play/record session back a couple of measures, so that you get a feel for the tempo before you start playing.

If you run out of tracks and need a spare one to record new takes, you have some options. Save your song file to a new file name. Take one of the less vital tracks and merge its data with another track. You will still have all of the notes, but the instrumental sound will be the same on each. Now you can delete the track and use it for scratch space.

When you are done with the scratch track, go to IMPORT and bring back both the track you erased, and the original track you merged to (without the added data).

It is uncommon to have more than eight instruments playing at one time. The usual reason for running out of tracks is that there are more than eight instrumental voices over the course of the song. Some voices come and go, but at any time there are less than eight playing. You can reduce the number of separate tracks required by recording MIDI Program Change data in a track. These MIDI commands will switch the sound (the "patch") that is produced by the synth responding to one of your tracks. This is the subject of the next section.

3.4 Other Uses for RECORD

There is no reason to restrict your use of the RECORD command to just MIDI note data. Any sort of MIDI information can be recorded.

As an example, let's say you have several synths. You want to be able to switch them all at once from one set of patches (selected sounds) to another set. Normally, you would have to go to the front panel of each synth and select the right patch. You can use MT to remember the settings.

The following will work as long as each synth is set to a different MIDI channel. You may have to select the right MIDI output option from your synth's control panel to turn transmission of program change messages on.

CLEAR all track data and then go to MT's RECORD menu. Move the cursor up to track 1 and make it *ACTIVE* by selecting the RECRD option. Move the cursor down to the lower left and select RECORD. MT is now recording all MIDI data to track 1. Go from synth to synth selecting certain patches. When you are done, go back to the computer keyboard and hit the ESC or SPACEBAR key to shut down recording. Note the COUNT value on track 1 shows that you recorded some data.

When you select a patch on your synthesizer, the synth sends out the patch number as a MIDI Program Change message. These Program Change messages are recorded by MT like any other MIDI data. When you PLAY the data on this track, MT sends the same Program Change messages out that it recorded. Your synthesizer(s) responds to the Control Change messages by changing the selected patch.

If you use certain patch selections frequently, record each one to a separate track and then save them all as a "song" file. You can LOAD this file and PLAY the right track any time you want the patch setup.

Control Change messages can also be embedded in your track data on a song. For example, while recording you may switch sounds (patches) from the front panel of the synth you are playing. This Control Change information will be recorded with the note data. The patch switch will occur when the song is played. If you do this routinely, you will find it convenient to start each track by selecting the right patch. That way, you will always start from the same place, regardless of what you had the synth set to before starting PLAY.

Some synths allow more elaborate external control through the use of MIDI Exclusive messages. Exclusive messages are specific to the make and model of equipment you are using. When transmitted, only that model will respond. MT can record Exclusive messages if the Exclusive On/Off toggle (lower right side of the RECORD menu) is set to On.

It is difficult to generalize as to what can be done with MIDI Exclusive messages. This is the "window" that the MIDI specification gives manufacturers to do their own thing. You may be able to set MIDI channels, record and transmit individual patch settings for unique sounds, etc. Check your synth's MIDI implementation documentation to see what is possible.

3.5 Examining MIDI Data

Most commercial sequencer/editors try to insulate the user from the low-level reality of MIDI commands. This is a good idea, as most users do not respond well to seeing a lot of hexadecimal numbers spill out on the screen. An example of hiding complexity is MT's Note Level Edit (NLE) screen. The reality behind all of those easy to change "notes" in front of the keyboard display is fairly complicated.

MT was designed for people who want to experiment with MIDI programming. If you fall in this group, you probably already have some ideas on how to improve or extend MT's capabilities. To help you trace and debug your efforts, MT provides two commands for seeing the

MIDI data in its raw form. Data Dump shows the MIDI data residing in the computer's memory. Data Trace displays the MIDI data as it is transmitted.

3.6 Data Dump

This command is available from both the RECORD and MLE screens. Data Dump starts at the current measure on all tracks, and displays data in hexadecimal. Here is an example for a few notes recorded to track 1 on MIDI channel 1:

Figure 3.6 Output of Data Dump Command

```
MIDI data in hex for tracks 1-8:

00f90000-00f90000-00f90000-00f90000-00f90000-00f90000-00f90000-00f90000-
f8000000-        -  .       -           -           -           -           -           -
1a903c30-        -           -           -           -           -           -           -
18903c00-        -           -           -           -           -           -           -
57903e36-        -           -           -           -           -           -           -
17903e00-        -           -           -           -           -           -           -
58f90000-        -           -           -           -           -           -           -
0390403c-        -           -           -           -           -           -           -
14904000-        -           -           -           -           -           -           -
f8000000-        -           -           -           -           -           -           -
57fc0000-        -           -           -           -           -           -           -
         -        -           -           -           -           -           -           -
         -        -           -           -           -           -           -           -
         -        -           -           -           -           -           -           -
         -        -           -           -           -           -           -           -
         -        -           -           -           -           -           -           -
         -        -           -           -           -           -           -           -
         -        -           -           -           -           -           -           -
         -        -           -           -           -           -           -           -
```

Hit space to continue, ESC to quit.

In this example only track 1 has data. The program file MPU401.H contains a list of all of the MPU-401 commands and their hexadecimal equivalent. Let's look at each line of data individually:

```
00 f9 00 00
```

F9 hex is the Measure End marker. MT uses the convention that all tracks start with a Measure End.

```
f8 00 00 00
```

F8 hex is the MPU-401 timing overflow message. The MPU's internal clock only counts to 239. After that it starts counting at 0. The MPU sends the F8 out every time 240 ticks pass without receiving any MIDI data so that the host computer can keep track of the timing.

```
1a 90 3c 30
```

The 1a is a timing byte. Twenty-six ticks (1a hex) passed between the receipt of the F8 and this MIDI message. The 90 hex is MIDI for Note On on channel 1. The 3c hex is the MIDI note number for middle C (see Appendix 1 for a table of MIDI note numbers in decimal and hexadecimal). The 30 hex is the key velocity value.

```
18 90 3c 00
```

After another eighteen hex ticks, the MPU received another MIDI Note On for note number 3c hex (middle C). In this case the velocity value is 00, so this is a Note Off.

```
57 90 3e 36
17 90 3e 00
```

These two lines show the Note On and Note Off for playing the D above middle C.

```
50 f9 00 00
```

After another fifty hex ticks the MPU-401 sent a Measure End message. The MPU keeps track of timing and transmits this message at the right point during recording.

```
03 90 40 3c
14 90 40 00
```

Note On and Note Off for note number 40 hex (E above middle C).

```
f8 00 00 00
```

Another timing overflow message. 240 ticks passed without data.

```
57 fc 00 00
```

FC hex is the Data End message. This marks the end of the track.

Note that Data Dump throws in extra 00s to pad out each data group to four bytes. The MPU-401 does not transmit all of these 00s. For example, the timing overflow (F8) message is just one byte when transmitted.

Data Dump is handy for seeing what is stored in memory. It does not show the commands sent between the computer and the MPU-401 to get various tasks started. To see exactly what data is exchanged, use the Data Trace command.

3.7 Data Trace

Go to the RECORD menu and set Data Trace to ON. Set up track 1 to record, all other tracks with PLAY OFF, and start recording. Hit a few keys on your synth. Shut down the record process by pressing the SPACEBAR on the computer's keyboard. You will see a display similar to this:

```
Data Trace Option - all data in hex.
rc=received, tc=trans command, td=trans data
```

```
tc=ff(ACK) tc=e0 tc=e0(ACK) td=64 tc=e6(ACK) td=4 tc=c5(ACK)
tc=e4(ACK) td=18 tc=ec(ACK) td=0 tc=b8(ACK) tc=a(ACK) tc=22(ACK)
rc=f8 rc=a rc=90 rc=3c rc=26 rc=2a rc=3c rc=0 rc=50 rc=3e rc=30
rc=26 rc=3e rc=0 rc=42 rc=f9 rc=10 rc=40 rc=38 rc=24 rc=40 rc=0
rc=f8 rc=bc rc=f9 tc=11(ACK) rc=73 rc=fc tc=84(ACK) tc=11(ACK)
tc=5(ACK) tc=b9 tc=b9(ACK)
```

```
Hit a key to return.
```

With Trace ON, MT displays everything it sends and receives as it happens. Each byte of data is shown in hexadecimal. To make it clear where the data came from, several codes are used:

`tc=` Transmitted command. This is a command that MT sent to the MPU-401. We will go over the common ones in a moment.

`td=` This is a data byte that MT sent. Data bytes frequently follow commands. For example, if the command was to set the MPU-401's metronome rate, the data byte would be a number reflecting that rate (100 for 100 beats per minute).

`rc=` Received data. This is a byte that came into the MPU-401's MIDI IN port. There is no distinction between data and commands for received data. The MPU-401 can only get commands from the computer.

`(ACK)` Acknowledgement. The MPU-401 acknowledges receipt of any command that it understands by sending an Acknowledgement byte (ACK) back to the computer. Sometimes the MPU-401 is not expecting a command, so the first transmission of the command is not understood. MT then resends the command until the ACK is received.

With this coding scheme we can follow what happened on our trace of recording a few notes. Let's take apart the first line from the trace:

```
tc=ff(ACK) tc=e0 tc=e0(ACK) td=64 tc=e6(ACK) td=4 tc=c5(ACK)
```

```
Command (In Hexadecimal) = Command Name (from MPU401.h file)
```

`ff = RESET`

The first command sent by MT was FF hex. This is the RESET command that puts the MPU-401 back to its start-up defaults.

`e0 + data byte = SET_TEMPO`

Next, MT sent E0 hex, the SET_TEMPO command. The MPU-401 did not acknowledge this command on the first try (recovering from the RESET), so MT resent it. The second time MT got the ACK. The SET_TEMPO command is followed by a data byte corresponding to the tempo in beats per minute. The data byte, 64 hex, corresponds to MT's default tempo of 100 beats per minute (6 x 16 + 4 = 100).

`e6 + data byte = METRO_MEAS`

MT then set the METRO_MEAS command (E6 hex) followed by a data byte of 4 hex. This set the MPU-401 metronome to four beats per measure. The next command (C5 hex, TB_120) sets the internal time base of the MPU-401 to 120 ticks per quarter note.

You probably get the general idea at this point. The remaining sequences are:

`e4 + Data Byte = MIDI_METRO`

Sets the metronome rate. A value of 24 (18 hex) gives the usual one metronome beep per quarter note. This is a fixed value in MT.

`eC + Data Byte = ACT_TRACK`

Activates the tracks set in the data byte. Each zero and one in the data byte represents one of the eight internal tracks in the MPU-401 logic. A data byte of 00000001 = 01 hex sets only track 1 on. 00000011 = 03 hex sets tracks 1 and 2 on. A zero data byte means no tracks are set to play.

`b8 = CLEAR_PCOUNT`

Clears all Play counters in the MPU-401 internal logic.

`Oa = START_PLAY`

Begins the Play process for any tracks set on by ACT_TRACK. In our example Data Trace, no tracks were set to play, so nothing happens.

`22 = START_REC`

Starts the Record process. The MPU-401 passes all MIDI data received on its MIDI IN port to the host computer. Timing data is also transmitted.

After line two, the MPU-401 has all of the commands it needs to start recording data. Let's examine each of the bytes on line three:

`f8 = TIME_OUT`

The MPU-401 internal clock can only count up to 239. After that it starts over from 0. Every time 240 ticks pass without the MPU-401 receiving any MIDI data, the MPU sends out an F8 so that the program can store this time period as part of the track data.

`a = A Timing Byte`

When the MPU-401 does get some MIDI data (next three bytes) the MPU first outputs the clock setting, then the MIDI bytes. In this case ten ticks (0A hex) passed from the point of the F8 transmitting until the MIDI data was received.

`90 = MIDI Note On - Channel 1`

This is standard MIDI coding for a Note On. Although people count MIDI channel numbers from 1 to 16, they are actually transmitted as values from 0 to 15. The channel number is added to 90 to come up with the full Note On command. If you transmit on channel 2, the Note On will be 91 hex.

```
3c = MIDI Note number
```

In this case the middle C key was pressed, which has the note number 3C hex. See Appendix 1 for a full list of note numbers in decimal and hexadecimal.

```
26 = MIDI Note Velocity (loudness)
```

Note velocities can be from 1 to 127 decimal. This was a fairly soft keypress.

This completes the first full receipt of the MIDI message. To cut down the amount of data transmitted to the computer (and make life a little more confusing), the MPU-401 keeps track of the last MIDI command transmitted. If the next command is the same, the MPU-401 does not bother to retransmit it. This is called "running status." In the example Data Trace, the next command turns off the middle C note using a MIDI Note On with key velocity equal to 0. This would normally be transmitted as:

```
Timing Byte     90     3c     0 = velocity
```

With running status, this gets shortened to:

```
Timing Byte     3c     0
```

when the data is transmitted to the computer. Internally, MT adds the running status byte back in and stores the full command. You will see all of the MIDI data in Data Dump.

Allowing for the missing running status bytes, you can follow three notes being turned on and off in the example sequence. Two bytes that do not follow this pattern mark a Measure End:

```
Timing Byte     f9 = MES_END
```

Since we told the MPU-401 we wanted four beats per measure and 120 ticks per beat, the measure end marks will occur every 480 ticks on this track. You can exercise your command of hexadecimal arithmetic by checking the example. (You can also use Sidekick's handy calculator which will do hex math.)

When the user hits a computer key, MT initiates the shutdown of the Record process by sending a STOP_REC command (11 hex). The MPU-401 will respond with a DATA_END mark:

```
Timing Byte     fc = DATA_END
```

When MT gets this message, MT sets off a general "shut down every-thing" set of commands. This includes shutting down the metronome (84 hex), stopping the Play process (05 hex), and clearing the internal MPU-401 Play map (b9 hex).

3.8 Memory Utilization

You may have noticed that when you start up MT, the first screen displays a message:

```
Free memory = 300 K bytes
```

where the number in place of 300 will depend on how much memory you have in your system. During start-up, MT calculates how much memory is available in 10K byte chunks. This is the number reported. MT does not add up all of the little bits of memory that may be available in smaller pieces.

On both the RECORD and MLE screens the Free Memory % is displayed and updated after each command that affects storage. If you experiment with MT, you will find that you can keep adding MIDI data to the point that MT goes not only to 0% free memory, but even to negative values. You will notice that MT becomes very sluggish when the Free Memory % drops below 0.

What happens is that at 0% free memory, all of the big chunks of memory have been used up. To find more, MT's memory allocation functions try to reorganize where things are stored to free up usable sized pieces. This takes time, and explains why MT slows down on editing functions such as Block Paste and Block Repeat when memory is low.

Another problem with operating with low memory is that you may not be able to use the NLE (Note Level Edit) screen. NLE makes a separate note list for the track you are editing. This speeds up note editing, but takes more memory. Only note data is stored for NLE, not controller or MIDI Exclusive messages. Still, you need memory to use NLE.

The moral is, keep an eye on the amount of free memory available. If things are getting too tight, save your tracks to a disk file and then edit down the remaining information. This might amount to breaking a very long song into two halves, or eliminating some tracks during editing. You can always use IMPORT to bring back a saved track after your edits are done.

3.9 End of the Tutorial

This brings us to the end of the description of the MT sequencer. The remainder of the book is devoted to explaining how the program is constructed.

PART 2

Sequencer Design

4

Sequencer Design

Designing a Sequencer Program

This chapter provides an overview of how sequencer programs are designed and constructed. This leads into the specific description of the MT sequencer starting in the next chapter.

4.1 MIDI Timing

Sequencer programs have a lot in common with data base applications. In both cases you store and retrieve data, add and subtract new items, provide editing features, and generally try to hide the complexity of the underlying program from the user.

The big difference with a MIDI sequencer is that data is not just added from the computer keyboard, it also comes into and flows out of the MIDI interface. That data has to not only be correct, it has to appear at the right time. In computer jargon, music is a "real time" application. Timing is the big issue with MIDI data.

MIDI time is measured in "ticks." This is an arbitrary division of one musical beat into smaller increments of time. Different sequencers divide time into different divisions. The MT sequencer uses 120 ticks per beat. Some sequencers allow the user to select the time increment to use, typically ranging from 96 to as high as 800 ticks per beat.

The advantage of using ticks as a time unit over seconds or milliseconds is apparent during playback. As ticks are relative to the tempo of the musical beat, speeding up the beat speeds up all of the MIDI data in proportion. If absolute time in milliseconds were used, speeding up playback would require changing all of the timing data in the entire song file. Absolute time formats are used in applications that need to match music to external real time devices such as film and video.

To keep track of time, MIDI data is preceded by a timing byte. The timing byte is the number of ticks between MIDI events. For example, the sequence of MIDI data:

```
───────────────────── MIDI Message ─────────────────
     35              90              3C              40 (hex)
 Timing Byte      Note On        Middle C        Key Velocity
```

has 35 hex MIDI ticks of time for a timing byte. If the tempo of playback is set to 100 beats per minute, and the sequencer uses 120 ticks per beat resolution, then 1 tick is equivalent to:

$$1 \text{ tick} \times \frac{1 \text{ beat}}{120 \text{ ticks}} \times \frac{1 \text{ minute}}{100 \text{ beats}} \times \frac{60 \text{ seconds}}{1 \text{ minute}} = 0.0050 \text{ seconds}$$

One thing to keep in mind when looking at the internal timing accuracy of the sequencer's MIDI clock is the limitation of the transmission speed used on the MIDI cables. The 31.25 KHz transmission rate specified by the MIDI standard works out to 320 microseconds per byte transmitted. As it takes three bytes to send a Note On (the best possible resolution for two notes, which the sequencer thinks of as occurring at the same time), this will actually result in the notes being separated by about 0.001 seconds. Other MIDI data on the channel will spread things out further.

MIDI information is always made up of bytes (1 byte = 8 bits), so the timing byte could express periods as long as FF hex (256 decimal) ticks. The usual practice is to limit timing bytes to below F0 hex (240 decimal), so that the numbers F0 to FF hex can be used as special

This means that the longest timing duration that a single timing byte can express is 240 ticks, or two musical beats (at 120 ticks per beat).

To express time durations longer than 240 ticks, the MPU-401 uses F8 hex as a "time out" or "timing overflow" message. This just means that 240 ticks went by without any other MIDI data. There can be long stretches of F8s in the MIDI data stream for long rests in the music, or long hold notes (the time between the Note On and Note Off sounding).

4.2 How Timing Data is Generated

The big advantage of the MIDI timing byte approach is that the sequencer program does not have to keep track of when the MIDI data arrived. The timing data is included with the MIDI information.

Somewhere in the system there has to be a clock keeping track of "real" time and generating those timing bytes. In our target system with a Roland MPU-401 or compatible interface, the clock resides in the interface. The MPU-401 internal clock tags each MIDI event it receives with a timing byte before passing it on to the computer. It also generates F8 hex Time Out messages if more than 240 ticks pass without a piece of MIDI data showing up at the interface.

If you end up working with a computer/interface system that does not have an internal clock like the MPU-401, you will need to use the computer's clock. During recording, the clock can be read and used to calculate a timing byte. As the target system for the MT sequencer uses the MPU-401 interface, all further discussion will assume that the timing bytes are generated by the MPU-401.

As a simple example of MIDI timing, imagine that the computer sends the MPU-401 the command to start recording MIDI data. The START_REC command (listed in the file MPU401.H as 22 hex) does this. The MPU-401 clock then starts ticking. If no MIDI data is received, the MPU-401 will send the computer a data stream looking like:

```
        MPU-401 Output in Record Mode
          (No MIDI data received)
F8                    <- Time Out marker
F8
0 F9                  <- Measure End marker, timing byte of 0
F8
F8
0 F9
...
```

The F8 hex values are the Time Outs. The 0 and F9 are a timing byte of 0, and a Measure End marker. These Measure Ends are also generated automatically by the MPU-401. In the default (start-up) mode the MPU-401 uses 120 ticks per beat and four beats per measure. This means that the Measure Ends fall every 4 x 120, or 480 ticks, exactly two Time Outs apart. This explains why the timing bytes for the Measure End markers are zero.[1]

Data received on the MIDI IN port of the MPU-401 is tagged with a timing byte and sent on to the computer. A typical sequence might be:

```
        MPU-401 Data in Record Mode
           (One note received)
F8
F8
0 F9
35 90 3C 64           <- MIDI Note On 35 hex ticks after beat
20 90 3C 00           <- MIDI Note Off (Note Off with velocity = 0)
F8
9B F9                 <- Next measure end, 480 ticks from last one.
```

---

[1] Chapters 10 and 11 of *C Programming for MIDI* (M&T Books, 1988) provide more details on timing bytes and an example program for testing the operation of the MPU-401 interface. The rate at which the MPU-401 sends out F8s depends on the tempo it is set for. The tempo can be adjusted by sending the MPU-401 the SET_TEMPO command (E0 hex) followed by a data byte for the tempo value.

```
F8
F8
0 F9
```

Here our musician has pressed the middle C key and held it for 20 hex ticks. The next Measure End is more than 240 ticks from the time the key is released, so the MPU-401 puts out a Time Out and then the Measure End. The timing bytes, plus 240 for every Time Out, continue to add up to the measure's 480 tick duration.

One additional complication arises from the MPU-401's use of running status. Running status reduces the number of bytes transmitted by not sending duplicate MIDI data. For example, if you are recording a track using MIDI channel 1, all of the Note On bytes will be 90 hex. The MPU-401 will send the first one to the computer, but the second and following ones will be skipped. This will continue until some other MIDI data type is sent, such as a pitch bend byte (E0 hex for channel 1). Here is what happens:

```
                       Running Status Examples


Synth Sends To MPU-401              MPU-401 Sends to Computer

90 3C 40   - first note on.         TB 90 3C 40
90 3C 00   - note off.              TB 3C 00        <- RS
90 3E 40   - second note on.        TB 3E 40        <- RS
E0 10 00   - pitch bend data.       TB E0 10 00
E0 15 10   - second pitch bend byte. TB 15 00       <- RS
90 3E 00   - second note off.       TB 90 3E 00

TB = timing byte, different for each data group.
RS = Running status in this data group.
90 = MIDI NOTE ON, channel 1.
3C = MIDI note number for middle C.
3E = MIDI note number for D.
40 = MIDI key velocity (volume) byte, medium hard keypress.
E0 = MIDI pitch bend on channel 1.
```

As you can see, any time the MIDI data changes, the running status must be updated, so the MPU-401 sends out what it receives. Only on duplicates is the data truncated. MT puts the running status bytes back into the stored data as it is received. This makes it much easier to make sense out of the stored data in memory.

4.3 Playing and Recording MIDI Events

The vertical separation in the two examples shown above between successive hexadecimal codes is not accidental. Each line in the example corresponds to one MIDI "event." Events can be from one to four bytes long. Byte 1 is the timing byte or Time Out marker. The remaining bytes make up the MIDI message. The length of the message is determined from the message type. See Appendix 5 for a full list of MIDI messages and their lengths.

The MIDI event is a basic element in a sequencer design. One event is the smallest meaningful parcel of MIDI data. You can think of a sequencer as a program that manipulates MIDI events.

Recording MIDI data is the process of storing incoming MIDI events into the computer's memory. The data is typically stored in a simple linear sequence in memory, sometimes called an "event list." More commonly, the list is referred to as a "track," making the analogy to a single track on a multi-track tape recorder. This is not a perfect analogy, but the terminology is clear enough for most users.

The data structure for an event will typically contain:

- One timing byte
- Three MIDI data bytes

The event data structure may also contain pointers to the next event in the event list.

There are a number of ways to store MIDI event data in memory. The technique of storing each event separately as it is received (as MT does), is the simplest method, but uses more memory than other techniques. Periods recorded when no MIDI data is received end up being long chains of events holding only F8 hex Time Out markers. These can be replaced in memory with a single (larger) numeric value to save space. Going further, timing can be expressed internally in other formats, such as relative to the measure and/or bar number. Note On/Off pairs can be combined in memory by storing the note duration rather than two separate Note On/Note Off events.

These options amount to a tradeoff between the efficiency of the storage format and the simplicity of the code for storing and playing back the data. As we will see in the next section, storage formats optimized for playing and recording may not be ideal for editing of the data.

Playing back the MIDI data is simply a matter of sending the MIDI events back to the MPU-401 interface in the right order. When the MPU-401 is in the Play mode, it requests MIDI data one event at a time from the computer. The first byte of the event is the timing byte (or Time Out). The MPU-401 waits that many ticks before sending the data out the MIDI OUT port (without the timing byte) and then requests the next event from the computer. This goes on until the computer sends an event with the DATA_END marker (FC hex). This lets the MPU-401 know that the Play process is over.

During playback periods when there is no MIDI activity, the sequencer must send F8 hex Time Out markers to the MPU-401 so that the interface can continue to keep time. This is simply a matter of sending back the Time Out markers that were recorded if the data is stored in a simple event list (like MT). More complex data storage formats require generating new Time Out markers in the playback logic to cover MIDI idle periods.

The MPU-401 can handle up to eight independent tracks of data in its internal logic. The MPU-401 will request data from the computer for each track individually using the Request Track Data codes F0 to F7 hex (for tracks 1 to 8, respectively). This is how the MT sequencer handles eight tracks. Using the internal MPU-401 tracks allows the interface to request ahead of time. This improves playback timing accuracy, particularly if a slow computer is supplying the MIDI data.

Many sequencer's ignore this feature of the MPU-401 and send all of the data to be played to one of the MPU-401 tracks (the "monster track" approach). Internal to the sequencer program, the transmitted data may reflect separate MIDI channels and instruments (tracks), but all of the data is requested by the MPU-401 in one data stream.

The most basic part of a sequencer program is the code for recording and playing back MIDI event lists. Recording is the process of adding new events to the end of an event list.

Figure 4.1 Generic Record Function Organization

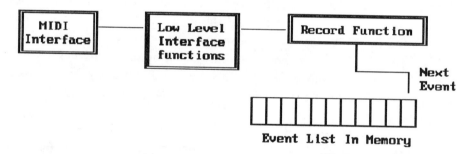

The low-level interface functions are normally written in assembly language. In MT, these are in the file MIO401.ASM. These pass data to and from the MIDI interface much the same way the C library functions *getchar()* and *putchar()* send and receive character data from the computer keyboard and screen.

There are two basic types of MIDI interface functions. MIO401.ASM contains "polling" functions. When called, these functions wait for MIDI data to show up. The program just loops until some MIDI data shows up or the process is halted, usually by the user hitting a computer key.

The alternative method is to use interrupt-driven interface functions. The MIDI interface will trip a computer interrupt when it receives a MIDI signal (the MPU-401 uses IRQ2). Program execution is passed to a short routine that responds to the interface signal before returning execution to whatever the main program was doing prior to the interrupt.

Interrupt-driven interfacing has the advantage of allowing the program to appear to do two things at once. For example, the user could change the MIDI volume on a track during playback, rather than having to stop the Play process to make a change. Again this amounts to a tradeoff between the complexity of the program and its power. MT uses the simpler polling functions [1]

Figure 4.2 Recording More Than One Track

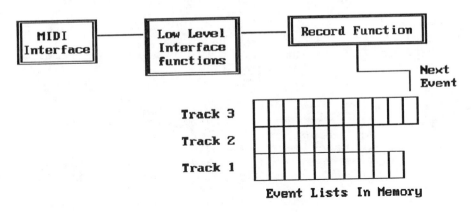

The Record function looks at the incoming bytes of data and breaks them into events. Each new event is then added to the end of the event list in memory.

---

[1] If you are interested in interrupt-driven functions on the IBM PC family, you will need to get the IBM technical reference manual for a description of communication with the interrupt controller via ports 20 and 21 hex. An example interrupt-driven C program is available on the MIDI Compuserve forum library (GO MIDI).

With one track of data recorded, the musician can now record a second instrument as a new track. Each new track recorded forms a separate event list in memory.

Only one track is recorded at a time. The tracks will have different lengths depending on the amount of MIDI data recorded on each one. Note that even a track that is recorded without any MIDI activity will contain Time Out and Measure End events.

During playback, the MIDI interface will request new data one event at a time. The Play function finds the events in the event lists and passes each event back to the the MIDI interface via the low level interface functions. Recording one track and playing back multiple tracks can be done simultaneously.

Figure 4.3 Recording and Playing Back Tracks

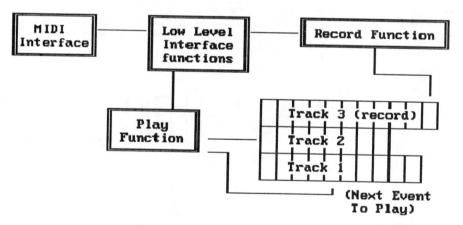

Figure 4.3 is an outline of the simplest sequencer program with only Play and Record functions. Any real program will also need to store and recall the track data from disk files. This is fairly simple, so I will not add it to the basic diagram.

The next step is to allow the event data in memory to be edited from the computer keyboard to fix mistakes, add new notes and so on.

4.4 Event Data Display Formats

The simplest form of event editing is to allow the user to directly edit the event data in either hexadecimal or decimal form. This is tedious for most applications, although it does have uses for experienced MIDI users. The MT sequencer will display the event data for all eight tracks (the Data Dump command), but does not allow direct editing.

The next, and perhaps most tempting way to display the event data is to convert it to conventional musical notation and allow the notation to be edited. This has the big advantage of displaying the data in a form that is understood by any trained musician. Screen images can be dumped to a graphics printer and immediately used. The notation format is also very compact. The drawbacks are:

1) Recorded event data tends not to be played exactly on the beat. As a result, when transcribed literally into musical notation, there tend to be a lot of odd-length notes, 64th rests, and other oddities. Even carefully played music ends up looking very different when directly converted. With a lot of smart programming, the screen can be cleaned up automatically, but at the cost of not displaying the actual event data correctly.

2) When you look at music notation from a programmer's point of view, all sorts of arbitrary aspects pop out that most musicians have long since forgotten. For example, the staffs are really set up for an eight note scale. The accidentals are added in via sharps and flats, which only exist for some notes. Even the positions on the staff are not evenly separated in pitch. Some transitions are a half step, some a full step.

These oddities in musical notation are due to the way in which notation was developed in the middle ages in Europe. All trained musicians quickly get used to it and take it for granted. For the programmer, these aspects complicate display and editing functions considerably. Although it can be done (Personal Composer is an outstanding example), the complexity of music notation makes its use an artificial intelligence application.

The third, and most common means of displaying event data, is to plot the MIDI "notes" on a time versus pitch plot on the screen. Usually pitch is the vertical axis and time is the horizontal. To orient the user, a piano keyboard is displayed on the left side to represent pitch divisions. Time is measured in MIDI ticks and broken down into measure and beat divisions.

On this type of display, the notes appear as horizontal lines. With the keyboard image on the left, the display ends up looking a lot like a player piano scroll. This has lead to the the common name for the image as a "piano roll" display. This is what the MT Note Level Editor uses.

Although the piano roll display is not as universal as music notation, it is quickly understood by users. It is also fairly simple to deal with for the programmer and lends itself to mouse-based "pointing" operations for adding and deleting notes.

There are some other event editing formats in use which are less common. Several sequencers provide an interface similar to a drum machine front panel. These sequencers are excellent for music that is repetitive, such as pop music, where the bass or drum lines follow a pattern that repeats, changes, and then reappears. (The MT sequencer addresses these applications by providing editing functions that operate at the measure level.)

The bottom line is that there is no single "best" method of displaying MIDI event data. Pick the format that suits the applications and users you are targeting.

4.5 Data Format for Editing

In the MIDI language, a musical note is composed of two events: one Note One, and one Note Off. Musicians think of a note as a single entity, one note with a given duration. This distinction is critical when it comes to editing event data. The user wants to add one note, not one Note On and one Note Off.

The event list data format mentioned above for recording and playing back MIDI data does not lend itself to editing data. There is no direct tie in the event list linking a Note On to a Note Off. You can always find the matching Note Off by tracing on in the event list until there is a match. This is a slow process if it has to be done every time a note is displayed, added, deleted, or modified.

To deal with this problem, many sequencers use a data format that stores the Note On/Note Off pairs together as a single entity. This is sometimes called the "single point" format. The data structure would contain something similar to:

- MIDI note number
- MIDI key velocity (loudness)
- Timing byte of Note On
- Duration of note

This type of data structure can be used instead of the simple event list to store all of the tracks of MIDI data. This is great for editing, and also saves space in memory, compared with the event list format. Unfortunately, the single point format makes recording and playback more complicated, as the data has to be decoded back to event format for those processes. Working with the other types of MIDI messages (pitch bend, controller, channel messages, etc.) also complicates things.

A compromise between using only the event format, or only the single point format, is to use both in the same sequencer. The event format works fine for recording, playing, and global editing functions. The single point format is used for note editing. After the edits are complete, the changes are written back to the event lists for playback and disk storage.

Typically, only one track is edited at the note level at any one time. This means that only one track needs to be translated into the single point format at any given time. If another track is to be edited, the memory used for the first edit session is freed, leaving room for the next track's edit data.

Our generic sequencer looks similar to Figure 4.4 with editing functions added in.

Figure 4.4   Adding Editing Functions

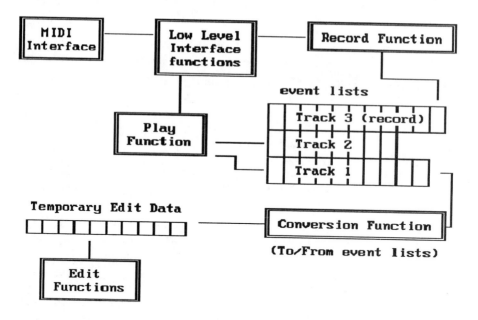

The MT sequencer follows the organization in Figure 4.4. MT uses both MIDI data representations. The event list format is used for everything except the Note Level Edit functions. When NLE is entered, the track to be edited is converted to a single point representation. This temporary data is freed from memory as soon as the NLE session is exited. More on this in Chapter 10.

4.6 Linked Lists

So far, we have just talked in general about storing event data in memory. Deciding the storage method and format is a key design decision for any sequencer. I will describe the method used by the MT sequencer here, and leave discussion of alternate formats for Chapter 12.

MT uses linked lists in memory to store recorded MIDI data, for note lists used by the Note Level Editor, and for screen images. The concept of a linked list is powerful, and can be applied to many programming problems. *The C Programming Language* by Kernighan and Ritchie includes a discussion of the subject and an example using a binary tree sorting algorithm.

As an example, consider the problem of storing a series of text lines in memory. The program does not know in advance how many lines there will be, or how many characters in each line. A brute force approach would be to set aside a large memory area and hope it is big enough. Another approach is to allocate a small memory area and keep enlarging it as needed.

The linked list approach is more elegant. The basic concept is to add each new line of text to the end of a chain in memory. To keep track of the chain's links we create a structure that has two pointers. One pointer points to the next link in the chain and the second pointer points to memory allocated for one text line.

This diagram shows how MT stores screen image data in memory. The screen files are read one line at a time from the disk. Each time a new line is added, the memory allocation function has to be called twice.

Once to allocate memory for the pointer structure, and a second time to allocate enough memory to hold the text line being stored.

Figure 4.5 A Linked List for Storing Text Lines

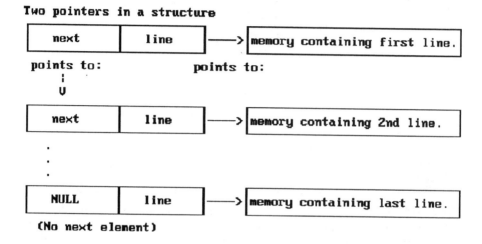

The data in a linked list is stored wherever the memory allocation function *malloc()* decides to put things. These physical addresses can all be scrambled in memory with no ill effects. The linked list keeps track of the order via the *next* pointers.

The advantage of the linked list over conventional memory structures such as arrays, is that the linked list makes no assumptions about how much data will be stored. Adding data to the middle of a list (insertion) is also simple. All you do is change an existing pointer in the list to point to the new node, and have the new node point back to the next link in the chain.

Adding the new node does not require moving any of the existing elements in the chain. The new node's address in memory is determined by the memory allocation function (*malloc()* in C). The *next* pointer in the element before the added node has its address changed to point to wherever the added node was placed in memory. The added node's *next* pointer is set to point back to the chain.

Figure 4.6 Adding Data to a Linked List

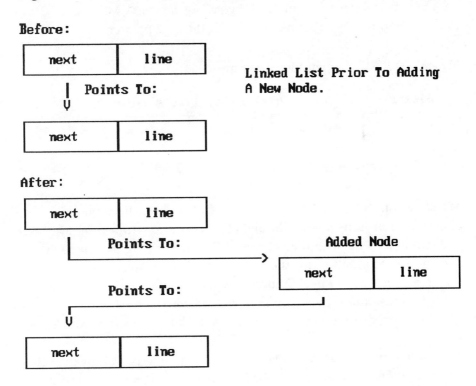

This ability to add and subtract elements without physically moving the other data items in memory makes linked lists useful in applications where the data will be changed frequently. Linked lists also work well when the size of each data item is variable.

The disadvantages of linked lists are the memory consumed by the pointers themselves, and the inability to find an element without going to the front of the list and working forward. The latter problem can be addressed by maintaining a second linked list as an index to the first. Pointers in the second list might point to every hundredth element in the primary list. MT does not use index files.

In storing MIDI events, the amount of the MIDI data for each event is known to be between one and four bytes. Each event's MIDI data bytes can be stored in one structure along with the *next* pointer.

Figure 4.7 A MIDI Event List Structure

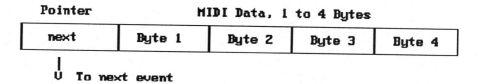

MT stores incoming MIDI event data in linked lists. Each new node is allocated as it is needed. The memory allocation functions are fast enough to keep up with the pace of MIDI data coming in. These event lists are the foundation for the Record, Play, and Measure Level Edit functions. For Note Level Editing, a separate (temporary) linked list of notes in single point data format is created for the track being edited. This list is freed from memory as soon as the NLE session is exited.

The event structure used in MT has one more byte per event than the structure shown in Figure 4.7. The extra byte (called *nbytes*) keeps track of how many of the four MIDI data bytes are used in any specific event. For example, an event consisting of just a Time Out marker (F8 hex) would only use one data byte. A MIDI Note On would use four. More on this in Chapter 6.

4.7 User Interface

One of the most important determinants of any program's commercial success is what it looks like on the screen. There are a lot of different approaches to take, including full screen menus, pull-down and pop-up menus, icons, graphics-based interfaces, etc.

MT uses the full screen menu approach almost exclusively. The basic concepts here are:

- All of the commands available from a screen are visible. The user does not have to remember key combinations or which function key to hit.

- Selection of a menu item is always by hitting the Return key. Deselection (escaping or quitting) is always via the ESC key. If a mouse is used, the left button selects and the right button deselects.

- User input is always prompted for at the bottom of the screen. Input can be aborted (deselected) by hitting the ESC key at any point during input. Range checking is immediate.

- Error and warning messages always appear at the bottom of the screen.

- Where the same or similar commands appear on different menus, they appear in the same order, position, and name.

This amounts to a simple, but consistent user interface. Pull down menus were not necessary in MT as all of the commands used fit on the screens without much cramming. If you add features to MT, you may find pull down menus preferable to adding more menu screens.

With the exception of the Note Level Edit screen, all of the screens in MT use the Character mode (not graphics). This improves the speed of screen updates, but limits the use of graphics; for icons, etc. The newer AT, and faster types of computers, have enough power to completely support graphics based programs. Requiring AT power greatly limits the potential market, as most users still have the basic PC and PC XT models.

The several video "standards" for the IBM PC world can pose a programming problem. MT deals with this by using an external INSTALL program that lets the user select what type of video equipment and screen colors he or she wishes to use. This data is written to a file that MT (or any other program) can read. This frees MT from having to include the video selection commands, which are normally only used the first time the program is used.

4.8 On to the Code

This completes the outline of a basic MIDI sequencer/editor program. The next chapter begins the detailed description of the MT program.

PART 3

Documentation of the MT Sequencer

5

Documentation of the MT Sequencer

Introduction to Program Documentation

This chapter begins the documentation of MT's nineteen program files. Techniques common to all of the program files are discussed, along with the mouse menu definition.

5.1 Compiler Considerations

C is a well standardized language, so the exact compiler used is not critical. Both Microsoft's C compiler version 5.1 and Borland's Turbo C version 2.1 were used to create and test MT. The minor differences between the two are handled in the source code with conditionals. If the word TURBOC is defined, the Turbo C code is compiled. Otherwise, the default (Microsoft) code gets compiled.

The one area where there is not complete standardization is in the functions added to allow control of the video display. Both Microsoft and Turbo compilers come with library functions to handle the display, but both versions are different.

To minimize the impact of the incompatibility, the low-level video functions are in one file called VIDEOFNC.C. This file contains the most TURBOC #defines, because all of the functions are video related. Once this file is compiled, the remaining files use the VIDEOFNC.C functions, rather than the raw compiler library versions. This also means that you only have to work over the VIDEOFNC.C functions if you change compilers.

If you are using a compiler that does not have a graphics function library, you can make your own using the assembly language/BIOS approach described in *C Programming for MIDI*.

MT takes advantage of function prototyping and the void data type, relatively recent additions to the C language. Function prototypes are all stored in the file MTDECLAR.H. Including this file at the top of every source code module allows the compiler to check to make sure that every reference to the function has the right parameter types passed to it.

```
/* function prototype - new style */
void getc_from_file(char *addr, int size, FILE *stream);
```

If your compiler does not support full prototyping, don't include the MTDECLAR.H file. Even without prototyping you will need to declare all functions with a returned type other than integer before they are used:

```
/* function declaration - old style */
long get_event_count();
```

If the void data type is not supported by your compiler, just delete the word *void* throughout the source code files. The void functions will be upgraded to integer functions, with minor impact on the performance of the program. Four functions [*get_from_file(), fget_from_file(), put_to_file(), fput_to_file()*] use the void data type as a parameter. For these functions substitute *char* for *void*. The functions will work equally well, but will generate compiler warning messages when used to store and recall data with other than the char data type. This is discussed in more detail in Chapter 11.

MT compiles to about 90K of .EXE file when complete. This is above the 64K maximum for the Small memory model. You should use the Medium memory model for all MT compiles. The only direct reference to memory models in the program code is in the MIO401.ASM code. To link properly to the C code, assembly language functions need to know which memory model is going to be used. Once assembled to make MIO401.OBJ (supplied on the source code disk), these functions will link with C programs compiled with the Medium memory model.

As we will see later, the choice of the Medium memory model (as compared to the Large or Huge models) does not limit the storage of note data to a 64K maximum. MT will use all available memory, up to 640K, in storing note data.

All pointers to note data are forced to *far* pointers (four bytes long) explicitly in the program code. The advantage of this technique is that only the note data addresses are four bytes long. All of the other variables are *near* pointers (two bytes long). This saves space and speeds execution times. The only disadvantage is that it forces the programmer to keep track of the couple of data types that are always *far*. More on this in the discussion of recording, playing, and editing of MIDI data.

5.2 Global Variables

In general, I try to avoid using global variables. Globals tend to make functions less portable, as you have to define the same names each time for all global variables referenced inside the function. On the other hand, globals are efficient, as you can reference them from within a function without having to pass the global value to the function as a *parameter* (the values within the parentheses following a function name are the parameters).

As the projects get bigger, the need for globals increases. Variables that are used in a large number of functions, such as video attributes, are good candidates for globals. Otherwise, you will have to put these values in the parameter heading for every function that uses them.

To make the global variables obvious, I precede each of their names with a *g_*. For example, *g_first_measure* is a global variable, while *first_measure* is not. This way you avoid the trap of using a global variable as a local variable within a function.

Another problem with globals is how to reference them in both the root module and dependent modules of the program. For example, in a program with two files that are separately compiled and then linked to produce the complete executable program, you would need the following lines to define the global variable to each module:

```
The Root Module File

int g_first_measure = 0;          /* allocates storage for one int */
main()
{
.....
}


The Second Module File

extern int g_first_measure;    /* tells compiler that variable is
                                  defined elsewhere */

functions()
```

Only the declaration in the root module allocates storage. The *extern* reference in all dependent modules lets the compiler know that the address of the variable will be specified by some other module at link time.

To avoid having to remember to put an extern at the top of each program file that uses the global variable, all of them are put in a header file. For MT this file is called MT.H. The `extern` references are automated by use of a conditional definition:

```
#ifdef ALLOCATE
    #define GLOBAL                  /* ...to nothing */
    #define INIT(x)    =x
#else
    #define GLOBAL     extern
    #define INIT(x)                 /* ...to nothing */
#endif
```

In the header file, all global variables are defined with a line that looks like:

```
GLOBAL int g_first_measure INIT(1);
```

Only the root module (MT.C) has the word ALLOCATE defined with the line:

```
#define ALLOCATE
```

All of the dependent module files lack this line. As a result, when the compiler sees the word GLOBAL in the root module, it is replaced with nothing, and the word INIT(1) is replaced with =1. This gives us the desired result of the line:

```
int g_first_measure =1;
```

The compiler allocates room for one int with the symbol name *g_first_measure* and initializes the variable to 1. In all of the dependent modules, the word ALLOCATE is not defined, so the exact same line in the header file gets expanded to:

```
extern int g_first_measure;
```

Look at the MT.H and VIDEO.H file listings for examples of these programming tricks.

5.3 Program File Naming Conventions

The full MT program consists of nineteen separate C program files (and a number of header files) that are separately compiled and then linked together. MT's individual program files are small (below 15K bytes in size), so that compiling after a change is fast. Small files also make editing faster.

The MT files are named in a reasonably consistent fashion:

`MT.C`

The central module. Contains *main()*. Initializes variables on startup and then controls overall program execution.

`MTRC1.C, MTRC2.C, MTRC3.C, MTRC4.C`

These contain the code for the 8-track MIDI recorder. MTRC1.C contains the menu control functions for the RECORD screen.

`MTED1.C, MTED2.C, MTED3.C`

The MLE (Measure Level Edit) functions that do the work are in these three files. MTED1.C does MLE screen control. MTED2.C and MTED3.C contain the functions for pasting, merging, and copying measures of data.

`MTSC1.C, MTSC2.C, MTSC3.C, MTSC4.C`

The NLE (Note Level Edit) functions are in these four files. MTSC1.C controls the menu functions. MTSC2.C, MTSC3.C, and MTSC5.C contain functions for building note lists and editing them.

`MTUT1.C, MTUT2.C, FILEFUNC.C`

These are utility functions, primarily for saving and recalling song file data. FILEFUNC.C contains general purpose file functions that are used in MT, but not specific to this application. MTUT1.C has the specific save and recall song functions. MTUT2.C controls the track import activities.

VIDEOFNC.C, WRITSCRN.C, CHAIN.C, INPUTF.C (SCREENF.LIB)

General purpose functions for controlling the video display. VIDE-OFNC.C has the lowest-level commands for drawing lines, writing words on the screen, etc. CHAIN.C has functions for loading and displaying screen files. It also has the fast console output functions that work by writing directly to the video memory. WRITSCRN.C contains the menu selection functions. INPUTF.C contains functions for getting user input of integers, floating point numbers, and character strings.

These four files are combined using the LIB program to make the SCREENF.LIB library file. This library is useful as a starting point for almost any large program development effort.

MIO401.ASM

The only assembly language file used in MT. The three functions in this module handle the lowest-level communication chores with the Roland MPU-401 interface. This file is set up to mesh with Medium and Large memory model C programs. It can be easily modified if you wish to use the Small memory model on a smaller project. An already assembled MIO401.OBJ file is included on the source code disk for those who do not want to use an assembler but need the MIDI interface functions.

In addition to the MT source code files, there are also five separate C program files for other purposes.

INSTALL.C

This is the general purpose installation program that allows the user to choose video modes and colors. INSTALL writes the data to a file called INSTALL.DAT (or another file name specified on the DOS command line). MT reads INSTALL.DAT every time it starts up.

BULDMENU.C

BULDMENU.C reads in a screen file and outputs a menu definition file in the form of an array of elements of type *selement*. This is how the menus in MTSCREEN.H were created. BULDMENU.C is discussed in Chapter 7.

MAKESONG.C

This is a simple demo program that writes a song with random note numbers centered on middle C. Although of no musical value, the file does provide a starting point for people interested in computer composition. The output of MAKESONG.C is a .SNG file that can be played and edited by MT.

MF_TO_MT.C

A separate program that converts from Standard MIDI Files 1.0 format to MT's .SNG format. This is handy for importing files from other sequencers and computers. The Small memory model is used, and total output file size is limited to 60K.

MT_TO_MF.C

A separate program for converting MT's .SNG files to Standard MIDI Files 1.0 format. The Small memory model is used. Individual tracks are limited to 30K of memory.

See Chapter 12 for details on usage of these conversion programs.

5.4 Header Files

The larger the program, the more important header files become. MT uses header files to define global variables and structures, to store screen menu data, and to provide readable names for the commands used by the MPU-401 interface and the video hardware. As discussed in Section 5.2, the same header file can be used to both define and reference global variables by use of the ALLOCATE definitions. This technique is used for both the video data global variables and the globals specific to MT.

STANDARD.H

This file defines names for common key codes used on the IBM PC family of computers. Examples are the function keys, arrow keys, ESC, etc. Besides making the code readable, these definitions make the program more portable. If you switch to another computer, changing this header file's numeric assignments will change the value associated with the arrow keys, etc., for every program compiled.

Note that function keys are not used in any part of MT. This is a personal preference. Function keys force the user to remember or look up key assignments. In MT, all of the commands available from any screen are visible on the screen.

SCREENF.H

This header file should be included any time the SCREENF.LIB function library is used for video and menu functions. The header file defines the structures used by the CHAIN.C and sprite functions. It also defines a couple of common video attributes for black and white characters. These are handy during startup of a program, before the video attribute data has been read. Function prototypes for all SCREENF.LIB functions are listed at the end of SCREENF.H.

MPU401.H

The MPU-401 interface has such a long list of commands and messages that they are difficult to remember in raw hexadecimal form. This header file defines an easier to remember name for each command/message.

VIDEO.H

This header file should be included in any file that makes use of video data stored by the INSTALL program. It defines the global variables used for the current video mode, attributes, screen width, height, and number of colors. The ALLOCATE #define "trick" is used to allow VIDEO.H to both define the globals in the *main()* module, and reference the globals in all other modules.

FILEFUNC.H

Include this header if you use FILEFUNC.C. It contains the menu data for displaying and selecting files.

MT.H

This is the main header file for MT's programs. Included are the definitions of a number of constants, global variables, and structures used throughout MT. At the end of the file is another #include command which references the file MTSCREEN.H. This is where the menu definitions for all MT screens are kept. It was made into a separate file just to keep the size of MT.H under control.

MTSCREEN.H

Menu definitions in the form of arrays of structures are stored here (Chapter 11 explains how menus are defined). The menu data was created with the BULDMENU.C program for each screen file. MTSCREEN.H is #included from within MT.H. Note that the external references to the arrays are at the bottom of MT.H while the actual data is in the MTSCREEN.H file.

MTDECLAR.H

This file has all of the function prototypes for every function in every module of MT. Defining the function type and the type of each parameter passed to the function helps eliminate the common programming error of passing the wrong type of data to/from a function.

MTSC.H

The NLE (Note Level Edit) screen uses sprites to make a cross shaped cursor and an M on the middle C key. These sprite definitions are in

MTSC.H. This file also has the structure data for *g_notes[]*, an array that allows MT to quickly figure out the location and name of each MIDI note on the screen. Again the ALLOCATE define is used to allow MTSC.H to both allocate and reference global variables.

5.5 Mouse Support

MT was designed from the start as a mouse-driven program. This is evident when you try to run the program without a mouse. Moving the cursor on the editing screens is much slower without a mouse.

All mouse activities start with loading the mouse driver. Microsoft and Logitech's mouse drivers are called MOUSE.COM. This program loads itself into memory and interprets mouse movement and mouse keys being pressed or released.

There are two ways to approach mouse support in a program. One is to "hard code" the mouse functions into the program. The 30 mouse functions use the CPU registers to interpret what the mouse is doing and move the cursor. Microsoft sells a programmer's reference guide to their mouse separately from the mouse hardware. This book contains examples and a full description of each function for several languages.

A simpler way to deal with the mouse is to let it emulate the cursor keys on the keyboard. This way, the programmer writes a program that will function without the mouse (vital in the PC world). If a mouse is available, the mouse "pretends" to be cursor keys, "fooling" the program. The mouse buttons can emulate the Return and ESC keys as well.

All mice come with a default mouse driver program that works along these lines. You may find that the default driver works fine with MT. If you want to create your own custom driver, read on. The examples are specific to the Microsoft mouse and software compatibles such as Logitech's.

The conversion of mouse movements to equivalent computer key presses is handled by loading a second program into memory—a mouse menu. The mouse menu is first defined in a simple mouse menu language. Here is the code for MT's menu definition for the Microsoft or Logitech mouse:

```
Mouse Menu Definition File - SIMPMOUS.DEF

Simple mouse menu functions to map arrow keys and ESC, Enter
and Del.; left mouse key is Enter, right (or both keys) is
Escape.

begin ent, es, both, lf, rt, up, dn, 32, 16

ent:        type enter
es:         type esc
both:       type esc
lf:         type 0, 75
rt:         type 0, 77
up:         type 0, 72
dn:         type 0, 80
```

With the Logitech three-button mouse, both the center and right buttons simulate hitting the ESC key with this menu.

This file is created with a text editor. The file name should have the suffix .DEF. The *begin* statement is followed by symbol names in the order left button, right button, both buttons, left movement, right movement, up movement, down movement, horizontal sensitivity, vertical sensitivity. Below this, each symbol is assigned to output ("type") a keyboard code. For example, the symbol ent is used for the left mouse button. It is mapped to the enter key. The arrow keys have a two-byte code on the IBM PC keyboard, the first byte being a zero.

Keycode 0, 75 is generated by pressing the left arrow key. This menu sends the identical code for a leftward mouse movement.

The menu definition file is converted to an executable menu file by the mouse menu compiler. Microsoft calls theirs MAKEMENU. Logitech calls theirs NEWMENU. Both read in the definition file and output a menu control file.

With a menu defined, getting the mouse menu activated is a two step process. First, the MOUSE.COM driver must be loaded into memory. Second, the mouse menu must be loaded into memory using the MENU.COM program. From DOS this looks like:

```
C:>MOUSE
C:>MENU SIMPMOUS
```

These commands are normally put in a batch file. When the program is done, the menu can be removed from memory with the command:

```
C:>MENU OFF
```

This leaves the basic mouse driver in memory, but removes the menu definition. Another menu definition can be loaded for the next program.

Mouse menus can be made much more complicated than the simple driver used for MT. Pop-up windows with cursor-selected commands are fairly simple to create and load into memory. I have not found this to be very useful. Programs for IBM PCs need to work without the mouse.

6

MT's 8-Track MIDI Recorder

This chapter describes the C functions that make up the MIDI record/playback operations of MT. The *main()* function in MT.C is also documented in this chapter.

6.1 Documentation Practices

The documentation is organized on a top-down basis. The highest-level functions are described first. Later chapters describe lower-level functions for screen displays, menu control, etc.

There are three levels of program documentation:

1) An overview of the purpose of the functions within each group of source code files at the beginning of the chapter. This will include a discussion of any unusual data types used, global variables, and header files.

2) A function-by-function description of each function in MT. These use the format:

   - Function type, name, and parameter list
   - Purpose
   - In File
   - Related Header Files
   - Returned Value
   - Discussion

   These descriptions are meant primarily for reference when you are reviewing the program code. Do not try to read each function description from first to last—they are dry reading. Use them later when you want to dig into the operation of a specific function.

3) Source code listings of all files and functions are in Part 3 of the book.

6.2 Data Structures for MIDI Data

MT stores recorded MIDI data in linked lists. Each link in the chain is a structure of type *event* defined in the file MT.H.

```
struct event{
    struct event far *next;
    unsigned char nbytes;
    unsigned char b[4];
};
```

Each next event in the list is found from the pointer *next*. Note that it is a *far* pointer, meaning that the address will be outside of the *near* memory area. This allows MT to use up to the full 640K of memory for storing MIDI data. The parameter nbytes is set to the number of bytes stored in any given event. The actual MIDI data is put into bytes labeled b[0] through b[3].

In most cases, the first byte (b[0]) will be a timing byte with a value less than 240. 240 is as high as the MPU-401 can count. If more than 240 ticks pass without receiving data, the MPU-401 sends out a TIME_OUT (F8 hex) byte and starts counting again at zero.

The leading timing byte determines how long the event will be stored in the MPU-401's track counter before it is sent. The MPU-401 will request the next event's MIDI data as soon as it sends the last group to its MIDI OUT port. The MPU-401 stays one event ahead by always keeping its active track counters supplied with data.

MT has eight tracks of data. The array *g_trackarray[]* holds each track's key parameters. Each element of *g_trackarray[]* is a structure:

```
struct trackdata {
    char name[TRACK_NAME_WIDE];
    int  midichan;
    long numevents;
    int  active;
    int  midivol;
    struct event far *first;
    struct event far *current;
    struct event far *last;
};

struct trackdata g_trackarray[8];
```

The *trackdata* structure holds the name, MIDI channel number, volume setting, active (play) status, and the number of events stored. In addition, each trackdata structure holds pointers to the first event, current event, and last event in each track's linked list of events.

As an example of how this works; to find the first byte of MIDI data on track 2:

```
data = g_trackarray[1].first->b[0];
```

Tracks are numbered internally from 0 to 7, not the 1 to 8 shown on the screen displays. This is why track 2 is shown with array reference [1]. The "first" pointer points to the start of the linked list of events. As it points to a structure event, we can use the indirection operator (->) to fetch the contents of the first byte of MIDI data, b[0]. The next byte is b[1], and so on, up to b[3].

The first byte in the second event can be referenced as:

```
data = g_trackarray[1].first->next->b[0];
```

In practice, this awkward notation is not used. The location of the next event is stored to a temporary variable:

```
struct event far *ep;

ep = g_trackarray[1].first;   /* ep points to first event*/
ep = ep->next;                /* ep points to second event*/
data = ep->b[0];              /* now read the data byte */
```

This may seem a little involved, but the payoff is easy access to the track data. *G_trackarray[]* is a global entity, so it can be referenced from within any function in MT. With this one variable name, all of the track data is accessible. Of course, to find a specific event it is frequently necessary to move from the start to the end of the linked list of events until the desired one is found.

As a programming convenience, MT starts each track with one event: a Measure End mark with a 0 timing byte. When MT starts up the first, current, and last pointers for each track, all point to the track's first event. As the track gets data, the pointers are updated.

6.3 Buffered Input/Output from the Interface

During both recording and playback, MIDI data is going both from the computer to the MPU-401 interface, and from the interface to the computer. This opens up the possibility of a data collision. To avoid this, MT uses a *data buffer*. Any data that is read during a period when MT is trying to send a command is placed on the buffer. The buffer is then read before any new data is fetched from the interface.

The functions that accomplish data buffering are in the file MTRC4.C. The buffer is a global array called *cmdbuf[]*. Figure 6.1 is a diagram of how the functions work around the buffer:

Figure 6.1 Block Diagram of RECORD.C Data Buffering

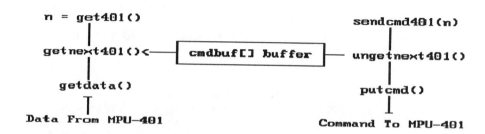

Getdata() and *putcmd()* are the assembly language functions described in IO401.ASM.

From a programmer's point of view, only the *get401()* and *send-cmd401()* functions are used directly. The rest are internal workings.

Once the MPU-401 has accepted a command from *sendcmd401()*, it will not send any additional requests for data to the computer until the interface has received the right number of data bytes. Transmission of data is, therefore, not buffered. The command *putdata401()* sends the data directly using the assembly language function *putdata()*.

If you look over the source code for these functions you will note that several of them print out the value of the data they are sending or receiving if the global variable *g_trace_on* is set non-zero. This is how the Trace command described in Chapter 3 is implemented.

6.4 Playing MIDI Data

Playing back recorded MIDI data is simpler than recording it, so I will describe the Play process first. The basic steps involved are:

1) Turn on the appropriate track counters in the MPU-401. The MPU-401 has eight internal track counters. Each holds the next MIDI command to be sent. In MT, each of the eight tracks corresponds to one track counter in the MPU-401. To turn on certain tracks, MT sends the command ACT_TRACK (EC hex), followed by a bit-mapped byte. This second byte has 1s for ON tracks and 0s for OFF tracks. The least significant bit is for the first track. For example, 00000101 (05 hex) would turn on tracks 1 and 3.

2) Turn the Play process on by issuing the START_PLAY (0A hex) command. As soon as START_PLAY is received, the MPU-401 will start requesting data for all active tracks. Each track counter has its own track request command, REQ_T1 (F0 hex) for the first track, REQ_T2 (F1 hex) for the second, etc.

3) Respond to track requests by sending the next event's MIDI data to the MPU-410. The number of bytes to send is stored in the nbytes parameter for each event.

4) The Play process will continue with alternating requests and transmittal of MIDI data until a track runs out of data. The last track event will contain an ALL_END (FC hex) byte. The MPU-401 will shut down this track once it receives an ALL_END.

   (Use the Data Dump command to look at the end of a track's data. The last line of data on each track will contain two bytes, a timing byte and an ALL_END byte (FC hex).)

5) When all of the active tracks are shut down, the MPU-401 will send an ALL_END message back to the computer. This marks the completion of playback of a song. The MPU-401 keeps track of all notes turned on on all MIDI channels. Any notes left on will be turned off right before the ALL_END is transmitted.

MT also allows the user to interrupt the Play process by hitting ESC or SPACEBAR on the computer's keyboard. To get an orderly shutdown of the Play process requires that the program shut down each track individually. Otherwise, notes may be left on.

MT keeps the Current Measure Number display up to date during the Play process. As all the active tracks have MEAS_END marks stored in their event data, only one track is followed to update the measure number. This is the highest numbered active track. The highest active track is updated as tracks are shut down (run out of data).

The *play()* function in MTRC2.C is the center of activity during the Play process. *Play()* has eight pointers to each track's data in *ep[]*. The pointers are initialized to point to the first events in the current measure by the function *init_401()*. *Init_401()* also calculates and returns the bit-mapped byte for the active tracks and sends out all of the commands necessary to put the MPU-401 in the Play mode with the right tempo, meter, etc.

Actual output of MIDI note data is accomplished by the *play_event()* function in MTRC3.C. This function scales the MIDI key velocity value:

$$\text{Old velocity value} \times \frac{\text{Track Volume}}{100} = \text{New velocity value}$$

The calculation is only done if one of the track volume settings (on the RECORD menu) is set to a value other than 100. This saves the calculation time in the normal case where all tracks are set to output at full MIDI volume.

Figure 6.2 Function Organization for *Play()*

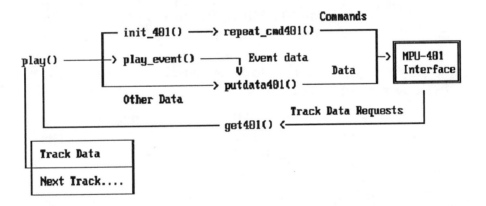

6.5 Recording MIDI Data

When recording, the MPU-401 also plays any tracks marked with PLAY ON. Only one track can record at a time.

Decoding of incoming commands from the MPU-401 is done in the *record_track()* function in MTRC2.C. Decoding is simplified by the way the MPU-401's commands are numbered. All of the commands have numeric values above 239 (E9 hex). Because of this, any value below

240 is a timing byte for a received MIDI message. Any value above 239 is some sort of MPU-401 message which the program will need to decode and/or store.

Depending on the message received, MT will store between one and four bytes of data in the next *event* location. The number of significant bytes is critical. Here is an outline of the decoding logic used in the *record_track()* function in file MTRC2.C:

MPU-401 Recorder Decode Logic

Byte 1 <= EF hex (239 decimal)—The byte must be a timing byte. The next byte is then fetched, leading to several possibilities:

1) Byte 2 <= 7F—This must be MIDI data where running status has allowed the MPU-401 to omit the MIDI message byte. MT stores the missing running status byte in memory to avoid later confusion. Byte 3 is then fetched and four bytes are saved (Byte 2 being the running status byte).

2) Byte 2 <= BF—This is four-byte MIDI data, so running status must have changed. The new running status byte is stored as the variable *mstatus* for later use. Bytes 3 and 4 are fetched, and all four are saved.

3) Byte 2 <= DF—MIDI program change and channel aftertouch messages have only three bytes to store.

4) Byte 2 <= EF—Pitch wheel data, handled just like the other four-byte MIDI data.

5) Byte 2 == F9—This is a Measure End mark, store it.

6) Byte 2 == FC—This is the Data End mark, so the Record process is done. Mark off the end of the track and then quit.

Anything else—Something is wrong, so print an error.

Byte 1 <= F7—This is a track data request. MT sends the next *event* of data to the MPU-401 so that the MPU can keep *playing* the tracks set with PLAY ON.

Byte 1 == F8—This is a timing overflow mark, meaning that more than 240 ticks have passed without getting MIDI data. The (single) byte is stored.

Byte 1 == F9—The MPU-401 requested conductor data. This is not expected as MT does not implement tempo changes in the middle of a song.

Byte 1 == FC—All end. The Record process should stop.

Byte 1 == FD—MPU sent a clock signal. Some sequencers take timing data directly from the MPU. As we will be using the MPU-401 timing logic exclusively, this message is not expected.

Byte 1 = FE—This is an ACK, ignore it.

The number of bytes to store is determined by the type of data. This number is stored for each event as the parameter *nbytes*. The actual data is stored in each event's data array b[0] through b[3].

During the Record process, MT is continually allocating memory for the incoming data. Each new track ends up forming a long list of linked event nodes stretching through memory. If you use your debugger to trace the memory locations where the events are stored, you will find that the events are not necessarily stacked one right after the other. The only way to trace a full track's worth of data is to start at the beginning and follow the chain of *next* addresses (see structure event definition in Section 6.1). This is exactly how MT finds the data in sequence for playing and editing.

Figure 6.3   Function Organization for *Record()*

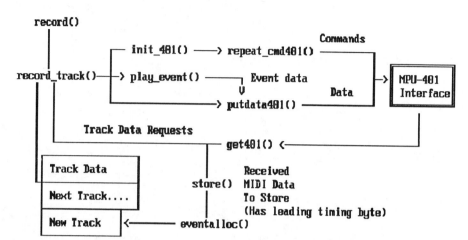

6.6 MT's Main() Module

The *main()* module for MT is in the file MT.C. *Main()* serves two purposes:

1) Initializes the program by loading in screen and video data, and by running several initialization functions.

2) Controls the MT primary menu. This menu directs execution to all other parts of MT, such as the RECORD, MLE, and SAVE functions.

Main() does not do any calculations itself, it just acts as a traffic director to and from the other modules of MT. *Main()* provides the only way to exit from MT, the QUIT command.

Function: `void main(void)`

Purpose: Central module for MT. Initializes data on start-up and controls the primary menu.

In File: MT.C

Related Header Files: MT.H, MTDECLAR.H, MTSCREEN.H, STANDARD.H, SCREENF.H, MT.H, MTSC.H, FILEFUNC.H, VIDEO.H

Returned Value: None.

Discussion: On start-up, *main()* displays a sign-on screen, loads the screen files from disk and runs several initialization functions. Once done, *main()* displays MT's primary menu. Based on user selections, *main()* passes execution to other modules such as the RECORD, EDIT, and SAVE functions.

6.7 RECORD Functions

Function: `void record_menu(void)`

Purpose: Controls the RECORD menu.

In File: MTRC1.C

Related Header Files: MT.H, MPU401.H

Returned Value: None (void).

Discussion: *Record_menu()* is much like *main()* in that it does not do anything complex, it just runs the RECORD menu. *Record_menu()* uses the *fdispchain()* function to put up the RECORD screen and calls *init_track_str()* to initialize the RECORD menu (MT2) with current character values for the PLAY, RECORD, and volume status settings.

The menu selection possibilities are numerous. In the top part of the RECORD menu are the individual track settings for the name, MIDI volume, etc., for each track. If the cursor is moved to this top area and the Return key is pressed, *record_menu()* calculates the track and parameter involved based on the menu item number returned by the cursor function *movescrn()*.

The MT2 menu data is in MTSCREEN.H. Unlike the primary menu's MT1 menu definition, the string values for the top of the RECORD menu items are left blank in the header file. This is because the menu items in this portion can change from ON to OFF, etc., based on the current status for each track.

The track's status information is stored in *g_trackarray[]*. This includes the MIDI volume, MIDI channel, and PLAY status (ON or OFF). The function *init_track_str()* does the work of putting the right characters into the MT2 menu based on the current track status in *g_trackarray[]*. Once initialized by *init_track_str()*, the *finitscrn()* menu function writes the current menu information to the screen.

The bottom half of the RECORD menu has a series of commands. In most cases execution is passed to a subfunction which does the work. These are described below.

_____

Function: void play(void)

Purpose: Plays back MIDI data on selected tracks.

In File: MTRC2.C

Related Header Files: MT.H, MPU401.H

Returned Value: None (void).

Discussion: Playing back the MIDI information is a matter of walking through each track's linked list one event at a time. The next event is fetched every time the MPU-401 sends a track data request.

Play() uses the *init_401()* function to set the bit map of the active tracks and to send out the initialization commands to the MPU-401 with the right tempo, meter, etc. After that, *play()* just feeds the MPU-401 MIDI data as it is requested by track request messages (REQ_T1...). The *play_event()* function does the actual transmission of the MIDI data, including scaling of the velocity data if the track volume setting is set to something other than 100.

The MPU-401 will send an ALL_END message when all tracks have been shut down. This tells *play()* to quit. *Play()* can also be stopped in the middle of a song by hitting a key on the computer. The *get401()* function detects the keypress and returns -1 instead of a MIDI byte when this happens. *Play()* then simulates reaching the end of each active track by sending out DATA_END messages in response to each track request. This shuts down each track in succession, prompting the MPU-401 to send the ALL_END message, and terminating the Play process.

———————————————————————————————————————

Function: void record(void)

Purpose: Checks to see if a track is active, then starts the Record process.

In File: MTRC2.C

Related Header Files: MT.H, MPU401.H

Returned Value: None (void).

Discussion: This is the starting point for the Record process. *Record()* checks to make sure a track has been selected for recording. It then starts recording by calling the *record_track()* function that does the work. When the Record process is stopped (user hits a key on the computer), *record()* changes all of the MIDI data received to the recorded track's current MIDI channel with a call to *change_channel()*. Finally, *record()* moves the track's Current Event pointer to a Measure End by calling *goto_measure()*.

Function: `struct event far *record_track(int track)`

Purpose: Does the work of recording a track while other tracks are set to PLAY.

In File: MTRC2.C

Related Header Files: MT.H, MPU401.H

Returned Value: *Far* pointer to last recorded event.

Discussion: *Record_track()* uses the logic described in Section 6.5 to decode the incoming data from the MPU-401 interface. The function also plays any tracks marked ON exactly the way the *play()* function operates so that one track can be recorded while a number of others are playing back already recorded data.

The Record process is stopped by the user hitting a key on the computer. The *get401()* detects this and returns a -1. *Record_track()* then sends out a STOP_REC command, but waits until the MPU-401 returns a DATA_END message before stopping execution.

Function: `void play_event(int track, struct event far *ep)`

Purpose: Sends one event's MIDI data to MPU-401; volume corrects MIDI Note On key velocity value transmitted.

In File: MTRC3.C

Related Header Files: MT.H, MPU401.H

Returned Value: None (void).

Discussion: *Play_event()* sends one event's data to the MPU-401 interface. This is in response to a track request message received during either the Play or Record (with tracks playing) processes. The number of bytes transmitted is determined by the event's *nbyte* parameter.

If the event is a MIDI Note On, and at least one of the tracks has the MIDI volume set to a value less than 100, *play_event()* will adjust the transmitted key velocity value (fourth byte) by the ratio of the track's MIDI volume to 100. This calculation is skipped if all tracks have the default MIDI volume setting of 100.

The global variable *g_track_vel_used* is set to TRUE by the *init_401()* function at the start of the Record and Play process if there is a MIDI volume less than 100. *Play_event()* uses *g_track_vel_used* to decide if the MIDI volume calculation is needed.

———————————————————————————————

Function: `void stop_401(int tracks_on)`

Purpose: Sends the MPU-401 commands to stop the Play/Record process and clear the internal MPU-401 Play map.

In File: MTRC3.C

Related Header Files: MT.H, MPU401.H

Returned Value: None (void).

Discussion: The commands in this function can be used any time you want the MPU-401 shut down. One trap here is that you should shut down all tracks individually by sending DATA_END messages before issuing the STOP_PLAY, STOP_REC commands. Otherwise, notes left on when you stop the Play process will continue to sound. The best way to stop the MPU-401 is to shut down each track individually, wait for the ALL_END message back from the MPU-401, and then issue shutdown commands.

If *tracks_on* is non-zero, *stop_401()* will send DATA_END messages for any tracks in the Play mode before shutting the MPU-401 down. If *tracks_on* is zero, no tracks are in the Play mode, so there are none to shut off (no chance of a "hung note").

Function: `int init_401(struct event far *ep[])`

Purpose: Performs initialization functions for setting up a Play or Record session.

In File: MTRC3.C

Related Header Files: MT.H, MPU401.H

Returned Value: Bit map for tracks on/off (trackbits).

Discussion: *Init_401()* does a number of chores which are needed to prepare for playing stored MIDI data. First, it makes a bit map for all tracks on/off. This ends up being the returned value. Next, it loads the *ep[]* array with the pointers for the events on each track from which to start the Play process. Using a separate array, *ep[]* saves pointer calculation time during playback, compared with the alternative of using the global array *g_trackarray[]*.

Init_401() then checks to see if any of the tracks have MIDI volumes set to other than the default value of 100. If so, the global variable *g_track_vel_used* is set TRUE to alert *play_event()* that volume correction should be calculated. Next, the MPU-401 is reset, and the start-up command sequences are sent out for turning on the metronome, allowing pitch bend data, etc.

Init_401() returns the bit map for the tracks with PLAY set to ON. Note that the bit map is returned as an integer, even though the bit map itself only occupies the least significant eight bits.

Function: `void maybe_measure_number(int track, int track-bits)`

Purpose: Writes the current measure number on the screen during the Play and Record processes.

In File: MTRC3.C

Related Header Files: MT.H, MPU401.H

Returned Value: None (void).

Discussion: Every track has MEAS_END markers. *Maybe_measure_number()* checks if the track parameter is equal to the highest active track marked ON in the *trackbits* bit map. If it is, the measure number is updated. If not, the function returns without action.

Function: `void erase_track(void)`

Purpose: Prompts the user for a track number, then erases all data in that track.

In File: MTRC3.C

Related Header Files: MT.H, MPU401.H

Returned Value: None (void).

Discussion: This function is used in both the RECORD and MLE screens to erase whole tracks.

Function: `void erase_one(int track)`

Purpose: Frees all memory associated with a track, and resets the track's pointers to the start-up values.

In File: MTRC3.C

Related Header Files: MT.H, MPU401.H

Returned Value: None (void).

Discussion: *Erase_one()* calls *clear_events()* to free all memory in the track's event list starting from the track's first event to the end. The starting event for the track is then set to be a Measure End, with no following next event (NULL pointer for next). The *g_trackarray[]* pointers "first," "current," and "last" are set to point to this starting event.

Function: `void erase_all(void)`

Purpose: Erases all data on all tracks.

In File: MTRC3.C

Related Header Files: MT.H, MPU401.H

Returned Value: None (void).

Discussion: This function is only activated from the primary menu's CLEAR command. It calls *erase_one()* eight times, once for each track.

_____

Function: `void init_track_str()`

Purpose: Updates the menu data for the top of the RECORD screen.

In File: MTRC3.C

Related Header Files: MT.H, MPU401.H, MTSCREEN.H

Returned Value: None (void).

Discussion: Unlike most menu items, the items at the top of the RECORD screen can be changed. For example, the track name, MIDI channel, MIDI volume, and Record/Play status settings can all be modified.

MT handles this by updating the *content* elements of the menu data structure. In this case the menu data array is *mt2[]*. The menu array structure is defined in the file MTSCREEN.H, but with blank *content* fields for the top menu items. *Init_track_str()* fills in those content fields based on the current name and status of each track. After that, the normal menu selection functions (*initscrn()*, *movescrn()* in MSCREENF.LIB) will allow the cursor to select any of the variable fields on the screen.

_____

Function: `long count_events(void)`

Purpose: Counts the number of events on each track in memory.

In File: MTRC3.C

Related Header Files: MT.H, MPU401.H

Returned Value: Long integer equal to the total number of events in memory.

Discussion: MT computes the amount of memory used based on the number of events stored in memory. The total for each track is stored as the *numevents* parameter in *g_trackarray[]*. The event count is also displayed on the RECORD menu as the *count* for each track.

Function: `void init_rec_val(void)`

Purpose: Updates the parameters at the bottom right of the RECORD menu.

In File: MTRC3.C

Related Header Files: MT.H, MPU401.H

Returned Value: None (void).

Discussion: All of the parameters at the bottom right of the RECORD menu are associated with global status variables. *Init_rec_val()* puts the current value for these variables on the screen. This includes the metronome rate, meter, current measure number, percent free memory, and on/off status for the metronome, pitchbend, exclusive, and trace toggles.

Function: `void calc_pct_free(void)`

Purpose: Calculates the percent of memory used.

In File: MTRC3.C

Related Header Files: MT.H, MPU401.H

Returned Value: None (void).

Discussion: The amount of available memory is estimated by *free_memory()* when MT starts up. The amount consumed is estimated by *used_memory()* which multiplies the number of events in each track times the size of an event in memory. The calculated value is stored in the global variable *g_pct_free_memory*.

_____

Function: `void write_on_off(int param, int column, int row)`

Purpose: Writes the word ON if param is non-zero, OFF if param equals zero.

In File: MTRC .C

Related Header Files: MT.H, MPU401.H, VIDEO.H

Returned Value: None (void).

Discussion: Several MT operations require that the word ON or OFF be displayed at a specific screen location. The word ON is written with the emphasized attribute *(g_emph_attrib)*, while OFF is written with the normal attribute *(g_norm_attrib)*.

_____

Function: `void all_notes_off(void)`

Purpose: Sends MIDI All Notes Off messages out on all sixteen channels.

In File: MTRC3.C

Related Header Files: MT.H, MPU401.H

Returned Value: None (void).

Discussion: This function is activated from the RECORD menu. It serves as a handy way to shut down all notes in complex MIDI setups where notes can "hang on."

––

Function: `void trace_header(void)`

Purpose: Writes the header information on the screen prior to Data Trace output display.

In File: MTRC3.C

Related Header Files: MT.H, MPU401.H

Returned Value: None (void).

Discussion: If the Data Trace option is turned on from the RECORD menu, all data to and from the MPU-401 is displayed as it is sent or received. This function clears the screen and puts the message:

```
Data Trace Option - all data in hex.
rc=received, tc=trans command, td=trans data
```

at the top of the screen. The data is then displayed as a long continuous line which will eventually scroll off of the screen.

––

Function: `struct event far *eventalloc(void)`

Purpose: Allocates enough memory to store one event.

In File: MTRC4.C

Related Header Files: MT.H, MPU401.H

Returned Value: *Far* pointer to allocated memory.

Discussion: This is the lowest-level memory allocation function. It reserves enough memory to store one event, and returns a pointer to that memory location.

———————————————————————————————

Function: `struct event far *store(struct event far node, int nbytes, int b0, int b1, int b2, int b3)`

Purpose: Puts the received MIDI data into an allocated event.

In File: MTRC4.C

Related Header Files: MT.H, MPU401.H

Returned Value: *Far* pointer to next allocated event.

Discussion: This function is constantly accessed during the Record process to store received data and to allocate storage for the next event. *Eventalloc()* is used to allocate memory for the new event. The data bytes are then written to this memory area.

———————————————————————————————

Function: `int getnext401(void)`

Purpose: Gets the next byte of data from either the MPU-401 or the data buffer (if there is data in the buffer).

In File: MTRC4.C

Related Header Files: MT.H, MPU401.H

Returned Value: The byte fetched, returned as int.

Discussion: This is the data fetch command mentioned in Section 6.3. If data is in the buffer, this is fetched in first in, first out order. Otherwise, the next byte of data is fetched from the MPU-401 interface.

The global array *cmdbuf[]* is used to store buffered data. The global integer *cmdbufp* is used to keep track of the position of the last byte in the buffer. Although these are globals, they are only used within the confines of the data fetching functions.

———————————————————————————

Function: `void ungetnext401(int n)`

Purpose: Puts a byte into the buffer.

In File: MTRC4.C

Related Header Files: MT.H, MPU401.H

Returned Value: None (void).

Discussion: In the case where there is a data collision, this function puts data temporarily in the buffer. See the discussion in Section 6.3.

———————————————————————————

Function: `int get401(void)`

Purpose: Get data from either MPU-401 or buffer.

In File: MTRC4.C

Related Header Files: MT.H, MPU401.H

Returned Value: Byte fetched, returned as int. Returns -1 if computer key is pressed.

Discussion: This is the top-level data fetch command mentioned in Section 6.3. *Get401()* first checks if a key on the computer was pressed. If so, a value of -1 is returned. Next, *get401()* calls *getnext401()* to fetch the next byte either from the MPU-401 or the buffer. If the data trace option is on (*g_trace_on*), the numeric value is written to the screen. *Get401()* then returns the byte fetched as an integer.

This is the function that all higher-level functions use to get data from the MPU-401.

_____

Function: `void putdata401(int n)`

Purpose: Sends a data byte to the MPU-401.

In File: MTRC4.C

Related Header Files: MT.H, MPU401.H

Returned Value: None (void).

Discussion: The MPU-401 requires a certain number of data bytes after each command. The MPU-401 will wait for the right number of bytes before continuing. Because of this, no buffering is needed for transmittal of data bytes. *Putdata401()* also writes the transmitted data to the screen if *g_trace_on* is TRUE.

_____

Function: `int sendcmd401(int n)`

Purpose: Sends a command to the MPU-401.

In File: MTRC4.C

Related Header Files: MT.H, MPU401.H

Returned Value: ACK (FE hex) if command was accepted, -1 otherwise.

Discussion: This is the top-level command transmission function mentioned in Section 6.3. If *g_trace_on* is TRUE, *sendcmd401()* will output the numeric value to the display. If the command is accepted, *sencmd401()* will also send (ACK) to the display.

If a data collision occurs, *sendcmd401()* will put the incoming data in the buffer and output (No ACK) if *g_trace_on* is true. The buffered data is then read on the next read cycle.

––

Function: `int repeat_cmd401(int n)`

Purpose: Determined send of command to MPU-401.

In File: MTRC4.C

Related Header Files: MT.H, MPU401.H

Returned Value: n, or -1 if unsuccessful.

Discussion: If the MPU-401 is not expecting a command, the first transmittal of a command can be missed. This typically happens right after a reset. *Repeat_cmd()* will try ten times to send the command. If unsuccessful, *repeat_cmd()* will return -1, otherwise, it echoes back the byte value sent.

In practice, the command will either be accepted within the first two tries, or not at all. The latter implies some sort of mechanical problem with the interface. With careful coding you can anticipate the MPU-401's state and avoid having to repeat a command. MT takes the brute force approach of just repeating the command.

––

Function: `int goto_measure(int measure)`

Purpose: Advances all track pointers to the specified measure.

In File: MTRC4.C

Related Header Files: MT.H, MPU401.H

Returned Value: The measure number advanced to.

Discussion: Tracks can contain any number of measures. *Goto_measure()* attempts to move the current event pointers (*g_trackarray[track].current*) on all tracks to a given measure number (*meas*). If a track does not have that many measures, *goto_measure()* will leave the current event pointer set to the last event on the track.

Goto_measure() returns the measure number it advanced to. If none of the tracks were as long as the measure specified, *goto_measure()* will return the measure number of the longest track. This is how the END TRACK command works. *Goto_measure(32000)* finds the end of every track (it is very unlikely that there will be 32000 measures on a track).

Function: `void change_channel(int track, int channel)`

Purpose: Adjusts all data on a track to one MIDI channel number.

In File: MTRC4.C

Related Header Files: MT.H, MPU401.H

Returned Value: None (void).

Discussion: MT does not allow more than one MIDI channel number to reside on a given track. During the Record process, MIDI data is accepted on all channels. Anything that makes its way to the MPU-401 MIDI IN port is saved. After the end of the Record process, *change_channel()* is used to adjust all of the data to the channel shown on the RECORD and MLE screens. Changing the channel on the RECORD or MLE screens also causes *change_channel()* to adjust all data on the specified track to the new MIDI channel number. The Block Paste and Repeat commands also use *change_channel()*.

Function: `void init_tracks(void)`

Purpose: Puts default values in for all tracks.

In File: MTRC4.C

Related Header Files: MT.H, MPU401.H

Returned Value: None (void).

Discussion: *Init_tracks()* is used on start-up and after the CLEAR command to set all tracks to their default values. This basically means that all values in the *g_trackarray[]* array are set. The track names are set to < >, track volumes to 100, MIDI channels equal to the track number, and the first event (only event) is set equal to a Measure End marker.

Function: `int free_memory(void)`

Purpose: Estimates the amount of memory available to store track data.

In File: MTRC4.C

Related Header Files: MT.H, MPU401.H

Returned Value: Number of K bytes free.

Discussion: *Free_memory()* works by seeing how many 10K chunks of data can be allocated after start-up. This is only a rough estimate of the amount of memory available as pieces of memory may be available with less than 10K room. After the estimate is made, *free_memory()* frees all of the 10K blocks it allocated.

Because of the conservatism with this form of memory space estimate, it is possible to end up with negative percent free memory when using

MT. Below ten percent, operation will be degraded as the memory allocation functions attempt to find pieces of free space. As a rule, avoid running at or below ten percent available memory.

_____

Function: `int used_memory(void)`

Purpose: Calculates the number of K bytes used by track data.

In File: MTRC4.C

Related Header Files: MT.H, MPU401.H

Returned Value: Number of K bytes used.

Discussion: *Used_memory()* estimates the amount of memory used in track data by multiplying the number of events stored by the amount of memory each event takes up.

_____

Function: `void data_dump(void)`

Purpose: Displays the data stored on all eight tracks in hexadecimal, starting with the current measure.

In File: MTRC4.C

Related Header Files: MT.H, MPU401.H

Returned Value: None (void).

Discussion: This function is available from both the RECORD and MLE menus. Data display starts from the Current Measure Number on each track. If off the end of the track data, the track will be blank. All four bytes in each event are shown in hexadecimal. Note that if the data is less than four bytes long, the empty bytes will be displayed as 00 on each track.

_____

Function: `void clear_forward(void)`

Purpose: Frees memory for all track data forward of the current measure.

In File: MTRC4.C

Related Header Files: MT.H, MPU401.H

Returned Value: None (void).

Discussion: This function is available from both the RECORD and MLE screens. The *clear_events()* function is used to free memory forward of the current measure. Once cleared, a single event is added at the end of the track with an ALL_END message. This becomes the new track terminator event.

_____

Function: `void clear_events(struct event far *start)`

Purpose: Frees memory for all events forward of pointer "start."

In File: MTRC4.C

Related Header Files: MT.H, MPU401.H

Returned Value: None (void).

Discussion: *Clear_events()* moves from event to event freeing memory. The data will still exist in RAM after the function is completed, but the space will be available for the next time memory is allocated.

Clear_events() does not add a track terminator event (ALL_END) or set the last event pointer *next* to NULL. These are the responsibility of the calling function.

_____

Function: `void wait_for_key(void)`

Purpose: Stops execution until a computer key is pressed.

In File: MTRC4.C

Related Header Files: MT.H, MPU401.H

Returned Value: None (void).

7

Measure Level Editing Functions

7.1 Measure Level Editing Overview

The measure is a basic unit in most music. Phrases usually find their beginning and ending at measure boundaries. Because of this, it is convenient to provide functions that work on groups of measures. We will also need to be able edit individual notes within a measure. That subject is covered in the next chapter.

The commands on MT's MLE screen are shown at the bottom of Figure 7.1.

Figure 7.1 MIDI Data Editor—Measure Level Edit Display

```
Measure:          1  2  3  4  5  6  7  8  9  10 11 12 13 14 15

       Track  │MIDI    Select a measure and hit Return to start Note Editor.
 1  <       >│ 2    [ ][ ][ ][ ][ ][ ][ ][ ][ ][ ][ ][ ][ ][ ][ ]
 2  bassguit │ 2    [◆][♫][♫][♫][♫][♫][♫][♫][♫][♫][♫][♫][♫][♫][♫]
 3  <       >│ 3    [ ][ ][ ][ ][ ][ ][ ][ ][ ][ ][ ][ ][ ][ ][ ]
 4  <       >│ 4    [ ][ ][ ][ ][ ][ ][ ][ ][ ][ ][ ][ ][ ][ ][ ]
 5  <       >│ 5    [ ][ ][ ][ ][ ][ ][ ][ ][ ][ ][ ][ ][ ][ ][ ]
 6  <       >│ 6    [ ][ ][ ][ ][ ][ ][ ][ ][ ][ ][ ][ ][ ][ ][ ]
 7  <       >│ 7    [ ][ ][ ][ ][ ][ ][ ][ ][ ][ ][ ][ ][ ][ ][ ]
 8  drums    │10    [♫][♫][♫][♫][♫][♫][♫][♫][♫][♫][♫][♫][♫][♫][♫]

  ┌─────────────────┬─────────────────┬──────────────────┐
  │ Start Block     │ Last Measure    │ Curnt Measure 1  │
  │ End Block       │ Fast Forwd >>   │ Erase Track      │
  │ Block Paste     │ Forward    >    │ Erase Forward    │
  │ Block Empty     │ Rewind     <    │ Data Dump        │
  │ Block Repeat    │ Fast Rewnd <<   │ Free Memory 95 % │
  │ Block Transp.   │ First Measure   │ QUIT Edit        │
  └─────────────────┴─────────────────┴──────────────────┘
                                                    mt3.scr
```

Only the commands on the lower left side are new. The center and right-hand side commands are all duplicates of the commands on the RECORD screen.

The Start Block and End Block commands allow one or more measures on a track to be marked off. From a coding point of view, blocks are controlled by four global variables:

`g_block_track`	The track number 0–7 of the block.
`g_block_on`	TRUE (1) if a block is marked, FALSE (0) if not.
`g_block_start`	The measure number for the start of the block.
`g_block_end`	The measure number for the end of the block.

Like track numbers, measure numbers are displayed to the user starting with measure number 1. Internal to MT, both tracks and measure numbers start with measure 0. This is consistent with standard C notation where all arrays and offsets start with element 0.

All of the note and empty measure symbols visible on the screen are menu items in the menu array *MT3[]*. This menu array (defined in MTSCREEN.H) includes the measure numbers at the top, the track names and MIDI channels on the left, the measures themselves and all of the commands at the bottom. Display of the note data, empty measures, and block symbols is handled by updating the *content* elements of the *MT3[]* menu. The menu functions then write the data on the screen.

The *init_meas_data()* function does the work of updating the *MT3[]* menu. The top measure numbers are added to the menu starting with the current measure number. This is the same global variable *g_current_measure* used in the RECORD menu, so both menus stay synchronized. The track names and MIDI channels are fetched from the global *g_trackarray[]* data, again assuring that any changes will show up on the RECORD menu. *Init_meas_data()* adds the block symbols, note, and empty measure symbols to the *MT3[]* menu data. The function *has_midi_data()* helps by determining if there are MIDI Note Ons in a given measure. If there are, the note symbol is displayed. If the measure has data, but no Note Ons, the empty measure symbol is displayed. If there is no data at all, the measure shows up blank.

The MLE commands are coordinated by the *edit_menu()* function, much like the *record_menu()* function handles the RECORD screen. Cursor movement on the screen is done with *movescrn()*. Once the user picks a spot (hits Return), *edit_menu()* decides what to do based on the user's selection. The most interesting selections have to do with pasting, repeating, and transposing blocks of measures.

7.2 Overview of Block Operations

Marking off the start and end measures for the block is facilitated by the *select_measure()* function. This function determines the measure and track number for the measure highlighted on the screen when the Return key was pressed. As there are two parameters to return (track number and measure number), *select_measure()* uses a simple structure of type "item" to return the two values. The item type is defined in MT.H as:

```
struct item {
    int track;
    int measure;
};
```

Once the start and end of the block are specified, the block operations can be used. Block Paste and Block Repeat are similar. Block Paste copies the block once to a destination while Block Repeat copies the block repeatedly starting at the destination measure.

There are a couple of considerations that make copying a block into a new measure more complex than it might seem at first:

1) If the block is copied past the end of a track, any gaps must be filled in with "empty" measures. Empty measures are measures that

include just timing information and MEAS_END bytes, no MIDI data.

2) If the block is copied into a track that already has MIDI data, both the existing and added data will have to have their timing adjusted to keep the notes sounding at the right time.

3) The MPU-401's inability to count above 239 ticks complicates things. TIME_OUTs (F8 hex) which mark 240 ticks without MIDI data may disappear after the block of data is merged.

4) If notes in the source block have their Note Offs outside of the block, pasting a copy will result in putting a Note On into the destination track without a matching Note Off. Without correction, this would result in a note left ON until the end of the song (called a "hung" note).

Let's look at a couple of examples. For simplicity, assume that the song was recorded with 4 beats per measure. This means that every measure will have 4 x 120 = 480 ticks before a Measure End mark. The marked block will only be one measure long. All notes will be on MIDI channel 1, so 90 hex is a Note On. Recall that F9 hex is the MEAS_END marker. Refer to MT.H for a full list of all MPU-401 commands and messages.

Figure 7.2 Example 1: Pasting into an Empty Measure

Marked Block Measure:

Ticks: 100 (64 hex)   160 (A0 hex)   220 (DC hex)

Message: Note On   Note Off   Measure End
In Hex: 64 90 3c 40   A0 90 3c 00   DC F9

```
                                         └ Velocity = 0, note off.
                       └ Velocity = 64 decimal, 40 hex.
                   └ Note number for middle C.
              └ MIDI Note On, channel 1.
           └ Timing Byte.
```

Destination Measure (Empty):

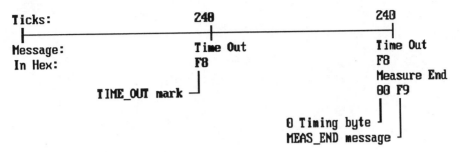

Result After Pasting Marked Block:

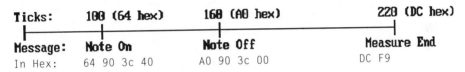

The "ticks count" above the line contains the timing byte information that would accompany each event as the first data byte. Ticks measure the time between events, not the cumulative time within the measure. The MPU-401 uses each timing byte to keep track of how long to wait before sending out the MIDI data and requesting the next event from memory.

In this example the destination measure is "empty." As the MPU-401 can only count up to 239, every 240 ticks the MPU-401 needs a TIME_OUT message to keep track of resets to the internal MPU-401 clock. The MEAS_END falls right on the second TIME_OUT, so the timing byte for the MEAS_END message is 00.

After the paste operation, both of the destination measure's TIME_OUT marks disappear. Also, one of the two MEAS_END marks must be ignored to avoid having two right next to one another. The sum of all the timing bytes in the destination measures remains 480.

Figure 7.3 Example 2: Pasting into an Active Measure

Marked Block Measure:

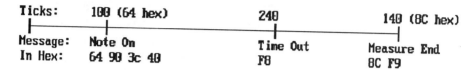

Destination Measure (Empty):

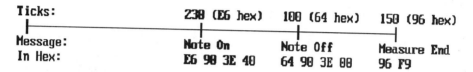

Result After Pasting Marked Block:

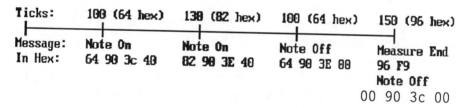

In this example the source block contains a Note On but does not have the matching Note Off. The Note Off must be in one of the measures after this one on the source track. If we paste this data without adding the Note Off, the result is a note left on until the track is over (a hung note).

To avoid the problem of hung notes, the paste operation must keep track of Note Ons, and then add in Note Offs at the end of the block. A similar, but less pressing problem, is that of a Note Off in the block, without a matching Note On. In this case, the event just wastes space in memory. These need to be purged to keep the track clean.

7.3 Block Functions

The central function in the paste and merge operations is the function *merge_measure()*. *Merge_measure()* is passed two pointers: one to the first event in the source measure, and one to the first event in the destination measure. *Merge_measure()* works forward, combining the two sets of events, until the Measure Ends are reached. *Merge_measure()* then returns a pointer to the last event in the destination measure.

G_note_array[] is used to make sure that every Note On has a matching Note Off. *G_note_array[]* has 128 elements, one for every MIDI note number. *Merge_measure()* adds 1 to *g_note_array[]* for every source Note On. The *g_note_array[]* values are all set to 0 by the function *init_note_array()* before the merge operation starts. After that, Note Ons result in adding 1 to the array, while Note Offs result in subtracting 1.

When *merge_measure()* is done, the function *add_note_offs()* looks over the *g_note_array[]* values. Any that are not zero are hung notes. *add_note_offs()* adds in Note Offs for all of these notes at the end of the last measure in the block. This results in all hung notes stopping abruptly at the last Measure End of the destination block. (Actually, the Note Offs are added right after the MEAS_END marker, with timing bytes of 0. Technically, they are in the next measure.)

The Block Repeat command is handled by repeating the Block Paste operation. The *block_repeat()* function asks the user two questions: where to start, and how many repetitions? Then *repeat_copy()* does the work of copying the blocks the requested number of times.

Transposing MIDI notes is simple. All you have to do is add or subtract the correct number of half-steps to the note number of any Note On and Note Off data within the block. Notes crossing the block boundaries are again a problem. If no correction is made, a Note Off within the block that shuts down a Note On in front of the block, will end up transposed. After transposition, the Note Off will no longer match the MIDI note number of the Note On, so the Note On will "hang." The same problem occurs if a Note On within the block has its matching Note Off outside the block.

Block_transpose() chops all notes off at the block boundaries to deal with the problem of mismatched Note On/Off pairs. *Add_note_offs()* is called at the beginning and end to shut down any notes that crossed the block boundaries.

The Empty Block command is also complicated by the need to avoid hung notes. Any notes left on at the start of the block have to be shut off at the beginning of the block. Any that start in the block but end after the block are removed.

Because of the addition of Note Offs at block boundaries to avoid hung notes, tracks can end up with the original Note Off being left as an orphan later in the track. Block paste operations that include the end of a track can also end up copying duplicate Track End markers onto the destination. Both of these types of extra data are purged from the track by the function *clean_track()*. This is called at the end of the Block Paste, Repeat, Empty, and Transpose commands. The *change_channel()* function is also called after the Block Paste and Repeat functions to adjust any added MIDI data to the track's current channel.

7.4 Edit Function Summary

Function: `void edit_menu(void)`

Purpose: Controls the MLE display.

In File: MTED1.C

Related Header Files: MT.H

Returned Value: None (void).

Discussion: *Init_meas_data()* does the work of updating the menu fields for the top part of the MLE display. With the menu updated, *edit_menu()* uses the normal *movescrn()* command to allow the user to highlight a measure number, measure, track name, track MIDI channel number, or command. Execution is then passed on to the proper subfunction based on the user's selection.

If one of the measures on the screen is highlighted, *edit_menu()* invokes the NLE (Note Level Editor) on that measure's data. This is the subject of the next chapter.

Function: void init_meas_data(void)

Purpose: Updates the MT3[] menu data array for *edit_menu()*.

In File: MTED2.C

Related Header Files: MT.H, MTSCREEN.H

Returned Value: None (void).

Discussion: All of the menu items in the top half of the MLE screen are variable. *Init_meas_data()* puts the right character strings in each menu element content field of the *MT3[]* menu array (defined in MTSCREEN.H). This allows the *finitscrn()* and *movescrn()* functions to handle writing the menu items to the screen.

The top line of the MLE display has the measure numbers. These are displayed starting with the value of *g_current_measure*. Track names and MIDI channel numbers are extracted from the *g_trackarray[]* data, and then written to the menu. The individual measures are updated with either a note, empty measure, block marker, or blank symbol. The function *has_midi_data()* looks through each measure's events for MIDI Note Ons. *Init_meas_data()* then adds block markers if appropriate, based on the status of the global block variables *g_block_on, g_block_track*, *g_block_track*, *g_block_start*, and *g_block_end*. Note that the characters for notes, empty measures, start, and end of blocks are defined in MT.H.

Function: `int has_midi_data(struct event far *measurep)`

Purpose: Determines if the measure starting with event *measurep* contains MIDI Note Ons.

In File: MTED2.C

Related Header Files: MT.H

Returned Value: 2 if measure has Note Ons; 1 if measure has data, but no Note Ons; 0 if measure is off end of track.

Discussion: This is a helper function for *init_meas_data()*. *Has_midi_data()* checks if any of the events in the measure starting with the event pointed to by *measurep* contain MIDI Note Ons. This is how *init_meas_data()* knows whether to put a note symbol, empty measure symbol, or just a blank in the measure part of the MLE display.

Init_meas_data() detects the end of a track by finding a NULL pointer. Once found, *has_midi_data()* returns a 0, and *init_meas_data()* knows that the end of the track has been reached, so no further calls to *has_midi_data()* are made on this track.

Function: `struct event far *increment_measure(struct event far *eventp)`

Purpose: Finds next MEAS_END marker event after *eventp*.

In File: MTED2.C

Related Header Files: MT.H

Returned Value: Pointer to next MEAS_END containing event, NULL if off end of data.

Discussion: This is a handy function for advancing to the next measure.

Function: `int select_measure(struct item *item)`

Purpose: Allow cursor movement to select a measure on MLE screen.

In File: MTED2.C

Related Header Files: MT.H, MTSCREEN.H

Returned Value: 1 if successful, 0 if aborted. The track and measure number are returned as elements of the item structure.

Discussion: The block operations require that the start and end measures be picked by moving the cursor to a measure marker and hitting the Return key. *Select_measure()* does this by using the *movescrn()* menu function for cursor movement. The selection takes into account that the MLE display starts with the *g_current_measure* as the left-most measure on the screen.

Rather than create a whole new menu structure for this operation, *select_measure()* uses part of the *MT3[]* menu data already defined in MTSCREEN.H for the whole MLE screen. The cursor is limited to the top half of the screen by passing *movescrn()* a "last" parameter equal to the last measure's menu number. This still allows the cursor to move to the left track name and MIDI channel which is not valid for selecting a measure.

If the user hits the ESC key or selects one of the track names or MIDI channel numbers, *select_measure()* returns a 0 value. If a valid measure is selected, *select_measure()* returns a 1. This still leaves the problem of how to return the measure number and track number.

To get the two values back, *select_measure()* writes them to a structure type "item." This is defined in MT.H. The calling function passes the address of the item to *select_measure()* as the parameter. On return, the calling function can look at the *item.track* and *item.measure* to find out which were selected.

Function: `struct event far *advance_to_measure(int track, int measure)`

Purpose: Returns a pointer to the event on a track starting the specified measure. Adds empty measures as needed to lengthen the track up to the specified measure number.

In File: MTED3.C

Related Header Files: MT.H

Returned Value: Pointer of type struct event far * to event. Returns NULL if out of memory during creation of new empty measures.

Discussion: This is a useful function, and shows up in many of the other MLE functions. If the track already has data up to and including the desired measure number, *advance_to_measure()* just advances to that point and returns the address of the starting event. More interesting is the case where the specified measure number is past the end of the track. *Advance_to_measure()* then adds empty measures to lengthen the track up to the desired measure. A track terminator event is then appended. The function *add_measure()* does the work of adding empty measures.

Function: `struct event far *add_measure(struct event far *ep)`

Purpose: Adds an empty measure starting from the event pointed to by *ep*. Overwrites *ep*. *Ep* must be at the end of the track.

In File: MTED2.C

Related Header Files: MT.H

Returned Value: Pointer to last event of added measure. Returns NULL if out of memory.

Discussion: The length of the added measure data has to match the number of ticks in the current song's meter. The global variable *g_meter* is used to calculate how many ticks are needed in a full measure. The empty measure is then built up by adding enough TIME_OUT marker events plus a MEAS_END mark to equal the measure's correct duration.

Function: `struct event far *merge_measure(struct event far *dest_p, struct event far *source_p)`

Purpose: Adds the event data from one measure into a second measure.

In File: MTED2.C

Related Header Files: MT.H

Returned Value: Returns pointer to last event of destination measure. Returns NULL if out of memory.

Discussion: The two event pointers passed to *merge_measure()* must point to the start of the destination measure (*dest_p*) and the start of the source measure (*source_p*). The basic logic during merging is:

1) Add up the ticks until the next source and destination events. This includes adding up all of the TIME_OUTs as 240 ticks each.

2) Determine whether the source or destination track has the next event in time sequence.

If the destination track's event is next, the event is already there.

If the source track's event is next, the source event must be added into the destination track. The next destination event's timing byte has to be reduced to compensate for the time accounted for in the new event.

3) If the timing of the next event in the merged track is over 239 ticks, TIME_OUT events must be added back to keep the measure's total tick count correct.

4) The global array *g_note_array[]* is updated with each added event to keep track of any notes that are turned ON but not OFF as a result of the merge operation.

Events are added to the destination measure by first creating the new event, and then setting the *next* pointers to incorporate the new event in the track's linked list. See Chapter 4 for more details on adding data to linked lists.

The problem of keeping track of the TIME_OUT marks is handled in *merge_measure()* by first eliminating all TIME_OUT marks, and then adding them back in if needed. The total time between events is kept track of for the source and destination events by the local variables *s_time* and *d_time*, respectively. *Merge_measure()* adds 240 for every TIME_OUT, plus the next event's timing byte to come up with the total amount of time between events. If *d_time* is less than *s_time*, the next event to add to the destination measure is already there—the destination event. If *s_time* is less than *d_time*, the next event to add is the source measure. This is added to the destination measure.

Function: `void init_note_array(void)`

Purpose: Sets all elements of *g_note_array[]* to 0.

In File: MTED2.C

Related Header Files: MT.H

Returned Value: None (void).

Discussion: *G_note_array[]* is defined in MT.H and has one element for every Note On the MIDI scale (128 notes). This array is used to keep track of notes that have been turned ON, but which lack a matching Note Off.

Function: `void fill_note_array(struct event far *start_event, struct event far *end_event)`

Purpose: Updates *g_note_array[]* for all MIDI Note On/OFF data between the events pointed to by *start_event* and *end_event*.

In File: MTED2.C

Related Header Files: MT.H

Returned Value: None (void).

Discussion: This function assumes that all of the notes on a track have the same MIDI channel number. *G_note_array[]* has one element for every MIDI note. *Fill_note_array()* adds or subtracts from the array using the note number as the array index. For example, a Note On for middle C would have a note number of 60 decimal. Array element *g_note_array[60]* would be incremented by one. A Note Off for middle C would reduce *g_note_array[60]* by one.

At the end of the scan, *g_note_array[]*s elements show the number of remaining Note Ons for every note in the MIDI scale.

Function: `struct event far *add_note_offs(struct event far *dest_event, int track)`

Purpose: Adds a Note Off event for every note shown as ON in *g_note_array[]*.

In File: MTED2.C

Related Header Files: MT.H

Returned Value: Returns pointer to last Note Off event added.

Discussion: *Add_note_offs()* does the work of adding any needed Note Off events to the track after the event pointed to by *dest_event*. Each array element in *g_track_array[]* is the number of pending Note Ons for that MIDI note number. For example, if *g_track_array[60]* = 3, there are three pending Note Ons for note number 60 (middle C). Three Note Offs need to be added.

Function: void `empty_block(int track, int channel, int b_start, int b_end)`

Purpose: Removes all MIDI data except TIME_OUTs and MEAS_ENDs between measure numbers *b_start* and *b_end* on the specified track.

In File: MTED3.C

Related Header Files: MT.H

Returned Value: None (void).

Discussion: All notes that are still on at the start of the block (left on from the previous measure) are shut off by a call to *add_note_offs()*. The elements within the block are all deallocated (freed) from memory, and new empty measures are added in their place using the function *add_measure()*. Any extra Note Offs are removed afterward with a call to *clean_track()*. After *empty_block()*, the measures marked as a block still exist as empty measures.

Function: `void block_repeat(void)`

Purpose: Runs the Block Repeat command operations.

In File: MTED3.C

Related Header Files: MT.H

Returned Value: None (void).

Discussion: *Block_repeat()* checks that the block is already marked off. The staring point for the repetitions is then specified with a call to *select_measure()*. Next, *block_repeat()* asks the user to specify how many times to repeat the block. Finally, the actual copying is initiated by calling the *repeat_copy()* function.

Note that no parameters or returned values are involved with this function. This is because the block status variables are all globals (*g_block_on, g_block_start, g_block_end, g_block_track*).

Function: `void repeat_copy(int source_meas, int source_track, int dest_meas, int dest_track, int n_meas, int reps)`

Purpose: Copies the marked block repeatedly, starting with the *dest_meas* on the *dest_track*.

In File: MTED3.C

Related Header Files: MT.H

Returned Value: None (void).

Discussion: Before events can be copied, the destination measures must exist. *Advance_to_measure()* creates new empty measures so as to extend the track to the length needed to hold all the copied measures. The *merge_measure()* function is called repeatedly to do the actual copying. During the copy operation, the repetition number is updated at the bottom of the screen so that the user can see that something is going on. Pressing the ESC key during the copy operation halts the process.

Function: `void transpose_block(void)`

Purpose: Transposes all note data within the marked block.

In File: MTED3.C

Related Header Files: MT.H

Returned Value: None (void).

Discussion: Transposition is accomplished by adding the designated number of half-steps to every MIDI note number within the block. All notes crossing the boundaries of the block are shut off at the boundary Measure Ends to avoid hung notes. This is done using *init_note_array()*, *fill_note_array()*, and *add_note_offs()*.

Function: `struct event far *find_event_before(int track, struct event *ep)`

Purpose: Finds the event right before the one pointed to by *ep* on the specified track.

In File: MTED3.C

Related Header Files: MT.H

Returned Value: Pointer to event before *ep*. Returns NULL if *ep* not found.

Discussion: This is a generally useful function, but only used in *transpose_block()* within MT.

Function: `void clean_track(int track)`

Purpose: Removes extra Note Offs and DATA_END events from the specified track.

In File: MTED3.C

Related Header Files: MT.H

Returned Value: None (void).

Discussion: Several of the block operations add new Note Offs at the block boundaries. This leaves the original Note Off event somewhere later in the track with no purpose. Also, if a block is marked for pasting that includes the end of a track, you can end up with two track end markers.

Although neither of these problems affects MT's other functions, they do waste space in memory. *Clean_track()* removes both types of duplicate events and frees the associated memory for reuse. Timing values for the events following the removed event are adjusted to keep the track's timing correct. In some cases this requires adding a new TIME_OUT event.

Clean_track() also converts from explicit MIDI Note Offs (80 hex) to implied Note Offs (Note Ons with key velocity values of zero). Not all synths respond to explicit Note Offs. As *clean_track()* is called any time a block is copied, copying one entire track to an empty track is a simple way to convert from explicit to implied Note Offs. This is useful when using files from other sequencers which may have been recorded using explicit Note Offs.

Function: `void block_paste(void)`

Purpose: Controls paste operation for MLE screen.

In File: MTED3.C

Related Header Files: MT.H

Returned Value: None (void).

Discussion: First, *block_paste()* checks to make sure a block of measures has been marked. The *select_measure()* function is used to locate the track and first measure to start the paste operation. To insure that the destination measures already exist, *advance_to_measure()* is used to advance all the way to where the end of the block will fall on the destination track.

The merging of the source and destination data is done by the *merge_measure()* function. Once done, any loose Note Ons are terminated at the end of the block with a call to *add_note_offs()*. The MIDI channel of the merged data is adjusted to match the track's current channel number by *change_channel()*. Finally, all *g_trackarray[]* current pointers are set to match the *g_current_measure* using *goto_measure()*.

8

Note Level Editing

The Note Level Editing functions require a different approach for storing and manipulating MIDI data. This chapter describes the data structures and functions involved.

8.1 Data Structures for Note Displays

All of the functions working with MIDI data so far have used the event data structure to store and recall track data. This structure closely matches the MPU-401's method of requesting and transmitting MIDI data and timing information, so the Record and Play processes are reasonably simple. The event structure also has the desirable characteristic of being able to store any kind of data received from the MPU-401. This includes notes, controller data, and exclusive messages.

The simple event structure runs into trouble when you want to provide the user with an edit screen for individual notes. People think of notes as single entities; one note, a tone of a given duration. MIDI looks at a note as two entities: a Note On, and a Note Off. The time separation between these two events is the duration of the note.

We want the program to function the way people think, not the way the MPU-401 "thinks," so some adjustments need to be made. MT uses a separate temporary data structure for the NLE (Note Level Edit) screen. This is the structure *note_time* defined in MT.H:

```
struct note_time{
    struct event far *on_event;
    int on_measure;
    int on_tick;
    int note_number;
    struct event far *off_event;
    int off_measure;
    int off_tick;
    struct note_time far *next;
};
```

This structure is used for only one track's data, and only when needed for an NLE session. Any changes are written back to the track's event list. The *note_time* data is freed from memory when the NLE session is finished.

The *note_time* structure contains three pointers. Two of these point to the track events that contain the Note On and Note Off data. The last pointer (called *next*) points to the next *note_time* data. The *note_time* data forms a linked list in memory.

The *note_time* structure also contains the timing of both the start and stop of the note and the note number. Timing information consists of the measure number and the number of ticks from the start of the measure. Both measure numbers and tick counts are stored as integers, providing plenty of precision for long tracks.

At the start of an NLE session, MT reads all of the events from the start to the end of the track being edited. During this reading process, MT calculates the timing (measure number and number of ticks) for each event containing a MIDI Note On. Those events marking the start of a note are held temporarily until the Note Off event with the same note number is found. Once the pair of events has been located, the new note is added to the *note_time* linked list. This continues until the end of the track is reached. Only note events are converted to the *note_time* structure. Controller data, exclusive messages, etc., are all ignored.

8.2 The Piano Roll Display

The next problem to face on the NLE display is how to show the *note_time* data on the screen. MT uses the "piano roll" type of display. A piano keyboard image is displayed on the left side of the screen. The lowest notes are at the bottom, and the highest are at the top. The horizontal scale is the time axis. Time is broken into measure numbers and MPU-401 ticks. The beat number is also shown on the display. MT uses 120 ticks per quarter note, and quarter notes are always one beat.

The keyboard display on the NLE screen is composed of rectangles. The "black" keys are five pixels high, while the "white" keys are eight pixels high. This is true regardless of the video mode. Lower resolution modes display fewer octaves.

The piano keyboard is not simple device. There are "missing" black keys between notes B and C, and notes E and F. To line up each note's display with the right key on the piano requires a little calculation.

MT uses the structure *note_map* defined in MT.H to simplify finding the right piano key.

```
struct note_map{
    char name[10];
    int up_dots;
    int down_dots;
};
```

The *up_dots* element defines how many pixels to move upward on the screen to reach the next note. *Down_dots* defines the number of pixels to move downward to reach the next lower note. The *name[]* element holds the character data for each note's name.

The data for this structure is defined in the *g_notes[]* array in MTSC.H. Here is an excerpt:

```
struct note_map g_notes[] = {
    { "C -5",      4, 0 },    /* 0 */   /* MIDI note number */
    { "C#/Db -5",  4, 4 },
    { "D -5",      4, 4 },
    { "D#/Eb -5",  4, 4 },
    { "E -5",      8, 4 },
    { "F -5",      4, 8 },             /* 5 */
    { "F#/Gb -5",  4, 4 },.....
```

G_notes[] has one element for every one of the MIDI notes (128 of them). The array index in *g_notes[]* maps to the MIDI note number, so *g_notes[0]* is C five octaves below middle C. Appendix 1 has a table of MIDI note values.

Note that the "missing" black key between notes E-5 and F-5 causes a separation of eight pixels between those notes. This is reflected in the *up_dots* element for E-5, and the *down_dots* element for F-5. The other note separations in this excerpt are all four pixels apart, as there are "black" keys between these notes. The lowest MIDI note, C-5, has a *down_dots* value of zero. There is no MIDI note lower than this element.

With *g_notes[]* defined, the vertical position of any note on the NLE screen can be found by starting from the top note and adding the number of *down_dots* for all of the notes from the top note to the note displayed. Two global variables are used to keep track of the top note displayed on the screen: *g_top_note* has the MIDI note number of the top note displayed; *g_top_note_line* has the pixel number for the vertical position of this note on the screen. All other notes are located relative to this top note.

8.3 Programming in Graphics Modes

NLE operates in a graphics video mode, not a text mode. The key to writing a program that uses graphics modes is to assume that the number of colors, pixels, etc., are variables, not constants. Every new piece of video equipment, from monochrome, CGA, EGA, to VGA, has introduced new video modes with differing physical characteristics. No end to this is in sight. MT's NLE display adapts to the resolution of the equipment available. More resolution allows more data to be displayed at once, but is not critical to the application.

MT reads the mode the user selected in the INSTALL program as the variable *g_graph_mode*. Each of the many graphics modes has different numbers of colors, pixel resolution, text lines, etc. INSTALL writes these to the following global variables defined in VIDEO.H:

`g_graph_mode`	The graphics mode number.
`g_graph_char_h`	The number of characters displayed horizontally in the graphics mode (number of columns).
`g_graph_char_v`	The number of characters displayed vertically in the graphics mode (number of rows).
`g_dots_v`	The number of vertical pixels.
`g_dots_h`	The number of horizontal pixels.
`g_graph_colors`	The number of possible colors.

Writing letters and numbers on the screen can be done with the C compiler library video output functions. Colors display just like in the text modes, but there is no equivalent to changing the background for a letter or word (no reverse video).

The functions for character output in VIDEOFNC.C (described in Chapter 10) work fine in the graphics modes. This includes:

`writeword()`	Writes a character string.
`movescrn()`	Handles menu selections.
`initscrn()`	Initializes menu items on screen.

In the text modes, the cursor is highlighted with reverse video. In the graphics modes, *movescrn()* highlights one item by underlining the command.

The sprite functions in VIDEOFNC.C are also used on the NLE screen. A cross-shaped cursor is used to mark the start and end of notes. Also a small letter M is written as a sprite to mark the middle C key on the piano keyboard. Both of these sprites are defined in MTSC.H.

8.4 Overview of Note Level Edit Functions

The NLE functions are in four files: MTSC1.C through MTSC4.C. MTSC1.C contains the *scrn_edit_control()* function that runs every aspect of NLE. This function is called from within MLE *edit_menu()* any time the user selects a measure on the MLE display.

The functions in MTSC2.C build the NLE graphics display. This includes displaying the piano keyboard, measure markers, and so forth. The most critical function is *build_note_list()*. This function reads all of the event data on one track, and converts any MIDI Note On/Off events to the structure *note_time* format. The *disp_notes()* function then draws lines on the screen for every note within the screen range. It also checks every note within ten measures of the screen area for notes that might carry over into the screen.

MTSC3.C contains the functions for finding and deleting notes. The pivotal function here is *select_note()* which allows the cursor to move on the screen.

In a number of places in the MTSC code, comparisons need to be made to see if a given note or the cursor is located before or after some other note. This can be done by comparing first the measure number, and second the tick number. The programming logic gets involved, since every comparison has to be made twice, once for the measure numbers, and once for the tick counts.

MT uses floating point numbers to do the comparison in one pass. The function *note_to_float()* converts the measure and tick count to a single floating point value. The tick number used as the decimal part of the floating point number, while the measure number is on the left side of the decimal. For example, say that the event in question is at tick 120 of measure 56, and the meter is set to four beats per measure. The floating point equivalent is:

```
56 + 120/(4 x 120) = 56.25
```

This would be accomplished with the function call:

```
/* float n; */
n = note_to_float(56, 120);
```

The *add_note()* function controls the overall operation of adding a note to a track from the NLE screen. *Add_note()* adds the Note On and Note Off events to the track event data. *Add_note_time()* adds the note to the temporary NLE *note_time* data to keep the piano roll display current.

The *change_vel()* function allows a crude form of velocity editing. Individual notes can have their velocity changed by using this function. More elaborate methods for velocity editing are discussed in Chapter 12.

8.5 NLE Function Descriptions

Function: `int scrn_edit_control(int track, int measure)`

Purpose: Central function for the Note Level Editor.

In File: MTSC1.C

Related Header Files: MT.H, MTSC.H, VIDEO.H

Returned Value: Returns the last measure edited.

Discussion: This function displays the NLE screen by calling subfunctions that create the piano keyboard image, note lines, etc. The bottom of the NLE screen is a menu of commands. *Scrn_edit_control()* directs control to the appropriate subfunction depending on the user's selection of a menu item.

During the course of an NLE editing session, the user can move forward and backwards in the track's data. When the user quits NLE, *scrn_edit_control()* returns the measure number the NLE session ended on. This allows the MLE screen cursor to highlight the measure number last edited.

Function: `void init_edit_param(void)`

Purpose: Initializes NLE global variables.

In File: MTSC1.C

Related Header Files: MT.H, MTSC.H, VIDEO.H

Returned Value: None (void).

Discussion: Because of differences in the resolution of different video cards, the number of octaves that can be displayed is variable. This also affects the placement of note information on the screen. To manage this, a number of global variables are used:

`g_oct_shown:`	The number of octaves displayed on the screen.
`g_top_note_line:`	The pixel line number of the top note displayed.
`g_bot_note_line:`	The pixel line number of the bottom note displayed.
`g_top_note:`	The MIDI note number of the top note displayed.
`g_bot_note:`	The MIDI note number of the bottom note displayed.

In addition, some of the video modes support having more than the default twenty-five lines of text on the screen. In this case, the menu items have to be moved down. The global variable *g_graph_char_v* (read in from INSTALL.DAT at the start of MT) contains the number of text lines on the graphics screen. If this is greater than twenty-five, *init_edit_param()* adjusts the *MT6[]* menu array elements.

Function: `void display_keyboard(void)`

Purpose: Puts the piano keyboard image on the left side of the screen.

In File: MTSC1.C

Related Header Files: MT.H, MTSC.H, VIDEO.H

Returned Value: None (void).

Discussion: The piano keyboard image is built up using rectangles. The "black" keys are filled in, while the "white" keys are displayed with just a border. The global variable *g_line_color* sets the display color for the keyboard.

Function: `void init_screen_box(int beat, int measure)`

Purpose: Master function to write the note display area on the NLE screen.

In File: MTSC2.C

Related Header Files: MT.H, MTSC.H, VIDEO.H

Returned Value: None (void).

Discussion: The NLE note display is all within a rectangular area on the screen. This area is cleared by filling the rectangle with the color *g_back_color,* and outlining it with the color *g_line_color. Init_screen_box()* also calls the *top_scale()* and *dottend_lines()* functions to complete the screen update.

Function: `void top_scale(int beat, int leftside, int topline, int rightside, int botline, int measure)`

Purpose: Puts the beat numbers and tick marks on the top of the NLE edit area.

In File: MTSC2.C

Related Header Files: MT.H, MTSC.H, VIDEO.H

Returned Value: None (void).

Discussion: The top scale consists of the beat numbers and the ruler lines marking off fractions of a beat. The ruler lines are added if the spot being marked is an even tick number.

Function: `void name_top_note(int oct_shown)`

Purpose: Writes the top note name in the lower right of the screen.

In File: MTSC2.C

Related Header Files: MT.H, MTSC.H, VIDEO.H

Returned Value: None (void).

Discussion: Normally, the middle C key serves as a reference. At the extreme ends of the MIDI scale, the middle C key will not be visible. As an added reference, MT keeps the name of the top note updated at the bottom-right side of the screen. The note name is fetched from the *g_notes[]* array defined in MTSC.H.

Function: `void name_measure(int measure)`

Purpose: Puts the current measure number in the upper-left corner of the NLE screen.

In File: MTSC2.C

Related Header Files: MT.H, MTSC.H, VIDEO.H

Returned Value: None (void).

Function: `void dotted_lines(int topx, int topy, int botx, int boty, int vspace, int hspace, int color)`

Purpose: Puts dotted lines on the NLE screen as a visual reference.

In File: MTSC3.C

Related Header Files: MT.H, MTSC.H, VIDEO.H

Returned Value: None (void).

Discussion: Without the dotted lines in the NLE editing area, it is difficult to see which keyboard key is in line with a note.

Function: `struct event far *build_note_list(int track)`

Purpose: Creates a temporary *note_time* structure linked list for one track's notes.

In File: MTSC2.C

Related Header Files: MT.H, MTSC.H, VIDEO.H

Returned Value: Far pointer to the start of the *note_time* linked list. Returns NULL if user interrupts by hitting ESC key.

Discussion: *Build_note_list()* starts from the beginning of the track event data and works to the end. When it encounters a MIDI Note On, *build_note_list()* stores the note temporarily in the array *on_array[]*. When the matching Note Off is found, the complete note's data is converted to structure *note_time* format and added to the linked list.

Build_note_list() does not make provisions for cases where two Note Ons follow each other on the same MIDI note number without an intermediate Note Off. In this case, the first Note On will be ignored. Only the second Note On will show up as a note on the NLE screen. This situation can occur if overlapping notes on different tracks are merged using the Block Paste or Block Repeat commands, or if the incoming data is from a MIDI merger device.

Function: `void free_note_list(struct note_time far *np)`

Purpose: Removes the *note_time* linked list from memory.

In File: MTSC2.C

Related Header Files: MT.H, MTSC.H, VIDEO.H

Returned Value: None (void).

Discussion: This function is called when NLE is exited to free all memory associated with the *note_time* data.

Function: `void disp_notes(struct note_time far *first_notep, int first_measure, int beat)`

Purpose: Puts the horizontal note lines on the NLE screen.

In File: MTSC2.C

Related Header Files: MT.H, MTSC.H, VIDEO.H

Returned Value: None (void).

Discussion: *Disp_notes()* reads from the start of the *note_time* linked list to the end. Each note is checked to see if it falls within the time range displayed on the screen. If so, the *draw_note()* function is called to put the note line on the screen. *Disp_notes()* only checks notes within ten measures of the measure(s) shown on the screen.

Function: `void draw_note(struct note_time *np, int color)`

Purpose: Puts a line on the NLE screen to represent one note.

In File: MTSC2.C

Related Header Files: MT.H, MTSC.H, VIDEO.H

Returned Value: None (void).

Discussion: *Draw_note()* checks to make sure the note is within the time range displayed on the NLE screen. *Find_note_line()* is called to determine the vertical pixel number. The horizontal pixel start and end points are calculated based on the starting measure/beat of the NLE display, and the current horizontal scale (*g_scale* parameter).

Function: `void mark_middle_c(int first)`

Purpose: Puts a small letter M on the keyboard for the middle C key.

In File: MTSC2.C

Related Header Files: MT.H, MTSC.H, VIDEO.H

Returned Value: None (void).

Discussion: The M has to be smaller than the standard characters on the graphics screen. A sprite pixel image called *little_m* is defined in MTSC.H. If the parameter *first* is true, the M is not already on the screen, so no effort is made to erase the old one. If *first* is zero, the old M is erased and a new one written to the screen.

A static variable *ypos* is used to keep track of the last M position. If this value is zero, the M is out of the displayed range.

Function: `int find_note_line(int note_no)`

Purpose: Determines the screen pixel line number for a given MIDI note.

In File: MTSC2.C

Related Header Files: MT.H, MTSC.H, VIDEO.H

Returned Value: The pixel line number.

Discussion: The notes are separated by either four or eight pixels, depending on where the note lies on the scale. *Find_note_line()* works its way from the *top_note_line* to the specified note. The number of pixels between each successive note is found in the *g_notes[]* array.

Function: `struct note_time far *delete_note(struct note_time far *first_notep, int measure, int beat, int track)`

Purpose: Deletes a note from the NLE display.

In File: MTSC3.C

Related Header Files: MT.H, MTSC.H, VIDEO.H

Returned Value: Pointer to start of note list, NULL if error.

Discussion: If the cursor is over a valid note, the address of the Note On and Note Off events are found via the *note_time* linked list. The two events are deleted and the note is also removed from the *note_time* list.

Delete_note() calls *select_note()* to find out which note the user is pointing to with the cross hairs cursor. If a note is selected, *remove_event()* is called twice to remove the Note On and Note Off events, and *remove_note()* is called once to remove the *note_time* structure for this note.

The note is erased from the screen by drawing the note's horizontal line over using the background color.

Function: `struct note_pos *select_note(struct note_time *first_notep, int measure, int beat, int option)`

Purpose: Controls cursor movement to select a note on the NLE screen.

In File: MTSC3.C

Related Header Files: MT.H, MTSC.H, VIDEO.H

Returned Value: Returns a pointer to a structure *note_pos*.

Discussion: If a valid note is located, *select_note()* needs to return the measure number, tick number, note number, and cursor position. The structure *note_pos* is used to return the data:

```
struct note_pos{
    int measure;
    int tick;
    int note;
    int sprite_x;
    int sprite_y;
}
```

Sprite functions are used to draw and remove the cursor. If the option parameter is true, the cursor is left on the screen after *select_note()* exits. Otherwise, the cursor is removed. During cursor movement the note name, measure number, and tick number are updated in the lower-right corner of the screen.

Select_note() uses a technique known as "wind up" to accelerate the cursor movement if the mouse or cursor keys are being moved rapidly. The keyboard input buffer is scanned for all cursor keypresses. If more than one is found in a given direction, the total displacement is multiplied by two to accelerate movement. Shift-array key combinations are also interpreted as fast cursor moves. Hitting ESC quits the function with a returned value of NULL, clearing the cursor.

Function: void clear_select_lines(void)

Purpose: Blanks out the note name, measure and tick number areas at the bottom right of the NLE screen.

In File: MTSC3.C

Related Header Files: MT.H, MTSC.H, VIDEO.H

Returned Value: None (void).

Function: `struct note_time far *find_note(struct note_time far *first_notep, int note, int measure, int tick)`

Purpose: Finds a given note in the *note_time* linked list.

In File: MTSC3.C

Related Header Files: MT.H, MTSC.H, VIDEO.H

Returned Value: Far pointer to note in *note_time* list. NULL if no match found.

Discussion: *Find_note()* walks through the *note_time* linked list starting with *first_notep*. If the note numbers match, and if *measure* and *tick* are within the note's duration, the note is found.

Function: `float note_to_float(int measure, int tick)`

Purpose: Converts the measure number and the tick number to a single floating point value.

In File: MTSC3.C

Related Header Files: MT.H, MTSC.H, VIDEO.H

Returned Value: Floating point value. The digits on the left side of the decimal point are the measure number; the decimal portion is the fraction of a full measure represented by the tick value.

Discussion: Converts the measure and tick numbers to a single floating point value. For example, measure 12, tick 240 would convert to 12.5 in a song with a four-beat meter (480 ticks per measure). This conversion makes comparisons for which note starts first, etc., simpler than first comparing measure numbers and then comparing tick numbers.

Function: `int remove_event(struct event far *eventp, int track)`

Purpose: Removes an event from the track's event data.

In File: MTSC3.C

Related Header Files: MT.H, MTSC.H, VIDEO.H

Returned Value: 1 if event removed; 0 if not found in track data.

Discussion: The removal of an event affects the next event's timing. If the sum of the removed event's timing byte plus the timing byte of the next event exceeds the MPU-401's limit of 239 ticks, a new TIME_OUT event is added in place of the removed event. The next event's timing byte is adjusted accordingly. Normally, only the next event's timing has to be adjusted to compensate for the removal of one event.

Function: `struct note_time far *remove_note(struct note_time far *first_notep, struct note_time far *notep)`

Purpose: Removes a note's data from the *note_time* linked list.

In File: MTSC3.C

Related Header Files: MT.H, MTSC.H, VIDEO.H

Returned Value: Pointer to start of *note_time* list; NULL if no match is found.

Discussion: One complication is that the note to be deleted can be the first note in the list. For this reason, *remove_note()* returns a pointer to the start of the list if it is successful at finding and deleting the note's data. The returned pointer then becomes the new beginning of the *note_time* linked list.

Function: `void add_note(struct note_time far *first_notep, int measure, int track)`

Purpose: Adds a note on the NLE screen.

In File: MTSC4.C

Related Header Files: MT.H, MTSC.H, VIDEO.H

Returned Value: None (void).

Discussion: *Add_note()* uses the *select_note()* function twice to allow the user to point to the start and end of the note on the screen. The user is then prompted to enter in a velocity value. A velocity of 64 is the default input if Return is pressed.

The note is then added to the track. As it is possible to edit a measure with no MIDI data, *advance_to_measure()* is called to build measures up to and including the end of the note added. The Note On and Note Off events are added to the track's event list with two calls to *add_event()*. The note is added to the *note_time* linked list with *add_note_time()*. Finally, the cursor is removed from the screen, and the note is displayed as a line by calling *draw_note()*.

Function: `struct event far *add_event(int track, int measure, int tick, int event_bytes, int b1, int b2, int b3)`

Purpose: Adds a new event to the track's event list.

In File: MTSC4.C

Related Header Files: MT.H, MTSC.H, VIDEO.H

Returned Value: Far pointer to the new event.

Discussion: In the most common case, the event is added to the event list, and the timing value of the next event reduced to compensate for the addition. If the next event is a TIME_OUT, the added event may eliminate the need for the TIME_OUT event.

Function: `struct note_time far *add_note_time(struct note_time far *first_np, struct event far *on_event, struct event far *on_meas, int on_tick, int off_event, int off_meas, int off_tick)`

Purpose: Adds a note to the *note_time* linked list.

In File: MTSC4.C

Related Header Files: MT.H, MTSC.H, VIDEO.H

Returned Value: Far pointer to the start of the *note_time* list.

Discussion: *Add_note_time()* puts the new note in the *note_time* linked list in time sequence based on the Note On timing. There is always the possibility that the added note will become the first note in the list, so the start of the list is the returned value.

Function: `void change_vel(struct note_time far *first_notep, int track)`

Purpose: Allows the user to pick a note and change its velocity.

In File: MTSC4.C

Related Header Files: MT.H, MTSC.H, VIDEO.H

Returned Value: None (void).

Discussion: Allows the user to enter a new velocity (or default value of 64) for a selected note. The note is located via *select_note()*.

The key velocity data is not stored in the *note_time* data. The *note_time* element contains a pointer to the Note On event. *Change_vel()* uses this pointer to find the fourth event byte (b[3]) and to change it to the new velocity value.

9

File and Utility Functions

This chapter concludes the description of MT's files and file-related functions.

9.1 MT File Format

MT stores track data in disk files differently from the method used to store the data in the computer's memory. The disk file format takes up less than half the number of bytes as the memory format. However, the disk files cannot be added to or edited without first reading the data into the more flexible memory format.

Song files on disk are built up from three parts: two fixed portions, and a variable portion that adjusts to the amount of track data in memory. Here is the format:

MT Song File Data Format

Bytes   **Contains**

Header (fixed size):

Bytes	Contains
51	Song title string.
2	Metronome rate, beats per minute (as int).
2	Meter, beats per measure (as int).
2	Pitchbend flag, 1 if on, 0 if not (as int).
2	Exclusive flag, 1 if on, 0 if not (as int).

Track Information (repeated eight times, once per track, fixed size)

9   Track name.

2   Track MIDI channel number (as int).

4   Track event count (as long int).

2   Track Play status, 1 if on, 0 if not (as int).

2   Track MIDI volume (as int)

Track Data (once for each event in track, variable size)

5 x event count Format of each group of 5 bytes:

        nbyte, b[0], b[1], b[2], b[3]

The header applies to all of the tracks in the file, so it is not repeated. The next group (track information) is repeated eight times, once for each track. Each track's data is placed immediately following the previous one. The key parameter in the track information group is the event count. This specifies how many events worth of data each track contains. Note that the long integer type is used to allow for very long tracks.

The actual event data for each track is written last. The only way to tell where one track's data ends and the next begins on the disk file, is to calculate the end of one track's data. Each event is five bytes long, so the event count times five gives the size of each track's event count.

Recall that in memory, MT stores each group of MIDI data as a structure event:

```
struct event{
    struct event far *next;
    char nbytes;
    char b[4];
}
```

The *next* element points to the next event in memory. When reading the song file off the disk, MT has to recreate the linked lists of events that make up the memory storage. This is done as the file is read. MT allocates one event's worth of memory and then reads the *nbyte* and *b[ ]* fields off the disk and right into the event. MT then sets the next pointer to the next memory space allocated for an event, reads in the next five bytes off of the disk, and so on.

The function *save_tracks()* writes the song data in memory to a disk file. *Recal_song()* reads the disk file back into memory, allocating memory for each event as needed. Both use the *put_to_file()* and *get_from_file()* functions to read and write data. MT reads and writes all five char bytes for each event (*nbytes* and *b[4]*) with one function call. This takes advantage of the assumption that the bytes are always right next to one another in storage. C compilers do not guarantee that all five bytes will be next to each other, so this speed-up trick is not 100 percent portable.

The disk file format is more compact than the memory format. The next pointers are eliminated on each stored event, saving four bytes. Also, bytes used by the memory allocation functions to keep track of storage space in memory are eliminated.

9.2 The IMPORT Menu

Importing a single track from memory is similar to loading a song file. The main difference is that only one track of data is loaded. The rest of the data in the file is skipped over.

When IMPORT is first activated, the user sees a list of all of the song files in the current drive/directory. The IMPORT menu is displayed when one song file is selected. IMPORT reads the header information from each track on the source file, but not the track data. This header information is displayed at the top of the IMPORT menu. Similar data for the tracks already in memory is displayed at the bottom to help the user avoid importing onto the wrong track.

The IMPORT menu is interesting. There are actually three independent menus on the screen. The bottom line is the first menu (*mt5[]*). If the user picks the Pick Source command, a second menu (*mt51[]*) on the track SOURC row is activated. This allows the user to select which track to import from the source file. Similarly, the DEST row is also a separate menu (*mt52[]*), used to pick the destination track. All menus are defined in MTSCREEN.H.

Figure 9.1 MT Import Menu

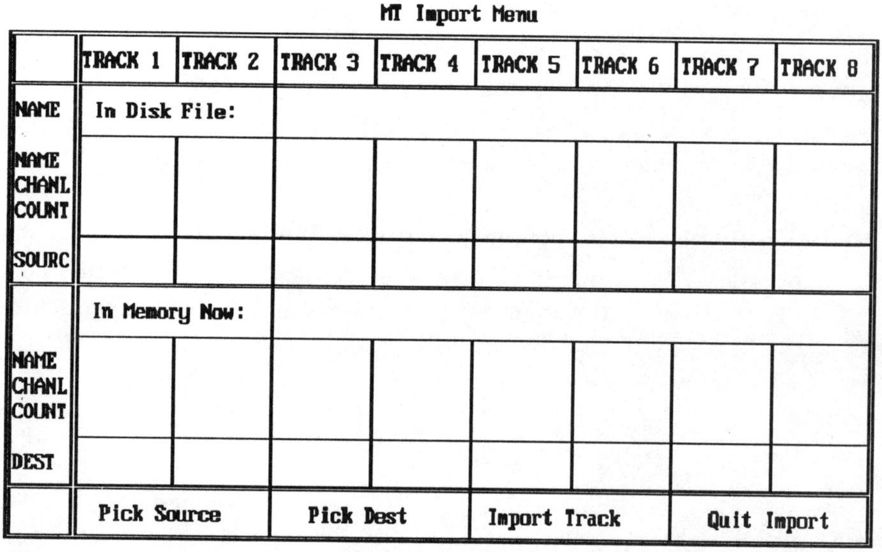

MT Import Menu

	TRACK 1	TRACK 2	TRACK 3	TRACK 4	TRACK 5	TRACK 6	TRACK 7	TRACK 8
NAME	In Disk File:							
NAME CHANL COUNT								
SOURC								
	In Memory Now:							
NAME CHANL COUNT								
DEST								
	Pick Source		Pick Dest		Import Track		Quit Import	

mt5.scr

Before the track of data is read from the source file, the existing data in the destination track is cleared from memory. IMPORT reads through the data in the disk file until it comes to the track data requested. This is then read one event at a time. New events are allocated in memory as needed until the end of the source track is read.

MT is not equipped to effectively handle tracks in memory with different *meters* (number of beats per measure). The *import_menu()* function checks to see if the meter in memory matches the meter in the source file. A warning is displayed if they do not match.

9.3 Low-Level File Access

MT uses four functions to move data between the disk and memory. Two functions work on *near* data in the default data segment, and two work on *far* data.

put_to_file()	Sends *near* data to the disk.
get_from_file()	Gets data from the disk and loads into *near* memory.
fput_to_file()	Sends *far* data to the disk.
fget_from_file()	Gets data from the disk and loads into *far* memory.

Let's take a look at the first function:

```
void                    /* put near data to stream */
put_to_file(void *addr, int size, FILE *stream)
{
    int i;
    char *addr2;

    addr2 = (char *)addr;
    for(i = 0; i < size; i++){
        fputc(*addr2++, stream);
    }
}
```

Put_to_file() is a somewhat unusual function, in that it uses the *(void *)* data type for a parameter. The reason for this is that we want to use *put_to_file()* to store any type of data in memory to the disk. Both Microsoft C version 5+ and Turbo C support the *(void *)* data type. If you are using an older C compiler that does not support *(void *)*, replace *void* with *char*. It will work fine, but may generate warning messages during compilation when *put_to_file()* and the other three functions are used to store and retrieve data other than type char.

The line:

```
addr2 = (char *)addr;
```

causes the address of the unspecified (void) type data to be coerced to type char for the *fputc()* function. Regardless of what type of data exists at *addr*, *fputc()* will send the data one byte (char) at a time to the output stream.

Let's look at how the *put_to_file()* function can be used for storing any type of data. We will use the int type as an example.

```
/* example of using put_to_file() to write integer data */

example()
{
    int i;
    FILE *stream;

    i = 8;
    stream = fopen("temp.dat", "wb");
    put_to_file(&i, sizeof(int), stream);
    fclose(stream);
}
```

In the IBM PC C compiler world, the int data type requires two bytes of data. Rather than write *put_to_file* (&i, 2, stream), the *sizeof()* function is used to compute the size of the data. This makes the program more portable.

Note that *put_to_file()* writes the bytes to the disk file in the same order that they exist in memory. The IBM PC family of computers store integers with the least significant bytes first. Other computer systems store integers with the least significant bytes last. Files written with these functions are therefore not directly readable with the same functions on other computers. If you need to exchange data with other families of computers it is best to use a data format that is specific down to the bit level. The Standard MIDI Files secification 1.0 fits this need. More on this in Chapter 12.

Put_to_file() is an example of how the improvements to the C language allow us to write more general functions and still maintain strong type checking. It will take improvements to our computers (getting rid of *near* and *far* data segments once and for all) before the ideal situation of needing only two of these functions is practical without added overhead. The C++ language provides means for overloading a function so that it can handle more than one data type. Conventional C does not allow this.

9.4 Function Descriptions

The FILEFUNC.C functions control both file selection and the reading of video data stored by INSTALL. These are general purpose functions, and can be used in many programs. The file display screens take advantage of a menu array *g_file_displ[]* defined in FILEFUNC.H. This array has room for ninety file names, including their three-letter extensions. The menu allows the normal *movescrn()* menu functions to control selection of a file.

Function: `int pick_file(char *dir, char *match_str, char *str)`

Purpose: Allows selection of a file from a list shown on the screen.

In File: FILEFUNC.C

Related Header Files: FILEFUNC.H, SCREENF.H

Returned Value: The selection element number in the *g_file_displ[]* array; -1 if nothing is selected.

Discussion: The *str* parameter is a header that is written at the top of the screen. All files in the drive/directory specified by the *dir* parameter which match the standard DOS wild card file specification in *match_str* are then displayed on the screen (ninety maximum). The user can then select a file by moving the cursor and then pressing Return. Pressing the ESC key exits this function with a returned value of -1.

Disp_files() is used to put the file names matching *match_str* on the screen. *Movescrn()* is used to run the menu selection.

Function: `int disp_files(char *dir, *match_str)`

Purpose: Displays file names in the *dir* drive/directory matching the *match_str* DOS wild card file specifier.

In File: FILEFUNC.C

Related Header Files: FILEFUNC.H, SCREENF.H

Returned Value: The number of files displayed; 0 if none found.

Discussion: Disp_files() builds a full drive/directory search string from the *dir* and *match_str* strings. The *find_first* and *find_next* library functions are used to put all matching file names into the *g_file_displ[]* menu array. *Finitscrn()* is then used to display the file names. A maximum of ninety file names can be displayed.

Function: `int get_drive(char *prodir, char *sampdir)`

Purpose: Prompts the user for a drive/directory to use for storing/retrieving song files.

In File: FILEFUNC.C

Related Header Files: FILEFUNC.H, SCREENF.H

Returned Value: 1 if OK; 0 if no selection.

Discussion: *Prodir* is a string containing the name of default drive/directory that MT started up on. *Sampdir* is the name of a drive/directory that songs should be read or written to.

Get_drive() is called from MT's primary menu to get the drive/directory used for loading and saving song files. Checks to make sure drive/directory exists before copying it to *sampdir*.

Function: `void put_to_file(void *addr, int size, FILE stream)`

Purpose: Writes size bytes starting at memory address *addr* in *near* memory to output device stream.

In File: FILEFUNC.C

Related Header Files: FILEFUNC.H, SCREENF.H

Returned Value: None (void).

Discussion: Be sure that all *size* bytes are in sequence in memory.

Function: `void fput_to_file(void far *addr, int size, FILE stream)`

Purpose: Writes *size* chars (bytes) to output device stream, starting at memory address *addr* in *far* memory.

In File: FILEFUNC.C

Related Header Files: FILEFUNC.H, SCREENF.H

Returned Value: None (void).

Discussion: This is the *far* memory version of *put_to_file()*.

Function: `void get_from_file(void *addr, int size, FILE stream)`

Purpose: Gets *size* bytes from input device stream and stores them into *near* memory starting at *addr*.

In File: FILEFUNC.C

Related Header Files: FILEFUNC.H, SCREENF.H

Returned Value: None (void).

Discussion: All *size* bytes should be in sequence in memory.

Function: `void fget_from_file(void far *addr, int size, FILE stream)`

Purpose: Gets *size* chars (bytes) from input device stream and stores them into *far* memory starting at *addr*.

In File: FILEFUNC.C

Related Header Files: FILEFUNC.H, SCREENF.H

Returned Value:

Discussion: This is the far memory version of *get_from_file()*.

Function: `void loadscrn(struct strchain *chain[], int number, char *namestr)`

Purpose: Loads a series of screen files into linked lists in memory.

In File: FILEFUNC.C

Related Header Files: SCREENF.H

Returned Value: None (void).

Discussion: One of the early lines in MT's *main()* module is:

```
loadscrn(g_chain, NSCREEN, "MT");
```

This loads the screen files MT1.SCR through MT6.SCR into memory. *Loadscrn()* assumes that the file names are in a numeric sequence starting with number 1, and that the file type is .SCR. The files are loaded into memory as linked lists of the type *strchain* (defined in SCREENF.H). The start of each linked list is kept in array *g_chain*. There are five screens to load, each starting with the letters MT.

Once *loadscrn()* is finished, other functions can display screens by calling *dispchain()* or *fdispchain()*. Failure to find a screen file causes an error message to be displayed, and calls *exit()* to abort the program.

The *strchain* structure is described in more detail in Chapter 11.

_____

Function: `void load_video_data(char *filename)`

Purpose: Loads the video parameters set by the INSTALL program into memory.

In File: FILEFUNC.C

Related Header Files: VIDEO.H

Returned Value: 1 if file found; 0 if not found.

Discussion: This is the counterpart to the INSTALL program. INSTALL writes all of the video parameters to a file. *Load_video_data()* reads them into global variables defined in VIDEO.H for use by all other parts of MT.

Function: void save_song(void)

Purpose: Control function for storing track data to disk.

In File: MTUT1.C

Related Header Files: FILEFUNC.H, SCREENF.H

Returned Value: None (void).

Discussion: *Disp_files()* is used to put all existing song file names on the screen. If a song file name has already been set, *save_song()* asks if this name should be kept. This is a convenient default. If a song file has not already been set, *getstr()* is used to prompt for input of a new file name. Assuming the file can be opened, *save_tracks()* writes the track data to disk.

During the file activity, the default directory is set to the *g_songdir* directory. Upon exit of *save_song()*, the default directory is set back to *g_prodir*, the directory active when the MT program was started.

Function: void save_tracks(FILE *stream)

Purpose: Writes current track data to stream.

In File: MTUT1.C

Related Header Files: FILEFUNC.H, SCREENF.H

Returned Value: None (void).

Discussion: This function does the work of writing a song file to disk.

Function: void load_song(void)

Purpose: Runs the file load operation.

In File: MTUT1.C

Related Header Files: FILEFUNC.H, SCREENF.H

Returned Value: None (void).

Discussion: *Pick_file()* is used to display the song files in the current drive/directory and allow a user selection. Once a song file is selected, *recal_song()* is used to load the data into memory.

Function: `void recal_song(FILE *stream)`

Purpose: Loads data from stream into memory.

In File: MTUT1.C

Related Header Files: FILEFUNC.H, SCREENF.H

Returned Value: None (void).

Discussion: Loading the data from disk requires that each event be allocated as it is needed to store track data. *Recal_song()* creates all new track event lists in memory whenever it is called.

Function: `void help_control(void)`

Purpose: Runs the HELP menu for MT.

In File: MTUT1.C

Related Header Files: FILEFUNC.H, SCREENF.H

Returned Value: None (void).

Discussion: The HELP command on the MT primary menu causes a HELP menu (MT4.SCR) to be displayed. The user selects a HELP topic and presses Return. *Help_control()* then displays the appropriate HELP screen file by calling *helpdisp()*. These screen files are cleared from memory right after being displayed.

Function: `void helpdisp(char *filename)`

Purpose: Displays a file on the screen, pauses for a keypress, then removes the screen file from memory.

In File: MTUT1.C

Related Header Files: FILEFUNC.H, SCREENF.H

Returned Value: None (void).

Function: `void import_menu(void)`

Purpose: Runs the IMPORT command menu for MT.

In File: MTUT2.C

Related Header Files: FILEFUNC.H, SCREENF.H, MTSCREEN.H

Returned Value: None (void).

Discussion: *Import_menu()* uses *pick_file()* to allow the user to select a song file. The file header and track information (but not the track data) is read in to fill out the top half of the IMPORT menu (MT5.SCR). These parameters are stored in local variables and *temp_trackarray[]*.

The current data in memory is shown at the bottom of the IMPORT menu.

The bottom line of the IMPORT screen is the IMPORT command menu, *mt5[]*, defined in MTSCREEN.H. If the user selects the Pick Source option, execution is passed to the *mt51[]* menu, which allows the user to select a source track. If the user selects the Pick Dest. option, the *mt52[]* menu is invoked, which allows the user to select a destination track. In all cases, the menus are updated by the *finitscrn()* function and selections controlled by *movescrn()*.

With the source and destination tracks selected, the user can select the Import Track option. *Import_menu()* uses the *import_track()* function to do the reading of the event data from disk.

Function: `void import_track(FILE *stream, int source_track, int dest_track, struct trackdata temp_trackarray[])`

Purpose: Reads one track's data off disk and into memory.

In File: MTUT2.C

Related Header Files: FILEFUNC.H, SCREENF.H

Returned Value: None (void).

Discussion: The header information in the song file was already read as part of *import_menu()*, so the DOS file pointer starts at the beginning of the track data when *import_track()* begins. Track data in the source file prior to the selected track has to be skipped over. *import_track()* uses the event counts passed in the *temp_trackarray[]* structure to determine how many bytes to skip over before the selected track's data begins.

During the reading of the source track data, new events are allocated in memory as each event is read from the disk. The pointer and event counts in MT's central *g_trackarray[]* structure are then updated.

Function: void show_source(int track)

Purpose: Highlights the source track on the IMPORT menu.

In File: MTUT2.C

Related Header Files: FILEFUNC.H, SCREENF.H, MTSCREEN.H

Returned Value: None (void).

Discussion: Works by updating the content element of the *mt51[]* menu data array.

Function: void show_dest(int track)

Purpose: Highlights the destination track on the IMPORT menu.

In File: MTUT2.C

Related Header Files: FILEFUNC.H, SCREENF.H

Returned Value: None (void).

Discussion: Works by updating the content element of the *mt52[]* menu data array.

10

Communication and Video Functions

This chapter describes the lowest-level functions used by MT for communication with the MPU-401 interface and the video display.

10.1 Communication with the MPU-401

All programs that work with MIDI data have to communicate with the MIDI interface. This is a low level task, and is usually handled in assembly language. The three functions used to talk to the MPU-401 interface are all in the file MIO401.ASM. This is the same file that was described in *C Programming for MIDI*, except that the Medium memory model is assumed.

Function: `int putcmd(int n)`

Purpose: Sends a command to the MPU-401 interface.

In File: MIO401.ASM

Related Header Files: MPU401.H

Returned Value: ACK (0xFE) if successful; -1 if not;

Discussion: The MPU-401 accepts a long list of commands. These are listed in the file MPU401.H along with their associated numeric value.

Typical commands turn the internal metronome beep on and off, set the tempo, start the Play process, etc.

Putcmd() sends the command to the MPU-401 interface. Normally, the command will be accepted and *putcmd()* returns a value of 0xFE which is the MPU-401 ACK (acknowledge) value. If the MPU-401 is not expecting a command, or if something mechanical is wrong, *putcmd()* will not get an ACK back from the interface. *Putcmd()* then returns an error value of -1.

————————————————————————————————————

Function: int getdata(void)

Purpose: Gets one byte of data from the MPU-401 interface.

In File: MIO401.ASM

Related Header Files: MPU401.H

Returned Value: Value fetched from MPU-401; -1 on error.

Discussion: This function fetches one byte from the MPU-401.

————————————————————————————————————

Function: int putdata(int n)

Purpose: Sends a data byte to the MPU-401 interface.

In File: MIO401.ASM

Related Header Files: MPU401.H

Returned Value: Returns byte value sent; -1 on error.

Discussion: Many of the MPU-401 commands require data to be transmitted after the command. For example, the SET_TEMPO command must be followed by a byte representing the tempo (100 for 100 beats per minute, etc.). *Putdata()* handles the communication of data bytes.

10.2 Video Attributes

MT supports user selection of colors for the screen displays. The selection of the colors is handled by a separate program called INSTALL that is described in Chapter 1. INSTALL writes a file called INSTALL.DAT that holds the chosen values for colors, video modes, etc. If INSTALL is started with a file name on the DOS command line, the output of INSTALL is written to that file. For example:

```
C:>INSTALL SECOND.DAT
```

would write the data to the file SECOND.DAT on the C: drive.

INSTALL can be used for providing video data to any program, including MT. Any program relying on INSTALL should use the same variable names for all of the video variables. These are defined in a file called VIDEO.H which is shown here:

```
/* video.h  header file for video attribute and mode data */
/* works in conjunction with install.c's output file install.dat */

#ifdef ALLOCATE
    #define GLOBAL                  /* to nothing */
    #define INIT(x)    =x
#else
    #define GLOBAL extern
    #define INIT(x)                 /* to nothing */
#endif


GLOBAL int g_text_mode;
GLOBAL int g_graph_mode;
GLOBAL int g_dots_v;               /* graphics pixels vertically */
GLOBAL int g_dots_h;               /* horizontally */
GLOBAL int g_norm_attrib;
GLOBAL int g_cursor_attrib;
```

```
GLOBAL int g_emph_attrib;
GLOBAL int g_let_dots_v;        /* character dot widths */
GLOBAL int g_let_dots_h;
GLOBAL int g_text_char_v;       /* number of char lines, text mode */
GLOBAL int g_text_char_h;       /* number of char columns */
GLOBAL int g_graph_char_h;      /* number in graphics mode for char */
GLOBAL int g_graph_char_v;      /* written to graphics screens */
GLOBAL int g_text_colors;       /* total number of colors available */
GLOBAL int g_graph_colors;

GLOBAL int g_line_color;
GLOBAL int g_back_color;
GLOBAL int g_emph_color;
```

As you can see, it takes a lot of numbers to fully define the video data. This is a side effect of the continuing evolution of video equipment for the IBM PC family.

The most frequently used of the global variables listed in VIDEO.H are the video *attribute* bytes. These are:

g_norm_attrib	The attribute for normal characters.
g_emph_attrib	The attribute for emphasized characters.
g_cursor_attrib	The attribute for letters highlighted by a moving cursor block.

Attributes are a concept the IBM PC family uses to keep track of the color of a letter and its background on the video screen when the display is in a text mode. Every letter position on the screen has two memory bytes associated with it: one for the ASCII code of the character being displayed, and the second for the attribute of the letter. The coding of the attributed byte is as follows:

Bit Position in Attribute   **Controls**

7 6 5 4 3 2 1 0

1	Blinking character on/off.
1	Red component of background.
1	Green component of background.
1	Blue component of background.
1	Intensity of foreground color.
1	Red component of foreground.
1	Green component of foreground.
1	Blue component of foreground.

The key thing to understand is that one attribute value controls both the color of the text letters, and the color of the background. Throughout the rest of the book, the *g_norm_attrib*, etc., variables will be used to pass the current color settings to output functions.

10.3 Video Modes

The IBM PC family of video adapters started out with several video display modes, and has gradually added new ones. Each mode has a different number of colors and pixels displayed on the screen. At the time of writing there are fifteen common video display modes, and a host of unusual ones supported by companies making video boards.

Figure 10.1 is a table of the common video modes.

Figure 10.1 Common Video Display Modes

Mode Number	Type	Colors	Columns	Rows	Resolution
0 CGA	Text	16	40 (of	25	
1 "	Text	16	40 text)	25	
2 "	Text	16	80	25	
3 "	Text	16	80	25	
4 "	Graph	4	40	25	320 × 200
5 "	Graph	4	40	25	320 × 200
6 "	Graph	2	80	25	640 × 200
7 Mono.	Text	2	80	25	
13 EGA	Graph	16	40	25	320 × 200
14 "	Graph	16	80	25	640 × 200
15 "	Graph	4	80	25	640 × 350
16 "	Graph	16	80	25	640 × 350
17 UGA	Graph	2	80	30	640 × 480
18 "	Graph	16	80	30	640 × 480
19 "	Graph	256	40	25	320 × 200
*15 Hercules	Graph	2	80	25	720 × 350

The Hercules graphics mode 15 is highlighted on the table because of its unusual status. Although this is not an "official" mode, and is not supported by the Microsoft C compiler graphics library, the Hercules card is so common that it should not be ignored. The INSTALL program recognizes that mode 15 can be either an EGA or Hercules mode. The ready-to-run version of MT.EXE on the program disk was compiled with the Microsoft compiler, and does not support Hercules graphics. See Appendix 4 for a discussion of how to use Hercules graphics by compiling with the Turbo C compiler.

The wide variety of video modes forces the programmer to deal defensively with video parameters. You must not assume that anything has a fixed value (such as screen height, width, number of colors). INSTALL sets the value of all of the video parameters based on the user's selection of video modes and colors. This frees you from having to worry about the video equipment in any application program that reads INSTALL's output file.

10.4 Video Functions

As mentioned earlier, controlling the screen display is not a standard part of the C language. To minimize the disruption, I put all of the low-level video functions in one file called VIDEOFNC.C.

Most of these functions are straightforward writing of text and graphics on the screen. Two of the functions deal with the less common problem of sprite images. Sprites are small video objects that can be moved around on the screen without disturbing the underlying image. Sprites are typically used as pointers for a moving cursor (mouse pointers), and for video animation. Only very limited use of sprites is made in MT, but the functions are of general value.

The data structure used to store a sprite is as follows:

```
struct sprite{
    int swide;
    int stall;
    unsigned char *sdata;
};
```

The *sdata* is a bit map of the sprite image. For example, a cross is used in MT as a moving cross hair. The cross is made up of binary data:

Example sprite bit map for a cross:

Binary	Hexadecimal
00001000 00000000	08 00
00001000 00000000	08 00
00001000 00000000	08 00
00001000 00000000	08 00
11111111 10000000	FF 80
00001000 00000000	08 00
00001000 00000000	08 00
00001000 00000000	08 00
00001000 00000000	08 00

This data is stored in the file MTSC.H as the *dcross*. This image is two bytes wide and nine bytes tall. Two and nine are the values for the *swide* and *stall* parameters within the sprite definition.

One of the standard tricks in manipulating sprites is to use the EXclusive OR operator (XOR). XOR has the property that if you do it twice, you end up with the same data you started with. Here is a truth table for XOR:

```
1 XOR 1 = 0                0 XOR 1 = 1
1 XOR 0 = 1                0 XOR 0 = 0
```

In the C language the XOR operator is the ^ symbol.

The *xsprite()* function uses the XOR concept to write a sprite on the screen. Using this function twice at the same location removes the sprite. To move a sprite on the screen, you first XOR it at the old location to remove it, then XOR it at the new location to make it reappear.

10.5 Functions in VIDEOFNC.C

Several of these functions work in all display modes. However, those that work on individual pixels only work in the graphics modes. I have indicated next to the function name if the function applies to "graphics only."

_____

Function: `void writeword(char *string, int x, int y, int attrib)`

Purpose: Writes a string to the screen at position column = x, row = y, with character attribute specified.

In File: VIDEOFNC.C

Related Header Files: VIDEO.H, SCREENF.H

Returned Value: None (void).

Discussion: Writing a group of characters on the screen is a common requirement. Most compiler libraries break this up into a process of setting the colors, positioning the cursor, and then writing the characters to the screen. *Writeword()* just rolls these up into one convenient function. See also the function *write_int()* which outputs an integer value much like *writeword()* outputs a string.

Most compiler libraries use the rather slow BIOS functions to write characters on the screen. This is OK for small amounts of writing, but bogs down if you have to write the whole screen. An alternative function, *fwriteword()*, is provided which writes directly to the video memory area.

————————————————————————————————

Function: `void clearscreen(int attrib)`

Purpose: Clears the screen.

In File: VIDEOFNC.C

Related Header Files: VIDEO.H, SCREENF.H

Returned Value: None (void).

Discussion: The screen color is set to the background value specified in the left four bits of the attribute byte. Besides clearing the screen, *clearscreen()* moves the cursor to the top-left corner.

————————————————————————————————

Function: `void csrplot(int x, int y)`

Purpose: Moves the cursor to column = x, row = y, on the screen.

In File: VIDEOFNC.C

Related Header Files: VIDEO.H, SCREENF.H

Returned Value: None (void).

Discussion: This function is seldom used, as the *writeword()* and similar functions do the same task. One use is when using the library function *printf()* for formatted output. *Printf()* starts printing from wherever the cursor was last placed, so you can precede *printf()* with a call to *csrplot()* to get the output in the right spot.

———————————————————————————————————————

Function: `void setvideomode(int mode)`

Purpose: Sets the video display mode.

In File: VIDEOFNC.C

Related Header Files: VIDEO.H, SCREENF.H

Returned Value: None (void).

Discussion: The INSTALL program lets the user select which modes to use for displaying text and graphics. Once these are chosen, an application program will normally only have to change modes when going to and from the graphics mode.

———————————————————————————————————————

Graphics only
Function: `void dotplot(int x, int y, int color)`

Purpose: Changes the color of the pixel at column = x, row = y, to color in a graphics video mode.

In File: VIDEOFNC.C

Related Header Files: VIDEO.H, SCREENF.H

Returned Value: None (void).

Discussion: Note that *dotplot()* will not work in a text mode. *Dotplot()* does not check to see if the (x, y) point is within the possible bounds of the video screen. The calling program can do this by comparing x and y to minimums of 0, and maximums of *g_dots_h* and *g_dots_v*, respectively (declared in VIDEO.H).

Graphics Only

Function: `void rectangle(int fill, int x1, int y1, int x2, int y2, int color)`

Purpose: Draws a rectangle on the graphics screen.

In File: VIDEOFNC.C

Related Header Files: VIDEO.H, SCREENF.H

Returned Value: None (void).

Discussion: (x1, y1) are the coordinates for the upper-left corner of the rectangle and (x2, y2) are the coordinates for the lower-right corner. If *fill* is TRUE (non-zero), the rectangle will be filled in with the specified color. Otherwise, only the border will be colored in. No checking is done to make sure that the (x, y) points are within the screen boundaries.

Graphics Only

Function: `void drawline(int x1, int y1, int x2, int y2, int color)`

Purpose: Draws a line from (x1, y1) to (x2, y2) on screen.

In File: VIDEOFNC.C

Related Header Files: VIDEO.H, SCREENF.H

Returned Value: None (void).

——————————————————————————————

Graphics Only

Function: `void wordul(int mode, char *string, int x, int y, int color);`

Purpose: Underlines the text at location (x, y) on the screen in a graphics mode.

In File: VIDEOFNC.C

Related Header Files: VIDEO.H, SCREENF.H

Returned Value: None (void).

Discussion: This function is a fast way to highlight a cursor position if you are running menus in a graphics mode. (x, y) is the character position on the screen, not the pixel position. The function calculates the pixel position based on the number of dots each character occupies in the given mode.

——————————————————————————————

Graphics Only

Function: `void draw_sprite(struct sprite spr, int xpos, int ypos, int line_color, int back_color)`

Purpose: Writes the sprite image at *(xpos, ypos)* on screen.

In File: VIDEOFNC.C

Related Header Files: VIDEO.H, SCREENF.H

Returned Value: None (void).

Discussion: This function writes the sprite image on the screen in the specified colors. The sprite must be specified using the sprite structure:

```
struct sprite{
    int swide;
    int stall;
    unsigned char *sdata;
};
```

Where *sdata* is the binary image of the object to be displayed (see the example in Section 10.4). Note that *draw_sprite* does not use the XOR technique, so the image cannot be erased by writing to the screen a second time at the same location. MT does not use this function, but it is included for completeness.

———————————————————————————————————

Graphics Only

Function: `void xsprite(struct sprite spr, int xpos, int ypos, int color)`

Purpose: Draws an XOR sprite at (*xpos, ypos*) on screen.

In File: VIDEOFNC.C

Related Header Files: VIDEO.H, SCREENF.H

Returned Value: None (void).

Discussion: This is the utility function for displaying a sprite image. The sprite is defined as a structure of type sprite (see Section 10.4). Each pixel on the video display is XORed with the sprite data. If the sprite bit image contains a 0, no change is made to the video data. If the sprite bit image contains a 1, the video data is XORed with the color parameter passed to *xspite()*.

Calling *xsprite()* once displays the sprite. Calling *xsprite()* again with the same location and color will erase the sprite image. MT uses this feature to allow a moving cursor on the graphics screen.

This completes the description of the lowest-level functions used in MT. Next, we will look at higher-level video functions—functions for displaying screens, and for cursor movement on menus.

11

Higher-Level Video Functions

This chapter covers the remaining functions for controlling screen images and menus. These will be combined to form a library file, SCREENF.LIB, that will provide standard video functions for the MT sequencer/editor.

11.1 Prompting User Input

MT frequently needs to prompt the user to input either a character string or a number. In the case of numbers, it is handy to check whether the number is within range before passing the value to the main program. In the case of strings, it is best to limit the input to a specified number of characters to avoid writing past the end of the string's memory area.

These basic input functions are provided in a file called INPUTF.C. Functions are provided for fetching an integer, a floating point number, and a string.

_____

Function: `int getfloat(int lineno, char *prompt, float *value, float min, float max, int norm_attrib, int emph_attrib);`

Purpose: Prompts user for input of a floating point number.

In File: INPUTF.C

Related Header Files: None.

Returned Value: 1 if input is received; 0 if user hits ESC or Return without input of a value.

Discussion: *Getfloat()* first clears the line *lineno*. It then prints the prompt string at the line number specified, starting at the left-most column. The prompt string is printed with the video attribute specified by *norm_attrib*. If the user enters a number and hits Return, *getfloat()* compares the value to *min* (the minimum acceptable value) and *max* (the maximum acceptable value). If the value is between min and max, *getfloat()* passes the entered number back via the pointer *value*. If the entered number is out of range, *getfloat()* prints the error message:

```
Value must be between XXX and YYY [hit a key]
```

where XXX is the min value, and YYY is the max value. The error message is printed with the *emph_attrib* video attribute.

Hitting the ESC key at any time stops *getfloat()*, and returns a value of 0. Hitting the Backspace key erases the previously typed characters. Hitting Return with no typed numerals showing stops *getfloat()* with a returned value of 0. The only way *getfloat()* will return a 1 is if a number between min and max is entered.

The most common problem with using *getfloat()* is to forget that it returns 0 or 1, not the floating point value input. The floating point value is stored at the memory address pointed to by *value*.

Function: `int getint(int lineno, char *prompt, int *value, int min, int max, int norm_attrib, int emph_attrib);`

Purpose: Prompts user for input of an integer number.

In File: INPUTF.C

Related Header Files: None.

Returned Value: 1 if input is received; 0 if user hits ESC or Return without input of a value.

Discussion: *Getint()* is identical to *getfloat()* except that the user is prompted for an integer. Again, the number input is stored at the address pointed to by *value*.

_____

Function: `int getstr(int lineno, char *prompt, char *string, int max, int attrib)`

Purpose: Prompts user for input of a character string.

In File: INPUTF.C

Related Header Files: None.

Returned Value: 0 if no string input; otherwise, the number of characters entered by the user is the return value.

Discussion: *Getstr()* is similar to the numeric input functions, except that there is no range checking for strings. The maximum number of characters the user can input is limited by the parameter max. Once the user types that many letters the cursor stops advancing, and further typing just overwrites the last character position.

Hitting ESC at any point in input stops *getstr()* with a returned value of 0. Hitting the Backspace key erases the previously typed letters. Hitting Return with no typed letters showing stops *getfloat()* with a returned value of 0.

The user's input is stored to the address pointed to by "string."

_____

Function: `int get_string(char *str, int max)`

Purpose: Gets at most, max characters from user input.

In File: INPUTF.C

Related Header Files: None.

Returned Value: The number of characters input by the user.

Discussion: This is a clean version of the standard library function *fgets()*. The reasons for not using standard *fgets()* versions are:

1) Standard versions of *fgets()* allow the user to type more than the maximum number of letters. Only the first *max* number is copied to the string, and it may be confusing to the user to find the result truncated.

2) *Fgets()* handling of the ESC key is not consistent with what the user would expect. In *fgets()*, hitting ESC will print a \ character and add a new line. In *get_string()*, hitting ESC exits the function immediately with return a value of 0.

Get_string() is used in *getint()*, *getfloat()*, and *getstr()*, but is not used alone in any part of the MT program.

11.2 Displaying Screen Image Files

MT's screen images are stored in a series of files called MT1.SCR, MT2.SCR, etc. These are loaded into the computer's memory when the program starts up. The HELP screens are also separate files, but are only loaded into memory when requested, and are then freed from memory (deallocated) when the HELP screen is cleared.

The screen files are stored as a linked list (see Section 4.6 for a discussion of linked lists). Each node in the list stores one line of the screen file. The structure *strchain{}* is used to store the data:

```
struct strchain {
    char *line;
    struct strchain *next;
}
```

The pointer *next* points to the next link in the chain. The last link is marked off with a NULL pointer.

The functions used to manipulate screen files are all in the file CHAIN.C. Once the screen files are loaded in memory, they have to be displayed. CHAIN.C contains both a standard library output function for display (*dispchain()*), and a faster version that writes directly to the video memory area (*fdispchain()*).

Both *dispchain()* and *fdispchain()* set the character attribute (color) for each character displayed. Areas on the screen that are not written to will not have their attributes changed. For a consistent screen image you will want to clear the screen with *clearscreen()*, using the same attribute used in *fdispchain()* or *dispchain()*.

Function: `struct strchain *inpchain(char *file, int maxlen)`

Purpose: Reads a file in from disk, stores as a linked list.

In File: CHAIN.C

Related Header Files: SCREENF.H

Returned Value: Returns pointer to the start of the linked list. Returns NULL if no file is found.

Discussion: Any file created in a text editor can be read, but the file should stay within the screen size of twenty-five lines by eighty characters. The file is read one line at a time into the near data segment.

Function: struct strchain *chain(struct strchain *p, char *w)

Purpose: Adds a string onto the end of a linked list.

In File: CHAIN.C

Related Header Files: SCREENF.H

Returned Value: Returns pointer to last node in the linked list.

Discussion: This is the workhorse function that adds the next line read by *inpchain()* to the linked list. The function reads its way to the end of the list recursively, allocates a new node with the *chainalloc()* function, and then puts the line into the node added.

Function: void dechain(struct strchain *p)

Purpose: Frees from memory a screen image stored as a linked list.

In File: CHAIN.C

Related Header Files: SCREENF.H

Returned Value: None (void).

Discussion: This function is used to purge HELP screens from memory after they have been viewed. This saves space for more MIDI data.

Function: void dispchain(struct strchain *p, int y, int attrib)

Purpose: Writes the screen file stored in memory as a linked list to the console.

In File: CHAIN.C

Related Header Files: SCREENF.H

Returned Value: None (void).

Discussion: The screen data is in a linked list pointed to by *p*. The first screen line number to start on is *y*. All characters are written with the character attribute *attrib*.

The standard (BIOS) functions are used to write to the screen. This makes *dispchain()* a bit slow. *Fdispchain()* is faster, but may show "snow" on CGA systems.

———————————————————————————————

Function: `struct strchain *chainalloc(void)`

Purpose: Allocates enough memory for one node on a linked list (chain).

In File: CHAIN.C

Related Header Files: SCREENF.H

Returned Value: Pointer to memory for holding next node.

Discussion: *Chainalloc()* uses the standard library function *malloc()* to allocate memory for one node. Note that memory for only the node is allocated. Additional memory for the string must be allocated separately with the function *strsave()*.

———————————————————————————————

Function: `char *strsave(char *s)`

Purpose: Stores a string of characters in memory.

In File: CHAIN.C

Related Header Files: SCREENF.H

Returned Value: Pointer to memory allocated for string.

Discussion: This function is straight out of *The C Programming Language* by Kernighan and Ritchie.

———————————————————————————————————

Function: `void fdispchain(struct strchain *p, int y, int attrib, int mode)`

Purpose: Rapidly writes the screen image stored in memory to the video display with the given character attributes.

In File: CHAIN.C

Related Header Files: SCREENF.H

Returned Value: None (void).

Discussion: The screen data is in a linked list pointed to by *p*. The first screen line number to start on is *y*. All characters are written with the character attribute *attrib*. Note that the video display mode is passed to this function. This is not the case with the sister function *dispchain()*.

Fdispchain() uses the fast output function *fwriteword()* in the file WRITSCRN.C. Output to the video display is fast because the function bypasses the BIOS and writes directly to the memory area that the video adapter uses to store the displayed characters.

11.3 Menu Function and Fast Video Output

The menu control functions revolve around a data structure called *se-lement* defined in SCREENF.H:

```
struct selement {
    int xpos;
    int ypos;
    char content[15];
    int nup;
    int ndown;
    int nleft;
    int nright;
    int key;
};
```

Each of these structures represents one menu item. The item is located at *xpos*, *ypos* (column, row) on the screen and contains up to fifteen characters (fourteen plus an ending zero) as stored in the *content[]* array. The *nup, ndown, nleft,* and *nright* elements specify which menu item to go to based on an up, down, left, or right arrow keypress. The last element (key) is used in applications where there is a one-on-one match between menu items and some numeric value in a program. This field is not used in the MT sequencer/editor.

For any real menu, there is more than one menu item and therefore more than one *selement{}* structure. To take a simple example, consider a screen with three menu items:

```
            Column
   123      10...
   Row  ─────────────────
   1
   2        FIRST
   3        SECOND
   4        QUIT
```

The data for this menu would be stored in a three-element array of selement structures:

```
struct selement example[3] = {
    {10, 2, "FIRST", 0, 1, 0, 0, 0},      /* example[0] */
    {10, 3, "SECOND", 0, 2, 1, 1, 1},     /* example[1] */
    {10, 4, "QUIT", 1, 2, 2, 2, 2},       /* example[2] */
};
```

The first element is at column 10, row 2, and contains the word FIRST. Pressing the up arrow key does nothing, as *nup* has the value of 0 (the same number as the *example[]* element). Pressing the down arrow key moves to the second item as *ndown* has a value of 1. Pressing either the right or left arrow key does nothing, again as these values are set to 0, the number of the *example[]* element.

Building these data arrays for even a simple menu is tedious. To cut down the work, a utility program called BULDMENU.C.C is included on the source code disk. BULDMENU.C reads an input file and writes the data array to an output file. It assumes anything surrounded in braces is a menu item. Remember that the maximum size of a cursor element is fourteen characters, so limit how much text you surround in braces (you could change this value by redefining the character array size *content* in structure *selement{}*).

As an example, if we take the example menu and add braces, we get:

```
            Column
   123        10...
   Row  ────────────────
   1
   2          {FIRST}
   3          {SECOND}
   4          {QUIT}
```

Let's assume this screen file is called SCREEN1. To run BULDMENU.C and create a data structure for use in your program, you would type the following command at the DOS prompt:

```
C:>BULDMENU.C SCREEN1 MENU1
```

This creates the file MENU1 with the following lines:

```
#define NPARAM  3

struct selement _____[NPARAM] = {
    { 10, 2, "FIRST",  0, 1, 0, 0, 0 },
    { 10, 3, "SECOND", 0, 2, 1, 1, 1 },
    { 10, 4, "QUIT",   1, 2, 2, 2, 2 },
};
```

BULDMENU.C leaves an underline in the place where you name the data array. In this case, you would erase the underline and replace it with the array name, like `example`:

```
struct selement example[NPARAM] = { ...
```

BULDMENU.C counts the number of data elements, and gives the count the name NPARAM. This is handy later when we want to know the number of the last element in the data array (NPARAM - 1).

After you are done running BULDMENU.C you can add the data array to a header file where you are keeping your menu data. For MT, all menu data is in the file MTSCREEN.H.

BULDMENU.C is not perfect. Although it will always produce a logical association from one cursor position to the next, sometimes you will want to limit cursor movement more than BULDMENU.C does. This is simply a matter of editing BULDMENU.C's output to suit your own taste.

With our menu data structure defined, we can take a look at the functions in the file WRITSCRN.C.

Function: `int movescrn(int vidmode, struct selement scrnarray[], int first, int last, int normal, int hilit)`

Purpose: Allows the user to pick a highlighted menu item by moving the cursor and pressing Return.

In File: WRITSCRN.C

Related Header Files: SCREENF.H, MTSCREEN.H

Returned Value: The number of the menu item selected. -2 if ESC key is hit, -3 if ? key is hit.

Discussion: *Movescrn()* is the primary function that controls cursor movement for menu selection. *Movescrn()* looks into the structure selement data to find the text heading that is printed under the cursor. It displays the text again with the *hilit* attribute (color) to show where the cursor is located. The text is converted back to the *normal* attribute when the cursor is moved to the next selection.

The menu is defined by an array of structures of type selement. The example in the text above is typical for a three-item menu. *Movescrn()* starts by highlighting the element number *first*. The function responds to the arrow keys, Tab, and Backspace as commands to move to the next element (as determined by the *nup, ndown*, etc., parameters). The Home and PgUp keys move to the first array element, while the End and PgDn move to the last.

If the user hits an alphanumeric key, *movescrn()* searches for the first menu item that starts with this letter and moves the cursor to it. Searching is on a left to right, top to bottom basis. Repeatedly hitting a letter key will cause the cursor to move from one matching menu item to the next, looping back to the first one when no other match can be found.

Movescrn() is exited in one of three ways. Hitting the Return key causes *movescrn()* to exit, returning the menu item number that was last highlighted. Hitting the ESC key causes *movescrn()* to exit with a return value of -2. Hitting the ? key causes *movescrn()* to exit with a return value of -3. This is handy if you want to build pop-up HELP screens into your program.

Function: `void to_new_csr(int vidmode, struct selement scrnarray[], int k, int oldk, int normal, int hilit)`

Purpose: Does the work of moving the cursor for *movescrn()*.

In File: WRITSCRN.C

Related Header Files: SCREENF.H, MTSCREEN.H

Returned Value: None (void).

Discussion: *To_new_csr()* is used only by *movescrn()*. It is used to move the highlighted element to the next selection. In the character-based video modes, this involves returning the last selection to the *normal* attribute, and setting the new selection to the *hilit* attribute.

In the graphics modes the cursor is displayed by underlining the selection. This is fast and convenient, but not as glamorous as using a picture of an arrow or a small hand to point to the selection. If you want this type of pointer, use the *xsprite()* function in place of *wordul()*.

Function: `void writerr(char *s, int lineno, int normal, int hilit)`

Purpose: Writes a message on line *lineno*. Pauses until a key is pressed.

In File: WRITSCRN.C

Related Header Files: SCREENF.H, MTSCREEN.H

Returned Value: None (void).

Discussion: *Writerr()* is most often used to display a one-line error message at the bottom of the screen. The message is displayed with the *hilit* attribute for all characters. Execution pauses until the user hits a key. The line is then cleared (with *normal* attribute blank characters) and execution resumes.

Function: `void clearline(int lineno, int attrib)`

Purpose: Clears the selected line on the screen.

In File: WRITSCRN.C

Related Header Files: SCREENF.H, MTSCREEN.H

Returned Value: None (void).

Discussion: Clearline() works by writing eighty blank characters with the attribute set to *attribute* on line *lineno*. Note that some of the EGA/VGA modes have more than eighty characters wide. This function will only clear the first eighty.

Function: `void initscrn(struct selement scrnarray[], int first,int last, int attrib)`

Purpose: Writes the menu items to the screen.

In File: WRITSCRN.C

Related Header Files: SCREENF.H, MTSCREEN.H

Returned Value: None (void).

Discussion: *Initscrn()* is usually used to put the menu items on the screen when a new screen is displayed. A certain range of menu items can be selected by setting the *first* and *last* parameters to something other than the usual 0 and NPARAM values. All menu items are written with the video attribute *attrib*.

Initscrn() uses the library character output functions. *Initscrn()* is slower than *finitscrn()*, but will work in all video modes, including the graphics modes.

——————————————————————————————

Function: `void finitscrn(struct selement scrnarray[], int first, int last, int attrib)`

Purpose: Writes the menu items to the screen.

In File: WRITSCRN.C

Related Header Files: SCREENF.H, MTSCREEN.H

Returned Value: None (void).

Discussion: Identical to *initscrn()* except the faster direct-to-video-memory function *fwriteword()* is used for character output. This works fine for everything except old CGA systems. Also, *finitscrn()* has not been expanded to cover the graphics modes.

——————————————————————————————

Function: `void fwriteword(char *string, int x, int y, int attrib, int mode)`

Purpose: Writes a string of characters to the video display at (x, y) with the specified video attribute.

In File: WRITSCRN.C

Related Header Files: SCREENF.H, MTSCREEN.H

Returned Value: None (void).

Discussion: This is the basic fast video output function. *Fwriteword()* determines where the video data is located in RAM based on the video mode in use. It then writes to the video memory area directly for both the characters and the specified attribute bytes.

Turbo C users should note that the default mode for video output from the Turbo C graphics library is the fast, direct-to-video-memory method. To maintain compiler compatibility, the Turbo C graphics functions are forced to the slower BIOS method in VIDEOFNC.C. *Fwriteword()* and *fdispchain()* are then provided for explicit use of fast video output. See Appendix 4 for further discussion.

————————————————————————————————————

Function: `void write_int(int value, int x, int y, int attrib)`

Purpose: Writes an integer number to the screen at (x, y) with the specified video attribute.

In File: WRITSCRN.C

Related Header Files: SCREENF.H, MTSCREEN.H

Returned Value: None (void).

Discussion: *Write_int()* uses the standard library output functions, so it will work on any video system without "snow."

11.4 The SCREENF.LIB Library File

The screen display and menu functions described in this and the previous chapter are so fundamental that essentially any program will use some of the functions. Therefore I put these functions in a library file called SCREENF.LIB. At link time, any functions that are needed are pulled out of the library file and added to the new program. Any functions in SCREENF.LIB that are not used in the new program are ignored.

To make library upkeep easy, I have included all of the commands needed to update the library in a MAKE file called SCREENF.MK5. It looks like:

```
----------------------------------------------------------
#make file for screenf.lib - medium memory model - Microsoft ver.

videofnc.obj:  videofnc.c
cl /c /AM  videofnc.c

chain.obj:     chain.c
cl /c /AM  chain.c

writscrn.obj: writscrn.c
cl /c /AM  writscrn.c

inputf.obj:    inputf.c
cl /c /AM  inputf.c

screenf.lib:   videofnc.obj chain.obj writscrn.obj inputf.obj
lib screenf -+videofnc.obj -+chain.obj -+writscrn.obj -
+inputf.obj,screenf.ndx;
----------------------------------------------------------
```

The Turbo C version, called SCREENF.TMK, looks like:

```
----------------------------------------------------------------

#screenf.tmk  Turbo C make file for screenf.lib

screenf.lib:   videofnc.obj chain.obj writscrn.obj inputf.obj
    tlib screenf -+videofnc.obj -+chain.obj -+writscrn.obj
        -+inputf.obj, screenf.ndx

chain.obj:      chain.c
    tcc -c -mm -DTURBOC=1 chain.c

videofnc.obj:   videofnc.c
    tcc -c -mm -DTURBOC=1 videofnc.c

writscrn.obj:   writscrn.c
    tcc -c -mm -DTRUBOC=1 writscrn.c

inputf.obj:          inputf.c
    tcc -c -mm -DTURBOC=1 inputf.c
----------------------------------------------------------------
```

Typing the command:

```
C:>MAKE SCREENF.MK5              /* Microsoft Make */
```

or

```
C:>MAKE -FSCREENF.TMK            /* Turbo Make */
```

at the DOS prompt causes any modified programs to be recompiled, and puts the latest versions of all of the functions into the library file. An index file called SCREENF.NDX is also created. This is handy for keeping track of which functions are included in the library file.

12

Conclusion and Suggestions

Here are a few ideas you may want to pursue to expand the usefulness of the basic MT sequencer/editor.

12.1 Using Data from Other Sequencers

A recent addition to the MIDI standard is the Standard MIDI Files 1.0 specification. This standard outlines a data format that allows sequencers to exchange data files. This opens up possibilities for exchanging and building upon sequencer files from your friends and associates. Even files created on different families of computers (Macs, Atari, IBM, etc.) can be exchanged if each sequencer supports the standard. Computer bulletin boards are an excellent, low-cost source of song files.

MT writes the sequencer data in a simple format close to MT's internal workings. Two utility programs are provided to convert MT files to the Standard MIDI Files format:

MT_TO_MF.C   Converts from MT to MIDI Files format.
MF_TO_MT.C   Converts from MIDI Files to MT format.

The usage of both programs is identical. One file is read in, and one file is created as output. As an example:

MF_TO_MT JSBACH.BIN JSBACH.SNG

converts the JSBACH.BIN file from MIDI Files format to MT .SNG format and stores the output in the file JSBACH.SNG.

One problem you may run into in using imported files has to do with explicit MIDI Note Offs. There are two ways to express a Note Off in the MIDI language. The most common is a Note On with a key velocity value of 0. A few synthesizers also transmit the velocity of the key release. This uses an explicit Note Off:

```
90 3C 00  <- Implied Note OFF, note = 3C, velocity = 0.
80 3C 40  <- Explicit Note OFF, note = 3C, release vel = 40.
```

MT will store, play, and display Note Off values in either format. However, some synthesizers will not recognize the explicit Note Offs. This leaves every note played ON until the end of the track. To convert from explicit to implied Note Offs, mark the entire track as a block and copy it to a spare track. During the Block Copy process, MT calls the *clean_track()* function which converts all explicit Note Offs to implied Note Offs. Otherwise, the track is not affected.

Some computers, such as the Macintosh, include a 128 byte header at the front of every file to store pointers and keep track of the file's extended name. MF_TO_MT.C skips past this header if it is present. During the reverse process, MT_TO_MF.C does not create the header when producing a Standard MIDI Files output. If the output of MT_TO_MF.C is read back into a Mac using Macbinary protocol, a new header is appended as the file is written to disk.

The Standard MIDI Files format is somewhat involved, and shows its roots as a Macintosh file standard. Readers who wish to dig into this aspect of sequencing should order a copy of the MIDI files specification for complete details (see Appendix 6).

12.2 Improvements to the Basic MT Program

As mentioned in the introduction, I had to make some compromises in building the MT program to keep the size and complexity of the code reasonable for a book. Some of the additions that would benefit MT are:

- Improved note velocity editing. MT allows editing of individual note velocities. Better still would be the ability to draw in a velocity curve on the NLE screen, and then have a range of notes adjusted. This would provide smooth changes in amplitude.

- Pitch Bend and controller editing. This data could be displayed on the NLE screen. Ideally, the user should be able to draw in a curve and have controller data added or adjusted to match.

- Tempo changes. The MPU-401 has built-in conductor logic that allows smooth changes to tempo. This would be a nice addition to the MLE screen.

- FSK and MIDI synchronization. If you are working with a multi-track tape recorder, it is vital to synchronize the MPU-401 to the tape speed. The MPU-401 always sends synchronized tones on the FSK line. To synchronize MT's playback to an incoming FSK signal requires that MPU-401 get the FSK_CLOCK command (81 hex). The default FSK to internal clock ratio will be fine, as MT uses the default 120 clicks per beat resolution. Synchronization to an external MIDI device (like a drum machine) is also possible. The MPU-401 accepts external, F8 hex, MIDI clocks as MIDI synchronization information after it receives the MIDI_CLOCK command (82 hex).

- If you envision controlling MT's playback from external MIDI devices, you will want to implement Song Position pointers. Song Position pointers allow you to start playback from any spot in a song. The MIDI 1.0 specification assigns the F2 hex system common message to this function. These messages should be ignored unless the sequencer is responding to external MIDI synchronization.

- Quantization. The idea is to make notes fall on the correct time interval or beat. To be useful, quantization must have several controllable parameters. You should be able to scale the adjustment to the nearest quarter note, eighth note, triplet, etc., down to a 64th note, depending on the needs of the user. Absolute quantization is often too mechanical. Several commercial sequencers allow percentage corrections. A fifty percent correction would adjust the note timing half-way to precision. Note On and Note Off data should be separately adjustable.

- Filters. Operations such as transposition and quantization can be made more powerful by limiting the range of notes affected. The selection of a block of measures is an example of a simple filter. Only the data within the block is affected by a block operation. This can be extended by having the block operations limited to certain ranges of notes, MIDI channel numbers, notes with a velocity in a given range, notes in a specified chord or scale, etc.

As an example, consider the problem of splitting the left- and right-hand data for a track recorded by a keyboard player. Splitting the data into two tracks allows you to assign a different sound to each track. To do this with filters, the track would be duplicated on a second track (Block Paste). A filter would be set to only allow notes above a certain value to be impacted. The Block Empty command would then only delete the upper notes on one track, leaving the lower ones unaffected. The opposite would be done with the second track to delete only the lower notes.

12.3 Adding More Tracks

Although eight tracks is enough for most musical activities, having more tracks available is handy for editing. Extra tracks allow you to keep bits and pieces of songs you are working on during edit sessions without having to write to the disk. Another factor is that software publishers have taken to using the number of tracks on their sequencer as an advertising ploy to differentiate their product from other sequencers. This has tended to make users overly conscious of the number of tracks, whether or not they will ever be used.

The MPU-401 is internally an 8-track device. This is unfortunate since the MIDI standard specifies that sixteen channels can coexist on the same MIDI cable. Many sequencers provide more than sixteen tracks, primarily for editing convenience. To get extra tracks requires that more than logical track use each of the MPU-401's eight track counters.

The simplest way to do this is to allow more than one MIDI channel to exist on each of the tracks in memory. Up to sixteen MIDI channels can coexist on each of the eight MPU-401 tracks. This potentially allows 8 x 16, or 128 tracks. Thirty-two tracks is probably more than enough for 99.9 percent of all users.

To make this work, the editing functions in MT have to be expanded to only pick up one MIDI channel's data from the physical track for each of the logical tracks displayed on the screen. The MEAS_END and TIME_OUT events will be common to all events on the track. Event timing for any one channel on a track has to consider the time taken by events on other MIDI channels, but otherwise, the editing logic is not affected. The existing playback routines will work fine after this change.

A more sophisticated way to handle additional tracks is to keep them completely separate in memory. During the playback process the next event on each track is compared. The event happening next is sent to the MPU-401.

The advantage of this method is that any number of tracks can have the same MIDI channel number. The disadvantage is that the playback routines have to poll between the several tracks being sent on one MPU-401 track number to find out which one is next. This amounts to sorting pending timing values among the competing tracks. The sorting must be done efficiently to avoid timing delays during playback.

Adding more tracks has some other side effects. Screens can get crowded if you try to show all of the tracks at once. One option is to have multiple "pages" for the EDIT and RECORD menu. Each page might display eight or sixteen logical tracks. Another option is to use windows to display tracks and commands only when needed.

12.4 Compressing Track Data

The *event* structure storage used by MT is convenient from the programmer's point of view. Each chunk of data to and from the MPU-401 occupies exactly one event. Adding new data is just a matter of inserting new events into the linked list. The new events can be placed anywhere in memory, as long as the *next* pointers connect each event to the linked list.

The drawback of the event structure is its consumption of memory. At most, each event contains four data bytes. Yet in memory, each event takes up twelve bytes. This is not obvious when you look at the event structure:

```
struct event {
    struct event far *next;
    unsigned char nbytes;
    unsigned char b[4];
};
```

Using char values instead of integers helps cut down the size of the event structure. The actual data is only one byte long, so no reason to use a two-byte integer.

The *nbytes* parameter is one extra byte. This makes playback of the events simple, as the number of significant bytes in the *b[]* array is stored in *nbytes* during Record. A more elaborate Play function could eliminate *nbyte* by looking at b[0] to determine the length of the event's data. Still, *nbyte* is only one byte.

The *far* pointer *next* requires four bytes. A *near* pointer would reduce this to two bytes, but would then limit the song storage to the 64K byte *near* data segment. The *near* data segment already contains our screen image files and variables, so not even the full 64K is available. *Far* pointers are necessary, but we have lost another four bytes.

The last source of inefficiency is the memory consumed by the *malloc()* memory allocation function's need to keep track of which bytes have been reserved. Remember that each event must have memory allocated for it. *Malloc()* sticks a two-byte number reflecting the amount of memory allocated at the end of the reserved area. Most versions of *malloc()* reserve memory in two- or four-byte chunks. The result of these losses is that our nine-byte structure event ends up taking twelve bytes in memory.

The above discussion points out that most of the memory space is occupied by pointers and *malloc()* information. To cut down the waste, the data structure has to be changed to reduce the number of pointers and the number of times *malloc()* is used. The largest savings occur when the full track of data is saved as one block of allocated memory. The sequencer just keeps track of a pointer to the start of the track's block, and the count of the number of events in it. In this case, an event would consist of only five bytes: the nbyte and b[4] data. Even larger savings are possible by eliminating *nbytes* and making each event's length a variable.

Recording and playing note data works fine with the continuous block of data approach. However, editing is difficult. To insert a new event, a "hole" has to be made in the track's data block. This pushes the end of the block forward five bytes. Unless it is the last track, the end of one track's data bumps right up against another, so that track has to be moved, and the next track, etc. Similarly, deleting events results in holes that have to be filled by reshuffling data.

Allocating data one measure at a time is a compromise between the linear block for the whole track, and an allocated block for each event. Each measure is an element in a linked list of measures. The size of each measure is variable, depending on the number of events in it.

Gaps tend to form in memory as this type of data structure is edited, but they can be filled later as new, small measures are added.

You can see from this discussion that there is not a single perfect memory structure for storing and editing track data. MT uses the event structure because of its simplicity for both recording, playing, and measure level editing. The inefficiency of the event structure is typically not a problem. MT itself takes up only about 110K bytes, including screen files. It takes a lot of song data to fill up a typical 512K or 640K computer. Editing becomes pretty slow on a 4.77 MHz PC if 400K of track data is recorded. Editing speed can also be improved with more complex memory structures (pointers to intermediate parts of each track's data, rather than just to the start and end), but again this makes the program more complex.

12.5 Computer Composition

There are several approaches to adding musical intelligence to MT. The MT program itself can be expanded upon to add compositional aids, or separate programs can be used to generate song files which MT then plays.

An example of adding intelligence to MT might be adding chord functions to the Note Level Edit commands. Pointing to a note and pressing a function key might generate new notes forming a Major fifth interval, Minor seventh, etc. MT does not use the function keys, although their keycodes are defined in STANDARD.H. A well thought out function would allow the user to define the meaning of the function keys. This might even be a limited macro-command capability to automate common keystrokes.

Computer composition is another interesting area to experiment with. You may find it easier to use a separate program to create synthetic song files, and then use MT to play and edit the results. A simple example of this is the MAKESONG.C program at the end of the source code

code listings. This program just writes a few measures of random quarter notes to a fixed file as track 1. Not at all musical, but it does provide an outline of the programming approach needed to create song files.

12.6 Final Comments

Electronic music and MIDI programming are still new fields. With the excellent hardware and computer languages now available, the limit is not what we can do, but what we can think of doing. I hope readers will find ways of using MT and other MIDI resources as starting points for projects that the rest of us have not yet imagined.

PART 4

Source Code Listings

```c
/* filefunc.h  empty struct selement to put file names into for selection */

#define NPARAM_FILE   90

#ifdef ALLOCATE

struct selement g_file_disp[NPARAM_FILE] = {
        { 2, 4, "                    ", 0, 5, 0, 1, 0 },
        { 18, 4, "                    ", 1, 6, 0, 2, 1 },
        { 34, 4, "                    ", 2, 7, 1, 3, 2 },
        { 50, 4, "                    ", 3, 8, 2, 4, 3 },
        { 66, 4, "                    ", 4, 9, 3, 4, 4 },
        { 2, 5, "                    ", 0, 10, 5, 6, 5 },
        { 18, 5, "                    ", 1, 11, 5, 7, 6 },
        { 34, 5, "                    ", 2, 12, 6, 8, 7 },
        { 50, 5, "                    ", 3, 13, 7, 9, 8 },
        { 66, 5, "                    ", 4, 14, 8, 9, 9 },
        { 2, 6, "                    ", 5, 15, 10, 11, 10 },
        { 18, 6, "                    ", 6, 16, 10, 12, 11 },
        { 34, 6, "                    ", 7, 17, 11, 13, 12 },
        { 50, 6, "                    ", 8, 18, 12, 14, 13 },
        { 66, 6, "                    ", 9, 19, 13, 14, 14 },
        { 2, 7, "                    ", 10, 20, 15, 16, 15 },
        { 18, 7, "                    ", 11, 21, 15, 17, 16 },
        { 34, 7, "                    ", 12, 22, 16, 18, 17 },
        { 50, 7, "                    ", 13, 23, 17, 19, 18 },
        { 66, 7, "                    ", 14, 24, 18, 19, 19 },
        { 2, 8, "                    ", 15, 25, 20, 21, 20 },
        { 18, 8, "                    ", 16, 26, 20, 22, 21 },
        { 34, 8, "                    ", 17, 27, 21, 23, 22 },
        { 50, 8, "                    ", 18, 28, 22, 24, 23 },
        { 66, 8, "                    ", 19, 29, 23, 24, 24 },
        { 2, 9, "                    ", 20, 30, 25, 26, 25 },
        { 18, 9, "                    ", 21, 31, 25, 27, 26 },
        { 34, 9, "                    ", 22, 32, 26, 28, 27 },
        { 50, 9, "                    ", 23, 33, 27, 29, 28 },
        { 66, 9, "                    ", 24, 34, 28, 29, 29 },
        { 2, 10, "                    ", 25, 35, 30, 31, 30 },
        { 18, 10, "                    ", 26, 36, 30, 32, 31 },
        { 34, 10, "                    ", 27, 37, 31, 33, 32 },
        { 50, 10, "                    ", 28, 38, 32, 34, 33 },
        { 66, 10, "                    ", 29, 39, 33, 34, 34 },
        { 2, 11, "                    ", 30, 40, 35, 36, 35 },
        { 18, 11, "                    ", 31, 41, 35, 37, 36 },
        { 34, 11, "                    ", 32, 42, 36, 38, 37 },
        { 50, 11, "                    ", 33, 43, 37, 39, 38 },
        { 66, 11, "                    ", 34, 44, 38, 39, 39 },
        { 2, 12, "                    ", 35, 45, 40, 41, 40 },
        { 18, 12, "                    ", 36, 46, 40, 42, 41 },
        { 34, 12, "                    ", 37, 47, 41, 43, 42 },
        { 50, 12, "                    ", 38, 48, 42, 44, 43 },
        { 66, 12, "                    ", 39, 49, 43, 44, 44 },
```

```
   { 2, 13, "                    ", 40, 50, 45, 46, 45 },
   { 18, 13, "                    ", 41, 51, 45, 47, 46 },
   { 34, 13, "                    ", 42, 52, 46, 48, 47 },
   { 50, 13, "                    ", 43, 53, 47, 49, 48 },
   { 66, 13, "                    ", 44, 54, 48, 49, 49 },
   { 2, 14, "                    ", 45, 55, 50, 51, 50 },
   { 18, 14, "                    ", 46, 56, 50, 52, 51 },
   { 34, 14, "                    ", 47, 57, 51, 53, 52 },
   { 50, 14, "                    ", 48, 58, 52, 54, 53 },
   { 66, 14, "                    ", 49, 59, 53, 54, 54 },
   { 2, 15, "                    ", 50, 60, 55, 56, 55 },
   { 18, 15, "                    ", 51, 61, 55, 57, 56 },
   { 34, 15, "                    ", 52, 62, 56, 58, 57 },
   { 50, 15, "                    ", 53, 63, 57, 59, 58 },
   { 66, 15, "                    ", 54, 64, 58, 59, 59 },
   { 2, 16, "                    ", 55, 65, 60, 61, 60 },
   { 18, 16, "                    ", 56, 66, 60, 62, 61 },
   { 34, 16, "                    ", 57, 67, 61, 63, 62 },
   { 50, 16, "                    ", 58, 68, 62, 64, 63 },
   { 66, 16, "                    ", 59, 69, 63, 64, 64 },
   { 2, 17, "                    ", 60, 70, 65, 66, 65 },
   { 18, 17, "                    ", 61, 71, 65, 67, 66 },
   { 34, 17, "                    ", 62, 72, 66, 68, 67 },
   { 50, 17, "                    ", 63, 73, 67, 69, 68 },
   { 66, 17, "                    ", 64, 74, 68, 69, 69 },
   { 2, 18, "                    ", 65, 75, 70, 71, 70 },
   { 18, 18, "                    ", 66, 76, 70, 72, 71 },
   { 34, 18, "                    ", 67, 77, 71, 73, 72 },
   { 50, 18, "                    ", 68, 78, 72, 74, 73 },
   { 66, 18, "                    ", 69, 79, 73, 74, 74 },
   { 2, 19, "                    ", 70, 80, 75, 76, 75 },
   { 18, 19, "                    ", 71, 81, 75, 77, 76 },
   { 34, 19, "                    ", 72, 82, 76, 78, 77 },
   { 50, 19, "                    ", 73, 83, 77, 79, 78 },
   { 66, 19, "                    ", 74, 84, 78, 79, 79 },
   { 2, 20, "                    ", 75, 85, 80, 81, 80 },
   { 18, 20, "                    ", 76, 86, 80, 82, 81 },
   { 34, 20, "                    ", 77, 87, 81, 83, 82 },
   { 50, 20, "                    ", 78, 88, 82, 84, 83 },
   { 66, 20, "                    ", 79, 89, 83, 84, 84 },
   { 2, 21, "                    ", 80, 85, 85, 86, 85 },
   { 18, 21, "                    ", 81, 86, 85, 87, 86 },
   { 34, 21, "                    ", 82, 87, 86, 88, 87 },
   { 50, 21, "                    ", 83, 88, 87, 89, 88 },
   { 66, 21, "                    ", 84, 89, 88, 89, 89 },
};

#else

extern struct selement g_file_disp[];

#endif
```

```
/* install.h */
/* menu deffinition for the INSTALL.C menu */

#define NPARAM  10

struct selement scrndata[NPARAM] = {
    { 3, 5, "Text Mode", 0, 1, 0, 0, 0 },
    { 3, 8, "Graphics Mode", 0, 2, 1, 1, 1 },
    { 3, 17, "Normal Letters", 1, 5, 2, 3, 2 },
    { 21, 17, "Cursor", 1, 6, 2, 4, 3 },
    { 50, 17, "Other", 1, 7, 3, 4, 4 },
    { 3, 18, "Background", 2, 8, 5, 6, 5 },
    { 21, 18, "Background", 3, 8, 5, 7, 6 },
    { 50, 18, "Background", 4, 8, 6, 7, 7 },
    { 3, 20, "Save Choices", 5, 9, 8, 6, 8 },
    { 3, 22, "Quit Install", 8, 9, 9, 6, 9 },
};
```

```
/* mpu401.h      header file */
/* mpu-401 command and message summary */

/* mpu marks */

#define NOP              0xf8      /* no operation */
#define MES_END          0xf9      /*  measure end */
#define DATA_END         0xfc      /*  end data */

/* mpu messages */

#define REQ_T1           0xf0      /* track data request track 1 */
#define REQ_T2           0xf1
#define REQ_T3           0xf2
#define REQ_T4           0xf3
#define REQ_T5           0xf4
#define REQ_T6           0xf5
#define REQ_T7           0xf6
#define REQ_T8           0xf7      /* track data request track 8 */
#define TIME_OUT         0xf8      /* timing overflow */
#define CONDUCT          0xf9      /* conductor data request */
#define ALL_END          0xfc      /* all end */
#define CLOCK_OUT        0xfd      /* clock to host */
#define ACK              0xfe      /* acknowledge */
#define SYS_MES          0xff      /* system message */

/* mpu commands */

#define STOP_PLAY        0x05
#define START_PLAY       0x0a
#define STOP_REC         0x11
#define START_REC        0x22
#define STOP_OVDUB       0x15
#define START_OVDUB      0x2A


#define NO_ALL_OFF       0x30      /* all notes off */
#define NO_RTIME         0x32      /* no real time */
#define THRU_OFF_CHAN    0x33      /* thru : off on channels */
#define WITH_TIME        0x34      /* with timing byte : on */
#define MODE_THRU        0x35      /* mode mes : on */
#define EXCL_THRU        0x36      /* exclusive thru : on */
#define COM_THRU         0x38      /* common to host : on */
#define REAL_THRU        0x39      /* real time to host : on */
#define UART             0x3f      /* uart mode */

/* channel reference table numbers are normally computed */

/*
40 - 4f sets channel reference table a
50 - 5f b
60 - 6f c
```

```
70 - 7f d
*/

#define INT_CLOCK       0x80    /* internal clock */
#define FSK_CLOCK       0x81    /* fsk clock */
#define MIDI_CLOCK      0x82    /* midi clock */
#define MET_ON_WOUT     0x83    /* metronome : on - w/o accents */
#define MET_OFF         0x84    /* metronome : off */
#define MET_ON_WITH     0x85    /* metronome : on - with accents */
#define BEND_OFF        0x86    /* bender : off */
#define BEND_ON         0x87    /* bender : on */
#define THRU_OFF        0x88    /* midi thru : off */
#define THRU_ON         0x89    /* midi thru : on */
#define DSTOP_OFF       0x8a    /* data in stop mode : off */
#define DSTOP_ON        0x8b    /* data in stop mode : on */
#define MEAS_OFF        0x8c    /* send measure end : off */
#define MEAS_ON         0x8d    /* send measure end : on */
#define COND_OFF        0x8e    /* conductor : off */
#define COND_ON         0x8f    /* conductor : on */
#define REAL_OFF        0x90    /* real time affecton : off */
#define REAL_ON         0x91    /* real time affection : on */
#define FSK_INT         0x92    /* fsk to internal */
#define FSK_MIDI        0x93    /* fsk to midi */
#define CLOCK_OFF       0x94    /* clock to host : off */
#define CLOCK_ON        0x95    /* clock to host : on */
#define EXCL_OFF        0x96    /* exclusive to host : off */
#define EXCL_ON         0x97    /* exclusive to host : on */

#define CHANA_OFF       0x98    /* reference table a : off */
#define CHANA_ON        0x99    /* a : on */
#define CHANB_OFF       0x9a    /* b : off */
#define CHANB_ON        0x9b    /* b : on */
#define CHANC_OFF       0x9c    /* c : off */
#define CHANC_ON        0x9d    /* c : on */
#define CHAND_OFF       0x9e    /* d : off */
#define CHAND_ON        0x9f    /* d : on */

/* reading data */

#define REQ_CNT0        0xa0    /* request play counter of track 1 */
#define REQ_CNT1        0xa1
#define REQ_CNT2        0xa2
#define REQ_CNT3        0xa3
#define REQ_CNT4        0xa4
#define REQ_CNT5        0xa5
#define REQ_CNT6        0xa6
#define REQ_CNT7        0xa7

#define REQ_REC_CNT     0xab    /* request record counter */
#define REQ_VER         0xac    /* request version */
#define REQ_REV         0xad    /* request revision */
```

```
#define REQ_TEMPO        0xaf    /* request tempo */

#define RES_RTEMPO       0xb1    /* resets relative tempo */
#define CLEAR_PCOUNT     0xb8    /* clear play counters */
#define CLEAR_PMAP       0xb9    /* clear play map - all notes off */
#define CLEAR_REC        0xba    /* clear record counter */

#define TB_48            0xc2    /* 48 timebase */
#define TB_72            0xc3
#define TB_96            0xc4
#define TB_120           0xc5
#define TB_144           0xc6
#define TB_168           0xc7
#define TB_192           0xc8

#define WSD0             0xd0    /* want to send data on track 1 */
#define WSD1             0xd1
#define WSD2             0xd2
#define WSD3             0xd3
#define WSD4             0xd4
#define WSD5             0xd0
#define WSD6             0xd6
#define WSD7             0xd7

#define WS_SYS           0xdf    /* want to send system message */

/* set conditions and values (follow by 1 byte data) */

#define SET_TEMPO        0xe0    /* set tempo */
#define SET_RTEMPO       0xe1    /* relative tempo */
#define SET_GRAD         0xe2    /* graduation */
#define MIDI_METRO       0xe4    /* midi clocks per metronome beep */
#define METRO_MEAS       0xe6    /* metro/meas */
#define INT_HOST         0xe7    /* int * 4 / clock to host */
#define ACT_TRACK        0xec    /* active tracks on/off */
#define SEND_PCOUNT      0xed    /* send play counter on/off */
#define CHAN_ON1         0xee    /* acceptable channels 1 - 8 on/off */
#define CHAN_ON2         0xef    /* acceptable channels 9 - 16 on/off */

#define RESET            0xff
```

```
/* mt.h    header file for mt.c */

/* there is a nested include file referenced in the body of this file: */
/* mtscreen.h  -  all screen menu data */

/* see also mtdeclar.h - contains all function declarations */


/* These defines to allow same header file to work for both initialization */
/*  and reference.  Only define the word ALLOCATE in the main() module. */

#ifdef ALLOCATE      /* GLOBAL defined equal to nothing */
    #define GLOBAL
    #define INIT(x)    =x
#else
    #define GLOBAL extern
    #define INIT(x)
#endif               /* INIT defined equal to nothing */


#define    NOTE_OFF          0x80    /* MIDI voice messages - channel 1 */
#define    NOTE_ON           0x90
#define    POLY_AFTERTOUCH   0xA0
#define    MODE_MESSAGE      0xB0
#define    PROGRAM_CHANGE    0xC0
#define    AFTERTOUCH        0xD0
#define    PITCH_WHEEL       0xE0
#define    ALL_NOTES_OFF     0x7B    /* channel mode message */

/* IBM PC character graphics symbol numbers for Measure Level Edit screen */

#define    NOTE_CHAR         14  /* character for measure with data */
#define    MEAS_CHAR         29  /* character for measure with no data */
#define    BLOCK_START       195 /* character for start of block */
#define    BLOCK_END         180 /* character for end of block */
#define    SMALL_BLOCK       199 /* character for 1 measure long block */

#define    NTRACK            8   /* number of tracks */
#define    NNOTES            128 /* number of possible MIDI note numbers */
#define    NCHANNEL          16  /* maximum number of MIDI channels */
#define    OCTIVE            12  /* number of MIDI notes in an octive */
#define    TRACK_NAME_WIDE   9   /* number of chars wide a name can be */
#define    TITLE_WIDE        51  /* number of chars for track title */
#define    N_TRACK_PARAM     7   /* number of menu items per track */
#define    NMEASURE_DISP     15  /* number of measures displayed (ed) */
#define    MAX_CLOCK         240 /* highest MPU-401 clock value */
#define    FMALLOC_BYTES     4   /* number of bytes used by fmalloc */

/* defines for mtsc modules */

#define    OCTIVE_HIGH    56      /* number of dots high in one octive */
```

```
#define      CROSS_HALF       4          /* cross sprite half hight (to center) */
#define      SC_TOP_LINES     2          /* space to reserve for text */
#define      SC_MENU_LINES    4          /* space at screen bottom - menu lines */
#define      SC_BOT_LINES     2          /* space at very bottom for messages */
#define      HALF_NOTE_DOTS   4          /* pixel hight of half key on screen */
#define      LEFT_BORDER      70         /* space in pixel dot widths */
#define      MIN_SPACE        3          /* min separation between MIDI tick */
#define      TICK_PER_BEAT    120        /* MPU tick per metronome beat */

#define      NSCREEN     5        /* number of screens */

/* defines the number of menu items on given screen */

#define      NPARAM1     10       /* main menu */
#define      NPARAM2     75       /* record menu */
#define      NPARAM3     168      /* measure level menu */
#define      NPARAM4     9        /* help menu */
#define      NPARAM5     4        /* import bottom menu */
#define      NPARAM51    8        /* source tracks on import */
#define      NPARAM52    8        /* distination tracks on import */
#define      NPARAM6     16       /* note level edit */

#define      DEFAULT_FILE_NAME    "NO_NAME.SNG"

/* global variables - all preceded by "g_" */

GLOBAL char g_prodir[50];            /* directory of program's files */
GLOBAL char g_songdir[50];           /* directory containing song data */
GLOBAL char g_filename[14] INIT(DEFAULT_FILE_NAME);
GLOBAL char g_songtitle[TITLE_WIDE] INIT(" ");

GLOBAL int g_free_memory INIT(0);        /* Kbytes of free memory at start */
GLOBAL int g_pct_free_memory INIT(0);    /* % of memory left to use */
GLOBAL int g_meton INIT(0);              /* toggle for metronome on/off */
GLOBAL int g_tick INIT(120);             /* tick number within measure */
GLOBAL int g_metrate INIT(100);          /* metronome rate */
GLOBAL int g_meter INIT(4);              /* beats per measure */
GLOBAL int g_midi_metro INIT(24);        /* MPU midi clocks per metro beat */
GLOBAL int g_pitchbend INIT(0);          /* toggle for pitchbend data thru */
GLOBAL int g_exclusive INIT(0);          /* toggle for exclusive data thru */
GLOBAL int g_current_measure INIT(0);    /* number of current measure */
GLOBAL int g_record_track INIT(-1);      /* track number set to record */
GLOBAL int g_bytes_used INIT(0);         /* number of kbytes used */
GLOBAL int g_trace_on INIT(0);           /* toggle for data trace option on */

/* globals for mted modules */

GLOBAL int g_block_on INIT(0);           /* toggle for block active */
GLOBAL int g_block_track INIT(-1);       /* track number for block */
GLOBAL int g_block_start INIT(-1);       /* measure number for block start */
GLOBAL int g_block_end INIT(-1);         /* measure number for block end */
```

```
/* globals for mtsc modules */

GLOBAL int g_scale INIT(4);            /* amount of compression of time */
GLOBAL int g_oct_shown;                /* number of octaves shown */
GLOBAL int g_top_note INIT(83);        /* MIDI note number of top note */
GLOBAL int g_top_note_line;            /* vert pixel number of top note */
GLOBAL int g_bot_note;                 /* MIDI note number of bottom note */
GLOBAL int g_bot_note_line;            /* vert pixel number of bottom note */
GLOBAL int g_first_measure INIT(0);    /* first measure number on screen */
GLOBAL int g_first_tick INIT(0);       /* first tick number on screen */
GLOBAL int g_sc_refresh INIT(1);       /* set true if note editor is left */

GLOBAL int g_note_array[NNOTES];    /* array to track which notes are left */
                                    /* on or off at end of a block */

GLOBAL int g_tracks_on[NTRACK];        /* tracks set to play */

GLOBAL int g_track_vel[NTRACK];        /* used to store velocity data for */
GLOBAL int g_track_vel_used INIT(0);   /* play module.  */

        /* structure definitions - for all modules in mt */

struct event {          /* structure used to store a midi data event */
    struct event far *next;
    unsigned char nbytes;
    unsigned char b[4];
};


struct trackdata {      /* structure to hold one track's data & pointers */
    char name[TRACK_NAME_WIDE];
    int midichan;
    long numevents;
    int active;
    int midivol;
    struct event far *first;
    struct event far *current;
    struct event far *last;
};


struct item {         /* temporary structure used to pass data from functions */
    int track;
    int measure;
};

/* structures used in mtsc modules */

struct note_map{        /* Structure to hold data about each MIDI note no. */
    char name[10];      /* Helps full screen display of piano, note name... */
```

```
    int up_dots;        /* = number of pixels to go up to next note */
    int down_dots;      /* = down to next note */
};

struct note_time{       /* note list structure used in full screen editing  */
    struct event far *on_event;
    int on_measure;
    int on_tick;
    int note_number;
    struct event far *off_event;
    int off_measure;
    int off_tick;
    struct note_time far *next;
};

/* structure used to keep track of note-ons when compiling note list */

struct on_event{
    struct event far *event;
    int measure;
    int tick;
    int vel;
};

/* temporary structure to pass measure/time/note of cursor position */

struct note_pos{
    int measure;
    int tick;
    int note;
    int sprite_x;
    int sprite_y;
};


/* the screen data definitions are too long for the INIT() approach, */
/* so different definitions are given depending on whether ALLOCATE is */
/* defined in the current module.  Look at the end of this file of the */
/* outline definitions for externals */

#ifdef ALLOCATE

                                  /* primary data array for tracks */
    struct trackdata g_trackarray[NTRACK];
                                  /* pointers to screen image data */
                                  /* plus 1 so screens start #1, #2 */
    struct strchain *g_chain[NSCREEN + 1];

    char g_note_char[2] = { NOTE_CHAR, '\0' };      /* char strings for */
    char g_meas_char[2] = { MEAS_CHAR, '\0' };      /* measure level edit */
    char g_blocks_char[2] = { BLOCK_START, '\0' };  /* symbols */
    char g_blocke_char[2] = { BLOCK_END, '\0' };
```

```
        char g_smallb_char[2] = { SMALL_BLOCK, '\0' };


#include "mtscreen.h"                    /* all menu data in this file */


#else       /* external references for dependant modules */

    extern struct trackdata g_trackarray[];
    extern struct strchain *g_chain[];
    extern struct selement mt1[];       /* the menu data referenced here */
    extern struct selement mt2[];       /* is in mtscreen.h */
    extern struct selement mt3[];
    extern struct selement mt4[];
    extern struct selement mt5[];
    extern struct selement mt51[];
    extern struct selement mt52[];
    extern struct selement mt6[];
    extern char g_note_char[2];
    extern char g_meas_char[2];
    extern char g_blocks_char[2];
    extern char g_blocke_char[2];
    extern char g_smallb_char[2];

#endif
```

```
/* mtdeclar.h  function declarations for all mt.c moudules */

/* mt.c */

void main(void);

/* mtrc1.c */

void record_menu(void);

/* mtrc2.c */

void play(void);
void record(void);
struct event far *record_track(int track);

/* mtrc3.c */

void play_event(int track, struct event far *ep);
void stop_401(int tracks_on);
int init_401(struct event far *ep[]);
void maybe_measure_number(int track, int trackbits);
void erase_track(void);
void erase_one(int track);
void erase_all(void);
void init_track_str(void);
long count_events(void);
void init_rec_val(void);
void calc_pct_free(void);
void write_on_off(int param, int column, int row);
void all_notes_off(void);
void trace_header(void);

/* mtrc4.c */

struct event far *eventalloc(void);
struct event far *store(struct event far *node, int nbytes, int b1, int b2,
     int b3, int b4);
int getnext401(void);
void ungetnext401(int n);
int get401(void);
void putdata401(int n);
int sendcmd401(int n);
int repeat_cmd401(int n);
int goto_measure(int meas);
void change_channel(int track, int channel);
void init_tracks(void);
int free_memory(void);
int used_memory(void);
void data_dump(void);
void clear_forward(void);
void clear_events(struct event far *start);
void wait_for_key(void);

/* mted1.c */
```

```
void edit_menu(void);

/* mted2.c */

void init_meas_data(void);
int has_midi_data(struct event far *measurep);
struct event far *increment_measure(struct event far *eventp);
int select_measure(struct item *item);
struct event far *advance_to_measure(int track, int measure);
struct event far *add_measure(struct event far *ep);
struct event far *merge_measure(struct event far *dest_p,
    struct event far *source_p);
void init_note_array(void);
void fill_note_array(struct event far *start_event,
    struct event far *end_event);
struct event far *add_note_offs(struct event far *dest_event, int channel);

/* mted3.c */

void empty_block(int track, int b_start, int b_end);
void block_repeat(void);
void repeat_copy(int source_meas, int source_track, int dest_meas,
    int dest_track, int n_meas, int reps);
void transpose_block(void);
struct event far *find_event_before(int track, struct event far *ep);
void clean_track(int track);
void block_paste(void);

/* mtsc1.c */

int scrn_edit_control(int track, int measure);
void init_edit_param(void);
void display_keyboard(void);

/* mtsc2.c */

void init_screen_box(int beat, int measure);
void top_scale(int beat, int leftside, int topline, int rightside,
    int botside, int measure);
void name_top_note(int oct_shown);
void name_measure(int measure);
void dotted_lines(int topx, int topy, int botx, int boty, int vspace,
    int hspace, int color);
struct note_time far *build_note_list(int track);
void free_note_list(struct note_time far *np);
void disp_notes(struct note_time far *first_notep, int first_measure,
    int beat);
void draw_note(struct note_time far *np, int color);
void mark_middle_c(int first);
int find_note_line(int note_no);

/* mtsc3.c */

struct note_time far *delete_note(struct note_time far *first_notep,
    int measure, int track);
```

269

```
struct note_pos *select_note(int measure, int option);
void clear_select_lines(void);
struct note_time far *find_note(struct note_time far *first_notep, int note,
    int measure, int tick);
float note_to_float(int measure, int tick);
int remove_event(struct event far *eventp, int track);
struct note_time far *remove_note(struct note_time far *first_notep,
    struct note_time far *notep);

/* mtsc4.c */

void add_note(struct note_time far *first_notep, int measure, int track);
struct event far *add_event(int track, int measure, int tick, int event_bytes,
    int b1, int b2, int b3);
struct note_time far *add_note_time(struct note_time far *first_np,
    struct event far *on_event, int on_meas, int on_tick,
    struct event far *off_event, int off_meas, int off_tick);
void change_vel(struct note_time far *first_notep, int measure);

/* mtut1.c */

void save_song(void);
void save_tracks(FILE *stream);
void load_song(void);
void recal_song(FILE *stream);
void help_control(void);
void helpdisp(char *filename);

/* mtut2.c */

void import_menu(void);
void import_track(FILE *stream, int source_track, int dest_track,
    struct trackdata temp_trackarray[]);
void show_dest(int track);
void show_source(int track);

/* filefunc.c */

int pick_file(char *dir, char *match_str, char *str);
int disp_files(char *dir, char *match_str);
int getdrive(char *prodir, char *sampdir);
void put_to_file(void *addr, int size, FILE *stream);
void fput_to_file(void far *addr, int size, FILE *stream);
void get_from_file(void *addr, int size, FILE *stream);
void fget_from_file(void far *addr, int size, FILE *stream);
void loadscrn(struct strchain *chain[], int number, char *namestr);
int load_video_data(char *filename);
```

```
/* mtsc.h  header data for screen editor portion of multi */

#ifdef ALLOCATE

/* data in hex for bit mapped images */
/* sprite structure defined in screenf.h */

unsigned char lm[] = {        /* bit map for small m used to mark middle C */
    0x82,
    0xc6,
    0xaa,
    0x92,
    0x82,
    0x82,
};

struct sprite little_m = { 1, 6, lm };

unsigned char dcross[] = {  /* bit map for cross for graphics cursor */
    0x08, 0x00,
    0x08, 0x00,
    0x08, 0x00,
    0x08, 0x00,
    0xF7, 0x80,
    0x08, 0x00,
    0x08, 0x00,
    0x08, 0x00,
    0x08, 0x00,
};

struct sprite cross = { 2, 9, dcross };


                           /* structure to hold note names and number of */
                           /* pixels to move up/down to get to next note. */
struct note_map g_notes[] = {
    { "C -5", 4, 0 },           /* 0 */                /* MIDI note number */
    { "C#/Db -5", 4, 4 },
    { "D -5", 4, 4 },
    { "D#/Eb -5", 4, 4 },
    { "E -5", 8, 4 },
    { "F -5", 4, 8 },
    { "F#/Gb -5", 4, 4 },
    { "G -5", 4, 4 },
    { "G#/Ab -5", 4, 4 },
    { "A -5", 4, 4 },
    { "A#/Bb -5", 4, 4 },
    { "B -5", 8, 4 },
    { "C -4", 4, 8 },           /* 12 */
    { "C#/Db -4", 4, 4 },
    { "D -4", 4, 4 },
```

```
{ "D#/Eb -4", 4, 4 },
{ "E -4", 8, 4 },
{ "F -4", 4, 8 },
{ "F#/Gb -4", 4, 4 },
{ "G -4", 4, 4 },
{ "G#/Ab -4", 4, 4 },
{ "A -4", 4, 4 },
{ "A#/Bb -4", 4, 4 },
{ "B -4", 8, 4 },
{ "C -3", 4, 8 },           /* 24 */
{ "C#/Db -3", 4, 4 },
{ "D -3", 4, 4 },
{ "D#/Eb -3", 4, 4 },
{ "E -3", 8, 4 },
{ "F -3", 4, 8 },
{ "F#/Gb -3", 4, 4 },
{ "G -3", 4, 4 },
{ "G#/Ab -3", 4, 4 },
{ "A -3", 4, 4 },
{ "A#/Bb -3", 4, 4 },
{ "B -3", 8, 4 },
{ "C -2", 4, 8 },           /* 34 */
{ "C#/Db -2", 4, 4 },
{ "D -2", 4, 4 },
{ "D#/Eb -2", 4, 4 },
{ "E -2", 8, 4 },
{ "F -2", 4, 8 },
{ "F#/Gb -2", 4, 4 },
{ "G -2", 4, 4 },
{ "G#/Ab -2", 4, 4 },
{ "A -2", 4, 4 },
{ "A#/Bb -2", 4, 4 },
{ "B -2", 8, 4 },
{ "C -1", 4, 8 },           /* 48 */
{ "C#/Db -1", 4, 4 },
{ "D -1", 4, 4 },
{ "D#/Eb -1", 4, 4 },
{ "E -1", 8, 4 },
{ "F -1", 4, 8 },
{ "F#/Gb -1", 4, 4 },
{ "G -1", 4, 4 },
{ "G#/Ab -1", 4, 4 },
{ "A -1", 4, 4 },
{ "A#/Bb -1", 4, 4 },
{ "B -1", 8, 4 },
{ "C Mid.", 4, 8 },         /* 60 - middle c */
{ "C#/Db 1", 4, 4 },
{ "D 1", 4, 4 },
{ "D#/Eb 1", 4, 4 },
{ "E 1", 8, 4 },
{ "F 1", 4, 8 },
```

```
{ "F#/Gb 1", 4, 4 },
{ "G 1", 4, 4 },
{ "G#/Ab 1", 4, 4 },
{ "A 1", 4, 4 },
{ "A#/Bb 1", 4, 4 },
{ "B 1", 8, 4 },
{ "C 2", 4, 8 },                /* 72 */
{ "C#/Db 2", 4, 4 },
{ "D 2", 4, 4 },
{ "D#/Eb 2", 4, 4 },
{ "E 2", 8, 4 },
{ "F 2", 4, 8 },
{ "F#/Gb 2", 4, 4 },
{ "G 2", 4, 4 },
{ "G#/Ab 2", 4, 4 },
{ "A 2", 4, 4 },
{ "A#/Bb 2", 4, 4 },
{ "B 2", 8, 4 },
{ "C 3", 4, 8 },                /* 84 */
{ "C#/Db 3", 4, 4 },
{ "D 3", 4, 4 },
{ "D#/Eb 3", 4, 4 },
{ "E 3", 8, 4 },
{ "F 3", 4, 8 },
{ "F#/Gb 3", 4, 4 },
{ "G 3", 4, 4 },
{ "G#/Ab 3", 4, 4 },
{ "A 3", 4, 4 },
{ "A#/Bb 3", 4, 4 },
{ "B 3", 8, 4 },
{ "C 4", 4, 8 },                /* 94 */
{ "C#/Db 4", 4, 4 },
{ "D 4", 4, 4 },
{ "D#/Eb 4", 4, 4 },
{ "E 4", 8, 4 },
{ "F 4", 4, 8 },
{ "F#/Gb 4", 4, 4 },
{ "G 4", 4, 4 },
{ "G#/Ab 4", 4, 4 },
{ "A 4", 4, 4 },
{ "A#/Bb 4", 4, 4 },
{ "B 4", 8, 4 },
{ "C 5", 4, 8 },                /* 108 */
{ "C#/Db 5", 4, 4 },
{ "D 5", 4, 4 },
{ "D#/Eb 5", 4, 4 },
{ "E 5", 8, 4 },
{ "F 5", 4, 8 },
{ "F#/Gb 5", 4, 4 },
{ "G 5", 4, 4 },
{ "G#/Ab 5", 4, 4 },
```

```
    { "A 5", 4, 4 },
    { "A#/Bb 5", 4, 4 },
    { "B 5", 8, 4 },
    { "C 6", 4, 8 },                    /* 120 */
    { "C#/Db 6", 4, 4 },
    { "D 6", 4, 4 },
    { "D#/Eb 6", 4, 4 },
    { "E 6", 8, 4 },
    { "F 6", 4, 8 },
    { "F#/Gb 6", 0, 4 },
};

#else

extern unsigned char dcross[];
extern struct sprite cross;
extern unsigned char lm[];
extern struct sprite little_m;
extern struct note_map g_notes[];

#endif
```

```
/* mtscreen.h */

/* screen data for cursor movement.      Format per movescreen() is: */
/* row, col, title, nup, ndown, nleft, nright, key, attribute */


struct selement mt1[NPARAM1] = {              /* main menu */
        { 5, 8, "DRIVE", 0, 1, 0, 0, 0 },
        { 5, 9, "LOAD", 0, 2, 1, 1, 1 },
        { 5, 10, "EDIT", 1, 3, 2, 2, 2 },
        { 5, 11, "RECORD", 2, 4, 3, 3, 3 },
        { 5, 12, "TITLE", 3, 5, 4, 4, 4 },
        { 5, 13, "SAVE", 4, 6, 5, 5, 5 },
        { 5, 14, "CLEAR", 5, 7, 6, 6, 6 },
        { 5, 15, "IMPORT", 6, 8, 7, 7, 7 },
        { 5, 16, "HELP", 7, 9, 8, 8, 8 },
        { 5, 18, "QUIT", 8, 9, 9, 9, 9 },
};

/* record menu */
/* key entry is track number */
struct selement mt2[NPARAM2] = {
        { 8, 5, "       ", 0, 8, 0, 1, 0 },
        { 17, 5, "       ", 1, 9, 0, 2, 1 },
        { 26, 5, "       ", 2, 10, 1, 3, 2 },
        { 35, 5, "       ", 3, 11, 2, 4, 3 },
        { 44, 5, "       ", 4, 12, 3, 5, 4 },
        { 53, 5, "       ", 5, 13, 4, 6, 5 },
        { 62, 5, "       ", 6, 14, 5, 7, 6 },
        { 71, 5, "       ", 7, 15, 6, 7, 7 },
        { 10, 6, "       ", 0, 16, 8, 9, 8 },
        { 19, 6, "       ", 1, 17, 8, 10, 9 },
        { 28, 6, "       ", 2, 18, 9, 11, 10 },
        { 37, 6, "       ", 3, 19, 10, 12, 11 },
        { 46, 6, "       ", 4, 20, 11, 13, 12 },
        { 55, 6, "       ", 5, 21, 12, 14, 13 },
        { 64, 6, "       ", 6, 22, 13, 15, 14 },
        { 73, 6, "       ", 7, 23, 14, 15, 15 },
        { 8, 7, "       ", 8, 24, 16, 17, 16 },
        { 17, 7, "       ", 9, 25, 16, 18, 17 },
        { 26, 7, "       ", 10, 26, 17, 19, 18 },
        { 35, 7, "       ", 11, 27, 18, 20, 19 },
        { 44, 7, "       ", 12, 28, 19, 21, 20 },
        { 53, 7, "       ", 13, 29, 20, 22, 21 },
        { 62, 7, "       ", 14, 30, 21, 23, 22 },
        { 71, 7, "       ", 15, 31, 22, 23, 23 },
        { 10, 8, "       ", 16, 32, 24, 25, 24 },
        { 19, 8, "       ", 17, 33, 24, 26, 25 },
        { 28, 8, "       ", 18, 34, 25, 27, 26 },
        { 37, 8, "       ", 19, 35, 26, 28, 27 },
        { 46, 8, "       ", 20, 36, 27, 29, 28 },
```

```
{ 55, 8, "      ", 21, 37, 28, 30, 29 },
{ 64, 8, "      ", 22, 38, 29, 31, 30 },
{ 73, 8, "      ", 23, 39, 30, 31, 31 },
{ 10, 9, "      ", 24, 40, 32, 33, 32 },
{ 19, 9, "      ", 25, 41, 32, 34, 33 },
{ 28, 9, "      ", 26, 42, 33, 35, 34 },
{ 37, 9, "      ", 27, 43, 34, 36, 35 },
{ 46, 9, "      ", 28, 44, 35, 37, 36 },
{ 55, 9, "      ", 29, 45, 36, 38, 37 },
{ 64, 9, "      ", 30, 46, 37, 39, 38 },
{ 73, 9, "      ", 31, 47, 38, 39, 39 },
{ 10, 10, "      ", 32, 48, 40, 41, 40 },
{ 19, 10, "      ", 33, 49, 40, 42, 41 },
{ 28, 10, "      ", 34, 50, 41, 43, 42 },
{ 37, 10, "      ", 35, 51, 42, 44, 43 },
{ 46, 10, "      ", 36, 52, 43, 45, 44 },
{ 55, 10, "      ", 37, 53, 44, 46, 45 },
{ 64, 10, "      ", 38, 54, 45, 47, 46 },
{ 73, 10, "      ", 39, 55, 46, 47, 47 },
{ 10, 11, "      ", 40, 56, 48, 49, 48 },
{ 19, 11, "      ", 41, 57, 48, 50, 49 },
{ 28, 11, "      ", 42, 57, 49, 51, 50 },
{ 37, 11, "      ", 43, 58, 50, 52, 51 },
{ 46, 11, "      ", 44, 58, 51, 53, 52 },
{ 55, 11, "      ", 45, 59, 52, 54, 53 },
{ 64, 11, "      ", 46, 59, 53, 55, 54 },
{ 73, 11, "      ", 47, 59, 54, 55, 55 },
{ 9, 14, "RECORD", 48, 63, 56, 57, 56 },
{ 23, 14, "Last Measure", 49, 60, 56, 58, 57 },
{ 41, 14, "Erase Track", 51, 61, 57, 59, 58 },
{ 61, 14, "Metronome", 54, 62, 58, 59, 59 },
{ 23, 15, "Fast Forwd >>", 57, 64, 63, 61, 60 },
{ 41, 15, "Erase Forward", 58, 65, 60, 62, 61 },
{ 61, 15, "Meter Bt/Mes", 59, 66, 61, 62, 62 },
{ 10, 16, "PLAY", 56, 69, 63, 64, 63 },
{ 23, 16, "Forward    >", 60, 67, 63, 65, 64 },
{ 41, 16, "Data Dump", 61, 67, 64, 66, 65 },
{ 61, 16, "Beats/Min.", 62, 68, 65, 66, 66 },
{ 23, 17, "Rewind    <", 64, 70, 63, 65, 67 },
{ 61, 17, "Pitch Bend", 66, 71, 65, 54, 68 },
{ 6, 18, "All Notes Off", 63, 72, 69, 70, 69 },
{ 23, 18, "Fast Rewnd <<", 67, 73, 69, 65, 70 },
{ 61, 18, "Exclusive", 68, 74, 65, 71, 71 },
{ 6, 19, "QUIT Record", 69, 72, 72, 73, 72 },
{ 23, 19, "First Measure", 70, 73, 72, 74, 73 },
{ 61, 19, "Data Trace", 71, 74, 73, 74, 74 },
};


struct selement mt3[NPARAM3] = {
      { 20, 3, " ", 0, 17, 16, 1, 0 },
```

```
{ 24, 3, " ", 1, 18, 0, 2, 1 },
{ 28, 3, " ", 2, 19, 1, 3, 2 },
{ 32, 3, " ", 3, 20, 2, 4, 3 },
{ 36, 3, " ", 4, 21, 3, 5, 4 },
{ 40, 3, " ", 5, 22, 4, 6, 5 },
{ 44, 3, " ", 6, 23, 5, 7, 6 },
{ 48, 3, " ", 7, 24, 6, 8, 7 },
{ 52, 3, " ", 8, 25, 7, 9, 8 },
{ 56, 3, " ", 9, 26, 8, 10, 9 },
{ 60, 3, " ", 10, 27, 9, 11, 10 },
{ 64, 3, " ", 11, 28, 10, 12, 11 },
{ 68, 3, " ", 12, 29, 11, 13, 12 },
{ 72, 3, " ", 13, 30, 12, 14, 13 },
{ 76, 3, " ", 14, 31, 13, 14, 14 },
{ 4, 6, "       ", 0, 32, 15, 16, 15 },
{ 14, 6, " ", 0, 33, 15, 17, 16 },
{ 20, 6, " ", 0, 34, 16, 18, 17 },
{ 24, 6, " ", 1, 35, 17, 19, 18 },
{ 28, 6, " ", 2, 36, 18, 20, 19 },
{ 32, 6, " ", 3, 37, 19, 21, 20 },
{ 36, 6, " ", 4, 38, 20, 22, 21 },
{ 40, 6, " ", 5, 39, 21, 23, 22 },
{ 44, 6, " ", 6, 40, 22, 24, 23 },
{ 48, 6, " ", 7, 41, 23, 25, 24 },
{ 52, 6, " ", 8, 42, 24, 26, 25 },
{ 56, 6, " ", 9, 43, 25, 27, 26 },
{ 60, 6, " ", 10, 44, 26, 28, 27 },
{ 64, 6, " ", 11, 45, 27, 29, 28 },
{ 68, 6, " ", 12, 46, 28, 30, 29 },
{ 72, 6, " ", 13, 47, 29, 31, 30 },
{ 76, 6, " ", 14, 48, 30, 31, 31 },
{ 4, 7, "       ", 15, 49, 32, 33, 32 },
{ 14, 7, " ", 16, 50, 32, 34, 33 },
{ 20, 7, " ", 17, 51, 33, 35, 34 },
{ 24, 7, " ", 18, 52, 34, 36, 35 },
{ 28, 7, " ", 19, 53, 35, 37, 36 },
{ 32, 7, " ", 20, 54, 36, 38, 37 },
{ 36, 7, " ", 21, 55, 37, 39, 38 },
{ 40, 7, " ", 22, 56, 38, 40, 39 },
{ 44, 7, " ", 23, 57, 39, 41, 40 },
{ 48, 7, " ", 24, 58, 40, 42, 41 },
{ 52, 7, " ", 25, 59, 41, 43, 42 },
{ 56, 7, " ", 26, 60, 42, 44, 43 },
{ 60, 7, " ", 27, 61, 43, 45, 44 },
{ 64, 7, " ", 28, 62, 44, 46, 45 },
{ 68, 7, " ", 29, 63, 45, 47, 46 },
{ 72, 7, " ", 30, 64, 46, 48, 47 },
{ 76, 7, " ", 31, 65, 47, 48, 48 },
{ 4, 8, "       ", 32, 66, 49, 50, 49 },
{ 14, 8, " ", 33, 67, 49, 51, 50 },
{ 20, 8, " ", 34, 68, 50, 52, 51 },
```

```
{ 24,  8,  "  ",  35,  69,  51,  53,  52 },
{ 28,  8,  "  ",  36,  70,  52,  54,  53 },
{ 32,  8,  "  ",  37,  71,  53,  55,  54 },
{ 36,  8,  "  ",  38,  72,  54,  56,  55 },
{ 40,  8,  "  ",  39,  73,  55,  57,  56 },
{ 44,  8,  "  ",  40,  74,  56,  58,  57 },
{ 48,  8,  "  ",  41,  75,  57,  59,  58 },
{ 52,  8,  "  ",  42,  76,  58,  60,  59 },
{ 56,  8,  "  ",  43,  77,  59,  61,  60 },
{ 60,  8,  "  ",  44,  78,  60,  62,  61 },
{ 64,  8,  "  ",  45,  79,  61,  63,  62 },
{ 68,  8,  "  ",  46,  80,  62,  64,  63 },
{ 72,  8,  "  ",  47,  81,  63,  65,  64 },
{ 76,  8,  "  ",  48,  82,  64,  65,  65 },
{  4,  9,  "       ",  49,  83,  66,  67,  66 },
{ 14,  9,  "  ",  50,  84,  66,  68,  67 },
{ 20,  9,  "  ",  51,  85,  67,  69,  68 },
{ 24,  9,  "  ",  52,  86,  68,  70,  69 },
{ 28,  9,  "  ",  53,  87,  69,  71,  70 },
{ 32,  9,  "  ",  54,  88,  70,  72,  71 },
{ 36,  9,  "  ",  55,  89,  71,  73,  72 },
{ 40,  9,  "  ",  56,  90,  72,  74,  73 },
{ 44,  9,  "  ",  57,  91,  73,  75,  74 },
{ 48,  9,  "  ",  58,  92,  74,  76,  75 },
{ 52,  9,  "  ",  59,  93,  75,  77,  76 },
{ 56,  9,  "  ",  60,  94,  76,  78,  77 },
{ 60,  9,  "  ",  61,  95,  77,  79,  78 },
{ 64,  9,  "  ",  62,  96,  78,  80,  79 },
{ 68,  9,  "  ",  63,  97,  79,  81,  80 },
{ 72,  9,  "  ",  64,  98,  80,  82,  81 },
{ 76,  9,  "  ",  65,  99,  81,  82,  82 },
{  4, 10,  "       ",  66, 100,  83,  84,  83 },
{ 14, 10,  "  ",  67, 101,  83,  85,  84 },
{ 20, 10,  "  ",  68, 102,  84,  86,  85 },
{ 24, 10,  "  ",  69, 103,  85,  87,  86 },
{ 28, 10,  "  ",  70, 104,  86,  88,  87 },
{ 32, 10,  "  ",  71, 105,  87,  89,  88 },
{ 36, 10,  "  ",  72, 106,  88,  90,  89 },
{ 40, 10,  "  ",  73, 107,  89,  91,  90 },
{ 44, 10,  "  ",  74, 108,  90,  92,  91 },
{ 48, 10,  "  ",  75, 109,  91,  93,  92 },
{ 52, 10,  "  ",  76, 110,  92,  94,  93 },
{ 56, 10,  "  ",  77, 111,  93,  95,  94 },
{ 60, 10,  "  ",  78, 112,  94,  96,  95 },
{ 64, 10,  "  ",  79, 113,  95,  97,  96 },
{ 68, 10,  "  ",  80, 114,  96,  98,  97 },
{ 72, 10,  "  ",  81, 115,  97,  99,  98 },
{ 76, 10,  "  ",  82, 116,  98,  99,  99 },
{  4, 11,  "       ",  83, 117, 100, 101, 100 },
{ 14, 11,  "  ",  84, 118, 100, 102, 101 },
{ 20, 11,  "  ",  85, 119, 101, 103, 102 },
```

```
{ 24, 11, " ", 86, 120, 102, 104, 103 },
{ 28, 11, " ", 87, 121, 103, 105, 104 },
{ 32, 11, " ", 88, 122, 104, 106, 105 },
{ 36, 11, " ", 89, 123, 105, 107, 106 },
{ 40, 11, " ", 90, 124, 106, 108, 107 },
{ 44, 11, " ", 91, 125, 107, 109, 108 },
{ 48, 11, " ", 92, 126, 108, 110, 109 },
{ 52, 11, " ", 93, 127, 109, 111, 110 },
{ 56, 11, " ", 94, 128, 110, 112, 111 },
{ 60, 11, " ", 95, 129, 111, 113, 112 },
{ 64, 11, " ", 96, 130, 112, 114, 113 },
{ 68, 11, " ", 97, 131, 113, 115, 114 },
{ 72, 11, " ", 98, 132, 114, 116, 115 },
{ 76, 11, " ", 99, 133, 115, 116, 116 },
{ 4, 12, "         ", 100, 134, 117, 118, 117 },
{ 14, 12, "  ", 101, 135, 117, 119, 118 },
{ 20, 12, " ", 102, 136, 118, 120, 119 },
{ 24, 12, " ", 103, 137, 119, 121, 120 },
{ 28, 12, " ", 104, 138, 120, 122, 121 },
{ 32, 12, " ", 105, 139, 121, 123, 122 },
{ 36, 12, " ", 106, 140, 122, 124, 123 },
{ 40, 12, " ", 107, 141, 123, 125, 124 },
{ 44, 12, " ", 108, 142, 124, 126, 125 },
{ 48, 12, " ", 109, 143, 125, 127, 126 },
{ 52, 12, " ", 110, 144, 126, 128, 127 },
{ 56, 12, " ", 111, 145, 127, 129, 128 },
{ 60, 12, " ", 112, 146, 128, 130, 129 },
{ 64, 12, " ", 113, 147, 129, 131, 130 },
{ 68, 12, " ", 114, 148, 130, 132, 131 },
{ 72, 12, " ", 115, 149, 131, 133, 132 },
{ 76, 12, " ", 116, 150, 132, 133, 133 },
{ 4, 13, "         ", 117, 151, 134, 135, 134 },
{ 14, 13, "  ", 118, 151, 134, 136, 135 },
{ 20, 13, " ", 119, 151, 135, 137, 136 },
{ 24, 13, " ", 120, 152, 136, 138, 137 },
{ 28, 13, " ", 121, 152, 137, 139, 138 },
{ 32, 13, " ", 122, 152, 138, 140, 139 },
{ 36, 13, " ", 123, 152, 139, 141, 140 },
{ 40, 13, " ", 124, 152, 140, 142, 141 },
{ 44, 13, " ", 125, 153, 141, 143, 142 },
{ 48, 13, " ", 126, 153, 142, 144, 143 },
{ 52, 13, " ", 127, 153, 143, 145, 144 },
{ 56, 13, " ", 128, 153, 144, 146, 145 },
{ 60, 13, " ", 129, 153, 145, 147, 146 },
{ 64, 13, " ", 130, 153, 146, 148, 147 },
{ 68, 13, " ", 131, 153, 147, 149, 148 },
{ 72, 13, " ", 132, 153, 148, 150, 149 },
{ 76, 13, " ", 133, 153, 149, 150, 150 },
{ 13, 16, "Start Block", 135, 154, 151, 152, 151 },
{ 32, 16, "Last Measure", 139, 155, 151, 153, 152 },
{ 50, 16, "Curnt Measure", 143, 156, 152, 153, 153 },
```

```
        { 13, 17, "End Block", 151, 157, 154, 155, 154 },
        { 32, 17, "Fast Forwd >>", 152, 158, 154, 156, 155 },
        { 50, 17, "Erase Track", 153, 159, 155, 156, 156 },
        { 13, 18, "Block Paste", 154, 160, 157, 158, 157 },
        { 32, 18, "Forward    >", 155, 161, 157, 159, 158 },
        { 50, 18, "Erase Forward", 156, 162, 158, 159, 159 },
        { 13, 19, "Block Empty", 157, 163, 160, 161, 160 },
        { 32, 19, "Rewind     <", 158, 164, 160, 162, 161 },
        { 50, 19, "Data Dump", 159, 167, 161, 162, 162 },
        { 13, 20, "Block Repeat", 160, 165, 163, 164, 163 },
        { 32, 20, "Fast Rewnd <<", 161, 166, 163, 162, 164 },
        { 13, 21, "Block Transp.", 163, 165, 165, 166, 165 },
        { 32, 21, "First Measure", 164, 166, 165, 167, 166 },
        { 50, 21, "QUIT Edit", 162, 167, 166, 167, 167 },
};


struct selement mt4[NPARAM4] = {                    /* help menu */
        { 4, 9, "GENERAL", 0, 1, 0, 0, 0 },
        { 4, 10, "MOUSE", 0, 2, 1, 1, 1 },
        { 4, 11, "FILES", 1, 3, 2, 2, 2 },
        { 4, 12, "EDITING", 2, 4, 3, 3, 3 },
        { 4, 13, "RECORDING", 3, 5, 4, 4, 4 },
        { 4, 14, "TITLES", 4, 6, 5, 5, 5 },
        { 4, 15, "CLEAR", 5, 7, 6, 6, 6 },
        { 4, 16, "IMPORT", 6, 8, 7, 7, 7 },
        { 4, 18, "QUIT", 7, 8, 8, 8, 8 },
};


struct selement mt5[NPARAM5] = {                    /* import bottom menu */
        { 11, 21, "Pick Source", 0, 0, 0, 1, 0 },
        { 29, 21, "Pick Dest.", 1, 1, 0, 2, 1 },
        { 46, 21, "Import Track", 2, 2, 1, 3, 2 },
        { 68, 21, "Quit", 3, 3, 2, 3, 3 },
};


struct selement mt51[NPARAM51] = {                  /* source track selection menu
*/
        { 8, 11, " ", 0, 0, 0, 1, 0 },
        { 17, 11, " ", 1, 1, 0, 2, 1 },
        { 26, 11, " ", 2, 2, 1, 3, 2 },
        { 35, 11, " ", 3, 3, 2, 4, 3 },
        { 44, 11, " ", 4, 4, 3, 5, 4 },
        { 53, 11, " ", 5, 5, 4, 6, 5 },
        { 62, 11, " ", 6, 6, 5, 7, 6 },
        { 71, 11, " ", 7, 7, 6, 7, 7 },
```

```
};




struct selement mt52[NPARAM52] = {                  /* destination selection menu
*/
        { 8, 19, " ", 0, 0, 0, 1, 0 },
        { 17, 19, " ", 1, 1, 0, 2, 1 },
        { 26, 19, " ", 2, 2, 1, 3, 2 },
        { 35, 19, " ", 3, 3, 2, 4, 3 },
        { 44, 19, " ", 4, 4, 3, 5, 4 },
        { 53, 19, " ", 5, 5, 4, 6, 5 },
        { 62, 19, " ", 6, 6, 5, 7, 6 },
        { 71, 19, " ", 7, 7, 6, 7, 7 },
};




struct selement mt6[NPARAM6] = {                     /* note editor menu */
        { 1, 20,  "Higher Octave", 0, 4, 0, 1, 0 },
        { 20, 20, "Next Meas. >>", 1, 5, 0, 2, 1 },
        { 42, 20, "Delete Note", 2, 6, 1, 3, 2 },
        { 61, 20, "Tick =", 3, 7, 2, 3, 3 },
        { 1, 21,  "Lower Octave", 0, 8, 4, 5, 4 },
        { 20, 21, "Next Beat  >", 1, 9, 4, 6, 5 },
        { 42, 21, "Add Note", 2, 10, 5, 7, 6 },
        { 61, 21, "Note =", 3, 11, 6, 7, 7 },
        { 1, 22,  "Expand <->", 4, 12, 8, 9, 8 },
        { 20, 22, "Prev Beat  <", 5, 13, 8, 10, 9 },
        { 42, 22, "Vel Change", 6, 14, 9, 11, 10 },
        { 61, 22, "Measure =", 7, 15, 10, 11, 11 },
        { 1, 23,  "Shrink >-<", 8, 12, 12, 13, 12 },
        { 20, 23, "Prev Meas. <<", 9, 13, 12, 14, 13 },
        { 42, 23, "Quit Edit", 10, 14, 13, 15, 14 },
        { 61, 23, "Top Note=", 11, 15, 14, 15, 15 },
};
```

```
/* screenf.h  header file for screenf.lib */
/* for writscrn.c, linedraw.c, chain.c  */

#define WHITE        1
#define BLACK        0
                            /* starting memory for video page */
#define CVIDMEM      0xB8000000L /* CGA text/graphics */
#define HVIDMEM      0xB0000000L /* monochrome/hercules text */
#define EVIDMEM      0xA8000000L /* ega/vga */

#define SCRNWIDE 80           /* usual width and hight of screen in chars */
#define SCRNTALL 25
                             /* codes for screen char attributes */

#define BWC   0x07  /* black and white */
#define ULC   0x01  /* underlined */
#define RVC   0x70  /* reverse video */
#define BRVC  0xF0  /* blinking reverse video */
#define BRBWC 0x0F  /* bright, black and white */

/* structures used in modules */
/* writscrn.c */

struct selement {   /* used by movescrn() for cursor element definition */
    int xpos;
    int ypos;
    char content[15];
    int nup;
    int ndown;
    int nleft;
    int nright;
    int key;
};

/* videofnc.c */

struct sprite{       /* sprite structure; sdata is bit map */
    int swide;
    int stall;
    unsigned char *sdata;
    };

/* chain.c   */

struct strchain {   /* used for linked list storage of screen displays */
    char *line;
    struct strchain *next;
};

/* old style func declarations

struct strchain *inpchain(),
                *chain(),
                *chainalloc();
char *strsave();                */
```

```
                  /* function prototypes */
/* videofnc.c */

void writeword(char *string, int x, int y, int attrib);
void clearscreen(int attrib);
void clearline(int lineno, int attrib);
void csrplot(int x, int y);
void setvideomode(int mode);
void dotplot(int x, int y, int color);
void draw_rectangle(int fill, int x1, int y1, int x2, int y2, int color);
void drawline(int x1, int y1, int x2, int y2, int color);
void wordul(int mode, char *string, int x, int y, int color);
void draw_sprite(struct sprite spr, int xpos, int ypos, int line_color,
    int back_color);
void xsprite(struct sprite spr, int xpos, int ypos, int color);

/* writscrn.c */

int movescrn(int vidmode, struct selement scrnarray[], int first, int last,
    int normal, int hilit);
void to_new_csr(int vidmode, struct selement scrnarray[], int k, int oldk,
    int normal, int hilit);
void writerr(char *s, int lineno,  int normal, int hilit);
void clearwind(int tx, int ty, int bx, int by, int attrib);
void initscrn(struct selement scrnarray[], int first, int last, int attrib);
void finitscrn(struct selement scrnarray[], int first, int last, int attrib,
    int mode);
void fwriteword(char *string, int x, int y, int attrib, int mode);
void write_int(int value, int x, int y, int attrib);

/* chain.c */

struct strchain *inpchain(char *file, int maxlen);
struct strchain *chain(struct strchain *p, char *w);
void dechain(struct strchain *p);
void dispchain(struct strchain *p, int y, int attrib);
struct strchain *chainalloc(void);
char *strsave(char *s);
void fdispchain(struct strchain *p, int y,  int attrib, int mode);

/* inputf.c */

int getfloat(int lineno, char *prompt, float *value, float min, float max,
    int normal, int hilit);
int getint(int lineno, char *prompt, int *value, int min, int max,
    int normal, int hilit);
int getstr(int lineno, char *prompt, char *string, int max,
    int attrib);
int get_string(char *str, int max);
```

```
/* standard.h      standard definitions for IBM PC */

#define TRUE         1
#define FALSE        0
#define CR           13
#define LF           10
#define FF           12
#define BELL         7
#define ESC          27
#define TABSPACE     8


#define BACKSP       8           /* keypress codes */
#define CTLC         3
#define TAB          9
#define BTAB         15          /* shift - tab for backtab */
#define SKUP         56          /* shift - arrow keys */
#define SKDOWN       50
#define SKLEFT       52
#define SKRIGHT      54


#define KUP          72          /* arrow keys */
#define KDOWN        80
#define KLEFT        75
#define KRIGHT       77
#define KHOME        71
#define KEND         79
#define KPGUP        73
#define KPGDN        81
#define KDEL         83
#define KINS         82


#define F1           59          /* function key codes */
#define F2           60
#define F3           61
#define F4           62
#define F5           63
#define F6           64
#define F7           65
#define F8           66
#define F9           67
#define F10          68
```

```
/* video.h  header file for video attribute and mode data */
/* works in conjuction with install.c's output file install.dat */

/* defines to allow same header file to work for both initialization */
/*  and reference.  Only define the word ALLOCATE in the main() module. */

#ifdef ALLOCATE
    #define GLOBAL
    #define INIT(x)   =x
#else
    #define GLOBAL extern
    #define INIT(x)
#endif


GLOBAL int g_text_mode;
GLOBAL int g_graph_mode;
GLOBAL int g_dots_v;                      /* graphics pixels vertically */
GLOBAL int g_dots_h;                      /* horizontally */
GLOBAL int g_norm_attrib;                 /* attribute for normal characters */
GLOBAL int g_cursor_attrib;               /*   for the cursor highlight */
GLOBAL int g_emph_attrib;                 /*   for emphasized characters */
GLOBAL int g_let_dots_v;                  /* character pixels vertical */
GLOBAL int g_let_dots_h;                  /* character pixels width */
GLOBAL int g_text_char_v;                 /* number of char lines, text mode */
GLOBAL int g_text_char_h;                 /* number of char columns */
GLOBAL int g_graph_char_h;                /* ditto in graphics mode for char */
GLOBAL int g_graph_char_v;                /* written to graphics screens */
GLOBAL int g_text_colors;                 /* total number of colors available */
GLOBAL int g_graph_colors;


GLOBAL int g_line_color;                  /* the color lines are drawn with */
GLOBAL int g_back_color;                  /* the background color */
GLOBAL int g_emph_color;                  /* line color for emphasis */
```

```
/* buldmenu.c  makes up a struct selement array from screen file */
/*  assumes that each screen element which should be a cursor choice */
/*  is surrounded by a pair of { } chars.  Close elements can use just { */
/*  jlc 6/88   rev 1 */
/*  9/88 converted to Microsoft graphics library row, col #'s */

/* #define TURBOC 1   Define if using TURBOC, leave out for Microsoft */

#include <stdio.h>
#include <string.h>

#ifdef TURBOC
    #include <alloc.h>
#else
    #include <malloc.h>
#endif

#include "standard.h"
#include "screenf.h"

#define MAXEL          500      /* max number of screen elements */
#define CONTENT_WIDE   15       /* char width of content, struct selement */
#define SCRN_PITCH     8        /* int ratio of row vs col dist on screen */
#define MINY_DIST      0        /* minimum significant vertical distance */
#define MINX_DIST      2        /* minimum significant horizontal distance */
/* (less and the items are considered to be on the same line vertically) */

/* the only function's prototype */

void write_instructions(void);


void
main(argc, argv)
int argc;
char *argv[];
{
    int *x, *y, i, j, numel, row, col, right_dis, left_dis, up_dis,
        down_dis, close_up, close_down, close_left, close_right, xdist,
        ydist, delx, dely;
    char c, *sp, nbuf[10], lbuf[SCRNWIDE], *str[MAXEL];
    FILE *infile, *outfile;

    if (argc < 2){          /* if no input file - put up help info. */
        write_instructions();
        exit();
    }
    else if (argc < 3){     /* default output is stdout */
        outfile = stdout;
    }
    else{
```

```
    outfile = fopen(argv[2], "w");
    if (outfile == NULL){
        fputs("\nCould not open output file.", stdout);
        write_instructions();
        exit();
    }
}

infile = fopen(argv[1], "r");
if (infile == NULL){
    fputs("\nCould not open input file.", stdout);
    write_instructions();
    exit();
}


x = (int *) malloc(MAXEL * sizeof(int)); /* allocate memory for arrays */
y = (int *) malloc(MAXEL * sizeof(int));
for (i = 0; i < MAXEL; i++){
    str[i] = (char *) malloc(CONTENT_WIDE * sizeof(char));
}

numel = 0;
col = row = 1;
while (1){                  /* main loop, runs through every char in file */
    c = fgetc(infile);
    switch(c){
    case('\t'):             /* expand tabs to blanks */
        while(!(++col % TABSPACE))
            ;
        break;
    case('{'):              /* start of a menu item */
        col++;
        x[numel] = col;
        y[numel] = row;
        sp = str[numel];
        i = 0;
        do {                /* read chars until }, { or out of space */
            c = fgetc(infile);
            if (c != '}' && c != '{')
                *sp++ = c;
            col++;
        } while (i++ < CONTENT_WIDE && c != '}' && c != '{' && c != EOF);
        *sp = '\0';
        numel++;
        break;
    case('\n'):             /* new line */
        col = 1;
        row++;
        break;
    case(EOF):              /* end of file, so compute neighbors distance */
```

```
                    fclose(infile);
                    fputs("\n#define NPARAM  ", outfile);
                    itoa(numel, nbuf, 10);
                    fputs(nbuf, outfile);
                    fputs("\n\nstruct selement _____[NPARAM] = {\n", outfile);
                    for (i = 0; i < numel; i++){
                        left_dis = right_dis = up_dis = down_dis = 32000;
                                            /* default nearest is same spot */
                        close_left = close_right = close_up = close_down = i;
                                            /* find nearest neighbors */
                        for (j = 0; j < numel; j++){
                            delx = x[j] - x[i];
                            dely = y[j] - y[i];
                                /* note the factor for screen not square */
                            xdist = abs(delx) + (SCRN_PITCH * abs(dely));
                            ydist = abs(delx) + abs(dely);
                            if (delx > MINX_DIST){              /* on right side ? */
                                if (xdist < right_dis){
                                    right_dis = xdist;
                                    close_right = j;
                                }
                            }
                            else if (delx < (-1) * MINX_DIST){  /* on left side ? */
                                if (xdist < left_dis){
                                    left_dis = xdist;
                                    close_left = j;
                                }
                            }
                            if (dely > MINY_DIST){              /* below ? */
                                if (ydist < down_dis){
                                    down_dis = ydist;
                                    close_down = j;
                                }
                            }
                            else if (dely < (-1) * MINY_DIST){  /* above ? */
                                if (ydist < up_dis){
                                    up_dis = ydist;
                                    close_up = j;
                                }
                            }
                        }
                    }
                    strcpy(lbuf, "\t{ ");   /* write the structure def. line */
                    itoa(x[i], nbuf, 10);
                    strcat(lbuf, nbuf);
                    strcat(lbuf, ", ");
                    itoa(y[i], nbuf, 10);
                    strcat(lbuf, nbuf);
                    strcat(lbuf, ", \"");
                    strcat(lbuf, str[i]);
                    strcat(lbuf, "\", ");
                    itoa(close_up, nbuf, 10);
```

```
            strcat(lbuf, nbuf);
            strcat(lbuf, ", ");
            itoa(close_down, nbuf, 10);
            strcat(lbuf, nbuf);
            strcat(lbuf, ", ");
            itoa(close_left, nbuf, 10);
            strcat(lbuf, nbuf);
            strcat(lbuf, ", ");
            itoa(close_right, nbuf, 10);
            strcat(lbuf, nbuf);
            strcat(lbuf, ", ");
            itoa(i, nbuf, 10);
            strcat(lbuf, nbuf);
            strcat(lbuf, " },\n");
            fputs(lbuf, outfile);
        }
        fputs("};\n", outfile);
        exit();
    default:            /* any other char - just move past it */
        col++;
        break;
        }
    }
}


void
write_instructions()
{
        fputs("\nBULDMENU - builds a cursor control file for use by
writscrn.c", stdout);
        fputs("\nfunction movescrn().  Normally the output file is added to
the", stdout);
        fputs("\nprogram's header file as a struct of type selement.",
stdout);
        fputs("\nEach element surrounded by { } characters becomes a menu
item.", stdout);
        fputs("\n\nUsage: buldmenu inputfile outputfile", stdout);
}
```

```
/* chain.c - screen file storage and display */
/* uses linked lists with each node defined as a struct strchain */
/* `MIDI Sequencing In C', Jim Conger, M&T Books, 1989 */

/* #define TURBOC 1    Define if using TURBOC, leave out for Microsoft */

#include <stdio.h>

#ifdef TURBOC
    #include <alloc.h>       /* Turbo C library file name */
#else
    #include <malloc.h>      /* Microsoft C library file name */
#endif

#include "standard.h"
#include "screenf.h"         /* contains structure definition */

/* read file into a linked list (chain) in near memory.  Returns a pointer */
/* to the start of the linked list. */
struct strchain
*inpchain(char *file, int maxlen)
{
    FILE *stream;
    struct strchain *root;
    char *strbuf;

    strbuf = (char *) malloc(maxlen + 1);        /* set asside input buffer */

    stream = fopen(file, "r");

    root = NULL;
    while(fgets(strbuf, maxlen, stream) != NULL){
        root = chain(root, strbuf);
    }

    fclose(stream);
    free(strbuf);                   /* free buff for other use */
    return(root);
}

/* add a string recursively to the end of a linked list.  Returns a */
/* pointer to the new node. */
struct strchain
*chain(struct strchain *p, char *w)
{
    if(p == NULL){
        p = chainalloc();
        p->line = strsave(w);
        p->next = NULL;
    }
    else{
        p->next = chain(p->next, w);
    }
    return(p);
```

```
}

/* free all memory reserved for the linked list (chain) pointed to by p */
void
dechain(struct strchain *p)
{
    struct strchain *q;
    if(p != NULL){
        q = p->next;
        free(p->line);
        free(p);
        dechain(q);
    }
}

/* write all lines of the linked list (chain) to stdout starting on line y. */
/* Standard console output version.  Characters written with color attrib. */
void
dispchain(struct strchain *p, int y, int attrib)
{
    if(p){
        writeword(p->line, 1, y, attrib);
        dispchain(p->next, ++y, attrib);
    }
}

/* Reserve memory space for next node in the linked list. */
struct strchain
*chainalloc(void)
{
    return((struct strchain *) malloc(sizeof(struct strchain)));
}

/* Save a string to memory.  Reserves memory and returns a pointer to start */
char
*strsave(char *s)
{
    char *p;
    if((p = (char *) malloc(strlen(s) + 1)) != NULL)
        strcpy(p,s);
    return(p);
}

/* Write all lines of list to console, FAST VERSION, y is start line */
/* p is pointer to start of linked list, mode is video mode. */
void
fdispchain(struct strchain *p, int y, int attrib, int mode)
{
    if(p){
        fwriteword(p->line, 1, y, attrib, mode);
        fdispchain(p->next, ++y, attrib, mode);
    }
}
```

```
/* filefunc.c    standard file utilities */
/* `MIDI Sequencing In C', Jim Conger, M&T Books, 1989 */

/* #define TURBOC 1   Define if using TURBOC, leave out for Microsoft */

#include <conio.h>               /* compiler library module headers */
#include <stdio.h>
#include <string.h>

#ifdef TURBOC
    #include <dir.h>
#else
    #include <dos.h>
#endif

#include "standard.h"            /* header files */
#include "screenf.h"
#include "video.h"
#include "filefunc.h"            /* must be included to use pick_file */

/* allow user to pick file matching wild card allow user to pick file  */
/* matching wild card string. Return number of choice in struct */
/* selement g_file_disp (see filefunc.h) */
int
pick_file(char *dir, char *match_str, char *str)
{
    char buf[SCRNWIDE];
    int num_files, pick;

    num_files = disp_files(dir, match_str);
    if (num_files == 0){
        strcpy(buf, "There are no files matching ");
        strcat(buf, match_str);
        strcat(buf, " on this drive/directory.");
        writerr(buf, g_text_char_v, g_norm_attrib, g_norm_attrib);
        return(-1);
    }
    fwriteword(str, 1, g_text_char_v - 1, g_emph_attrib, g_text_mode);
    pick = movescrn(g_text_mode, g_file_disp, 0, num_files - 1, g_norm_attrib,
        g_cursor_attrib);
    if (pick >= num_files)
        return(-1);
    else
        return(pick);
}


/* display file names matching str, returns # of files displayed */
int
disp_files(char *dir, char *match_str)
{
```

```
    char buf[SCRNWIDE], *s;
    int i, status;
#ifdef TURBOC
    struct ffblk ffblk;              /* define in dir.h */
#else
    struct find_t c_file;            /* defined in dos.h */
#endif

    for (i = 0; i < NPARAM_FILE; i++){
        strcpy(g_file_disp[i].content, " ");
    }

    clearscreen(g_norm_attrib);
    strcpy(buf, "Files matching ");
    strcat(buf, match_str);
    strcat(buf, " on your selected drive (");
    strcat(buf, dir);
    strcat(buf, "):\n");
    writeword(buf, 1, 1, g_emph_attrib);

    strcpy(buf, dir);        /* build up full path\:*.XXX string for DOS */
    s = (char *)strchr(buf,'\0');
    if(*(--s) != '\\'){      /* add '\' if necessary*/
        *(++s) = '\\';
        *(++s) = '\0';
    }
    strcat(buf, match_str);


#ifdef TURBOC
    status = findfirst(buf, &ffblk, 0);
#else
    status = _dos_findfirst(buf, _A_NORMAL, &c_file);
#endif
    if (status){
        return(0);
    }
#ifdef TURBOC
    strcpy(g_file_disp[0].content, ffblk.ff_name);
#else
    strcpy(g_file_disp[0].content, c_file.name);     /* copy file names to */
#endif
                                                     /* screen data array */
    i = 1;
    do {
#ifdef TURBOC
        status = findnext(&ffblk);
#else
        status = _dos_findnext(&c_file);
#endif
```

```
        if (status)
            break;
        else
#ifdef TURBOC
            strcpy(g_file_disp[i].content, ffblk.ff_name);
#else
            strcpy(g_file_disp[i].content, c_file.name);
#endif
    } while (++i < NPARAM_FILE);

    finitscrn(g_file_disp, 0, i - 1, g_norm_attrib, g_text_mode);
    return(i);
}



int                     /* prompt for drive/directory to store data */
getdrive(char *prodir, char *sampdir)
{
    char tmpdir[51], errbuf[80];

    while(1){
        if(getstr(g_text_char_v - 1, "Enter drive/directory ->", tmpdir, 50,
            g_norm_attrib)){

            if (tmpdir[1] == '\0'){      /* convert C to C: */
                tmpdir[1] = ':';
                tmpdir[2] = '\0';
            }
            if (tmpdir[2] == '\0'){      /* convert C: to C:\ */
                tmpdir[2] = '\\';
                tmpdir[3] = '\0';
            }

            if(chdir(tmpdir) != -1){     /* make sure directory exists */
                strcpy(sampdir, tmpdir);
                chdir(prodir);
                return(1);
            }
            else{
                chdir(prodir);
                strcpy(errbuf,"Could not open directory ");
                strcat(errbuf, tmpdir);
                writerr(errbuf, g_text_char_v, g_norm_attrib, g_emph_attrib);
            }
        }
        else{
            return(0);
        }
    }
}
```

```
void                                    /* put near data to stream */
put_to_file(void *addr, int size, FILE *stream)
{
    int i;
    char *addr2;

    addr2 = (char *)addr;
    for(i = 0; i < size; i++){
        fputc(*addr2++, stream);
    }
}


void                                    /* put far data to stream */
fput_to_file(void far *addr, int size, FILE *stream)
{
    int i;
    char far *addr2;

    addr2 = (char far *)addr;
    for(i = 0; i < size; i++){
        fputc(*addr2++, stream);
    }
}


void                /* get data from stream, put into near memory */
get_from_file(void *addr, int size, FILE *stream)
{
    int i;
    char *addr2;

    addr2 = (char *)addr;
    for(i = 0; i < size; i++){
        *addr2++ = fgetc(stream);
    }
}


void                    /* get data from stream, put into far memory */
fget_from_file(void far *addr, int size, FILE *stream)
{
    int i;
    char far *addr2;

    addr2 = (char far *)addr;
    for(i = 0; i < size; i++){
        *addr2++ = fgetc(stream);
    }
```

```
}


/* Load screen files into memory as linked lists. */
void
loadscrn(struct strchain *chain[], int number, char *namestr)
{
    int i;
    char nbuf[10], buf[50];

    fputs("\nLoading screen images....\n",stdout);

    for(i = 1; i <= number; i++){
        strcpy(buf, namestr);          /* screen names are "namestr"1.scr,... */
        nbuf[0] = '0' + i;
        nbuf[1] = '\0';
        strcat(buf,nbuf);
        strcat(buf,".scr");
        chain[i] = inpchain(buf,SCRNWIDE + 1);
    }

    for(i = 1; i <= number; i++){
        if(chain[i] == NULL){
            fputs("Failed to load screen file ",stdout);
            fputs(namestr, stdout);
            itoa(i+1, buf, 10);
            fputs(buf, stdout);
            fputs(".scr\n", stdout);
            fputs("Be sure you run the program from the default drive.",
                stdout);
            exit(0);
        }
    }
}


/* Load values from filename into global data defined in video.h.  This */
/* is the counterpart to the INSTALL program that builds a video data file. */
int
load_video_data(char *filename)
{
    FILE *infile;

    infile = fopen(filename, "r");

    if (infile == NULL)
        return(0);

    get_from_file(&g_text_mode, sizeof(int), infile);
    get_from_file(&g_graph_mode, sizeof(int), infile);
    get_from_file(&g_dots_v, sizeof(int), infile);
```

```
    get_from_file(&g_dots_h, sizeof(int), infile);
    get_from_file(&g_norm_attrib, sizeof(int), infile);
    get_from_file(&g_cursor_attrib, sizeof(int), infile);
    get_from_file(&g_emph_attrib, sizeof(int), infile);
    get_from_file(&g_let_dots_v, sizeof(int), infile);
    get_from_file(&g_let_dots_h, sizeof(int), infile);
    get_from_file(&g_text_char_h, sizeof(int), infile);
    get_from_file(&g_text_char_v, sizeof(int), infile);
    get_from_file(&g_graph_char_h, sizeof(int), infile);
    get_from_file(&g_graph_char_v, sizeof(int), infile);
    get_from_file(&g_text_colors, sizeof(int), infile);
    get_from_file(&g_graph_colors, sizeof(int), infile);

    if (g_graph_colors >= 4){
        g_line_color = g_norm_attrib & 0x0F;
        g_back_color = (g_norm_attrib & 0xF0) >> 4;
        g_emph_color = g_emph_attrib & 0x0F;
    }
    else{                       /* for black/white display modes */
        g_line_color = 1;
        g_back_color = 0;
        g_emph_color = 1;
    }

    fclose(infile);
    return(1);
}
```

```
/* inputf.c    functions for prompting user input */
/* `MIDI Sequencing In C', Jim Conger, M&T Books, 1989 */

#include <conio.h>        /* compiler library module headers */
#include <stdio.h>
#include <stdlib.h>
#include <ctype.h>

#include "standard.h"           /* header files */
#include "screenf.h"


/* Get floating point no. from user.  Return enters value, ESC quits. */
/* Prompt string is printed on line number lineno with norm_attrib. */
/* If input is not >= min or <= max, error message is printed on */
/* lineno with emph_attrib, and user is given another try. */
/* Returns 1 if number was input, 0 if process was escapted. */
int
getfloat(int lineno, char *prompt, float *value, float min, float max,
         int norm_attrib, int emph_attrib)
{
    char input[20], minbuf[20], maxbuf[20], message[SCRNWIDE];
    int n;
    float tempval;

    while(1){
        while(kbhit())
            getch();           /* clear any stray keypress */
        clearline(lineno, norm_attrib);
        writeword(prompt, 1, lineno, norm_attrib);
        n = get_string(input, 19);
        if (n == 0)
            return(0);
        tempval = atof(input);

        if(tempval > max || tempval < min){
            gcvt(min, 3, minbuf);
            gcvt(max, 3, maxbuf);
            strcpy(message, "Value must be between ");
            strcat(message, minbuf);
            strcat(message, " and ");
            strcat(message, maxbuf);
            writerr(message, lineno, norm_attrib, emph_attrib);
        }
        else{
            *value = tempval;
            return(1);
        }
    }
    return(0);
}
```

```
/* Get integer value from user.  Return enters value, ESC quits. */
/* Prompt string is printed on line number lineno with norm_attrib. */
/* If input is not >= min or <= max, error message is printed on */
/* lineno with emph_attrib, and user is given another try. */
/* Returns 1 if number was input, 0 if process was escapted. */
int
getint(int lineno, char *prompt, int *value, int min, int max,
    int norm_attrib, int emph_attrib)
{
    char input[20], minbuf[20], maxbuf[20], message[SCRNWIDE];
    int tempval, n;

    while(1){
        while(kbhit())
            getch();         /* clear any stray keypress */
        clearline(lineno, norm_attrib);
        writeword(prompt, 1, lineno, norm_attrib);
        n = get_string(input, 19);
        if (n == 0)
            return(0);
        tempval = atoi(input);

        if(tempval > max || tempval < min){
            itoa(min, minbuf, 10);
            itoa(max, maxbuf, 10);
            strcpy(message, "Value must be between ");
            strcat(message, minbuf);
            strcat(message, " and ");
            strcat(message, maxbuf);
            writerr(message, lineno, norm_attrib, emph_attrib);
        }
        else{
            *value = tempval;
            return(1);
        }
    }
    return(0);
}

/* Get input string of no more than max chars from user */
/* Prompt string is printed on line number lineno with norm_attrib. */
/* Returns number of characters input. */
int
getstr(int lineno, char *prompt, char *string, int max, int attrib)
{
    int n;

    clearline(lineno, attrib);
    while(kbhit())
        getch();
    writeword(prompt, 1, lineno, attrib);
```

```
    n = get_string(string, max);
    clearline(lineno, attrib);
    return(n);
}

/* Clean version of fgets().  Returns no. of chars read, up to max.*/
/* Returns 0 for just ENTER or if ESC is hit at any time. */
int
get_string(char *str, int max)
{
    int i, c;

    i = 0;
    while (1) {
        c = getch();
        if (c == ESC || (c == '\n' && i == 0)){
            *str = '\0';
            return(0);
        }
        else if (c == 0)          /* ignore arrow or function keys */
            getch();
        else if (c == '\r')       /* do not put a CR in string */
            break;
        else if (c == BACKSP){    /* rub out on back space */
            if (i > 0){
                *(--str) = ' ';
                i--;
                putch(BACKSP);
                putch(' ');
                putch(BACKSP);
            }
        }
        else if (iscntrl(c))
            ;                      /* do not process other control chars */
        else{
            if (i < max){         /* do not advance past max chars */
                i++;
            }
            else{
                str--;             /* just overwrite last char position */
                putch(BACKSP);
            }
            putch(c);
            *str++ = c;
        }
    }
    *str = '\0';
    return(i);
}
```

```
/* install.c  allows user to pick the type of monitor and addaptor in use */
/* and the color of the foreground, background and emphasized letters. */
/* writes values to a file specified on command line, default: install.dat */
/* link with screenf.lib */

/* MIDI Sequencing In C, Jim Conger, M&T Books, 1989 */

/* #define TURBOC 1   Define if using TURBOC, leave out for Microsoft */

#include <stdio.h>
#include <conio.h>

#include "standard.h"
#include "screenf.h"
#include "install.h"

/* function declarations */

void init_colors(void);
void put_to_file(void *addr, int size, FILE *stream);
void get_from_file(void *addr, int size, FILE *stream);
void set_text_attrib(int mode);
void set_graph_attrib(int mode);
int load_video_data(char *filename);

/* globals - these variables will normally be globals in a program */

int  g_text_mode, g_graph_mode, g_dots_h, g_dots_v, g_let_dots_v,
     g_let_dots_h, g_norm_attrib, g_emph_attrib, g_cursor_attrib,
     g_text_char_h, g_text_char_v, g_graph_char_h, g_graph_char_v,
     g_text_colors, g_graph_colors;


void
main(argc, argv)
int argc;
char *argv[];
{
    int ans, pick, lastpick, color_let, let_bak, color_emph, emph_bak,
        color_cursor, cursor_bak;
    char nbuf[10], filename[15];
    FILE *outfile;
    struct strchain *chain;

    g_text_mode = 3;                        /* default values (CGA assumed) */
    g_graph_mode = 6;
    set_text_attrib(g_text_mode);           /* initialize variables */
    set_graph_attrib(g_graph_mode);
    g_norm_attrib = 7;
    g_emph_attrib = 0x0F;
    g_cursor_attrib = 0x70;
```

```
clearscreen(BWC);
chain = inpchain("install.scr", SCRNWIDE + 1);
if (chain == NULL){
    fputs("\nCould not open file install.scr - not on default disk?",
        stdout);
    exit();
}

if (argc > 1)        /* get output file from command line or use default */
    strcpy(filename, argv[1]);
else
    strcpy(filename, "install.dat");

ans = load_video_data(filename);
if (!ans)
    writerr("First time installation - no install file.", 15, BWC, BWC);

color_let = g_norm_attrib & 0x0F;
let_bak = (g_norm_attrib & 0xF0) >> 4;
color_cursor = g_cursor_attrib & 0x0F;
cursor_bak = (g_cursor_attrib & 0xF0) >> 4;
color_emph = g_emph_attrib & 0x0F;
emph_bak = (g_emph_attrib & 0xF0) >> 4;

pick = 0;
while (1){
    g_norm_attrib = (let_bak << 4) + color_let;
    g_cursor_attrib = (cursor_bak << 4) + color_cursor;
    g_emph_attrib = (emph_bak << 4) + color_emph;
    clearscreen(g_norm_attrib);
    dispchain(chain, 1, g_norm_attrib);
    init_colors();
                                    /* display example lines for attrib */

    writeword("Normal letters will look like:", 21, 20, BWC);
    writeword("These letters.", 57, 20, g_norm_attrib);
    writeword("Cursor letters will look like:", 21, 21, BWC);
    writeword("These letters.", 57, 21, g_cursor_attrib);
    writeword("Emphasized letters will look like:", 21, 22, BWC);
    writeword("These letters.", 57, 22, g_emph_attrib);

    write_int(g_text_mode, 7, 6, BRBWC);     /* put numeric values on */
    write_int(g_graph_mode, 7, 9, BRBWC);    /* screen by selection */
    write_int(color_let, 17, 17, BRBWC);     /* menu item */
    write_int(let_bak, 17, 18, BRBWC);
    write_int(color_cursor, 46, 17, BRBWC);
    write_int(cursor_bak, 46, 18, BRBWC);
    write_int(color_emph, 75, 17, BRBWC);
    write_int(emph_bak, 75, 18, BRBWC);
```

```
/* allow cursor movement to select a menu item, pick is item chosen */

pick = movescrn(g_text_mode, scrndata, pick, NPARAM - 1,
    g_norm_attrib, g_cursor_attrib);
switch (pick){
case (0):
    getint(SCRNTALL - 1, "Enter text mode number ->", &g_text_mode,
        2, 7, BWC, BRBWC);
    set_text_attrib(g_text_mode);
    break;
case (1):
    getint(SCRNTALL - 1, "Enter graphics mode number ->",
        &g_graph_mode, 6, 18, BWC, BRBWC);
    set_graph_attrib(g_graph_mode);
    break;
case (2):
    getint(SCRNTALL - 1, "Enter normal letter attribute number ->",
        &color_let, 0, 15, BWC, BRBWC);
    break;
case (3):
    getint(SCRNTALL - 1, "Enter cursor letter attribute number ->",
        &color_cursor, 0, 15, BWC, BRBWC);
    break;
case (4):
    getint(SCRNTALL - 1, "Enter emphasized letter attribute number -
>",
        &color_emph, 0, 15, BWC, BRBWC);
    break;
case (5):
    getint(SCRNTALL - 1,
        "Enter normal letter background attribute number ->",
        &let_bak, 0, 15, BWC, BRBWC);
    break;
case (6):
    getint(SCRNTALL - 1,
        "Enter cursor background attribute number ->",
        &cursor_bak, 0, 15, BWC, BRBWC);
    break;
case (7):
    getint(SCRNTALL - 1,
        "Enter emphasized background attribute number ->",
        &emph_bak, 0, 15, BWC, BRBWC);
    break;
case (8):                    /* save */
    outfile = fopen(filename, "w");
    if (outfile == NULL){
        fputs("\nCould not open output file ", stderr);
        fputs(filename, stderr);
        fputc('\n', stderr);
        clearscreen(BWC);
        exit();
    }
```

```
            else{
                put_to_file(&g_text_mode, 1, outfile);
                put_to_file(&g_graph_mode, 1, outfile);
                put_to_file(&g_dots_v, 1, outfile);
                put_to_file(&g_dots_h, 1, outfile);
                put_to_file(&g_norm_attrib, 1, outfile);
                put_to_file(&g_cursor_attrib, 1, outfile);
                put_to_file(&g_emph_attrib, 1, outfile);
                put_to_file(&g_let_dots_v, 1, outfile);
                put_to_file(&g_let_dots_h, 1, outfile);
                put_to_file(&g_text_char_h, 1, outfile);
                put_to_file(&g_text_char_v, 1, outfile);
                put_to_file(&g_graph_char_h, 1, outfile);
                put_to_file(&g_graph_char_v, 1, outfile);
                put_to_file(&g_text_colors, 1, outfile);
                put_to_file(&g_graph_colors, 1, outfile);
                fclose(outfile);
            }
            clearscreen(BWC);
            exit();
        case (-2):                 /* ESC */
        case (9):                  /* quit */
            pick = 0;
            writeword("Don't forget to save data. Quit ? (Y/N)->",
                1, SCRNTALL, BWC);
            ans = getche();
            if(toupper(ans) != 'Y'){
                break;
            }
            else{
                clearscreen(BWC);
                exit();
            }
        default:
            writerr("Use arrow keys to move cursor, ret to select.",
                SCRNTALL - 1, BWC, BRBWC);
            break;
        }
    }
}


void
init_colors()          /* show each attribute as a number */
{
    int i, x;
    char str[3];

    for (i = 0; i < 16; i++){
        itoa(i, str, 10);
```

```
        x = 24 + (3 * i);
        writeword(str, x, 13, BWC);
        writeword(str, x, 14, i);
        writeword(str, x, 15, i << 4);
    }
}



void
set_text_attrib(mode)          /* set globals based on text mode selected */
int mode;
{
    switch(mode){
    case(2):
    case(3):
        g_text_char_h = 80;
        g_text_char_v = 25;
        g_text_colors = 16;
        break;
    case(7):
        g_text_char_h = 80;
        g_text_char_v = 25;
        g_text_colors = 4;
        break;
    default:
        g_text_mode = 3;
        writerr("Text screen must be mode 2, 3, or 7.",
            SCRNTALL, BWC, BRBWC);
        break;
    }
}



void
set_graph_attrib(mode)          /* set globals based on graphics mode selected */
int mode;
{
    char nbuf[10];

    switch(mode){
    case(4):
    case(5):
        g_dots_h = 320;
        g_dots_v = 200;
        g_let_dots_v = 8;
        g_let_dots_h = 8;
        g_graph_char_h = 40;
        g_graph_char_v = 25;
        g_graph_colors = 4;
```

```
            break;
      case(6):
            g_dots_h = 640;
            g_dots_v = 200;
            g_let_dots_v = 8;
            g_let_dots_h = 8;
            g_graph_char_h = 80;
            g_graph_char_v = 25;
            g_graph_colors = 2;
            break;
      case(13):
            g_dots_h = 320;
            g_dots_v = 200;
            g_let_dots_v = 8;
            g_let_dots_h = 8;
            g_graph_char_h = 40;
            g_graph_char_v = 25;
            g_graph_colors = 16;
            break;
      case(14):
            g_dots_h = 640;
            g_dots_v = 200;
            g_let_dots_v = 8;
            g_let_dots_h = 8;
            g_graph_char_h = 80;
            g_graph_char_v = 25;
            g_graph_colors = 4;
            break;
      case(15):                  /* can be either Hercules or EGA */
          writeword("Hercules mono or EGA ? (H/E) ->", 0, SCRNTALL - 1,
              BWC);
          gets(nbuf);
          if (toupper(*nbuf) == 'H'){
              g_dots_h = 720;
              g_dots_v = 348;
              g_let_dots_v = 14;
              g_let_dots_h = 9;
              g_graph_char_h = 80;
              g_graph_char_v = 25;
              g_graph_colors = 2;
          }
          else if (toupper(*nbuf) == 'E'){
              g_dots_h = 640;
              g_dots_v = 350;
              g_let_dots_v = 14;
              g_let_dots_h = 8;
              g_graph_char_h = 80;
              g_graph_char_v = 25;
              g_graph_colors = 4;
          }
          else{
```

```
            writerr("Must be either E or H.", SCRNTALL - 1, BWC, BRBWC);
        }
        break;
    case(16):
        g_dots_h = 640;
        g_dots_v = 350;
        g_let_dots_v = 14;
        g_let_dots_h = 8;
        g_graph_char_h = 80;
        g_graph_char_v = 25;
        g_graph_colors = 16;
        break;
    case(17):                    /* VGA modes */
        g_dots_h = 640;
        g_dots_v = 480;
        g_let_dots_v = 16;
        g_let_dots_h = 8;
        g_graph_char_h = 80;
        g_graph_char_v = 30;
        g_graph_colors = 2;
        break;
    case(18):
        g_dots_h = 640;
        g_dots_v = 480;
        g_let_dots_v = 16;
        g_let_dots_h = 8;
        g_graph_char_h = 80;
        g_graph_char_v = 30;
        g_graph_colors = 16;
        break;
    case(19):
        g_dots_h = 320;
        g_dots_v = 200;
        g_let_dots_v = 8;
        g_let_dots_h = 8;
        g_graph_char_h = 40;
        g_graph_char_v = 25;
        g_graph_colors = 256;
        break;
    default:
        writerr("Graphics screen must have a valid mode number.",
            SCRNTALL - 1, BWC, BRBWC);
        break;
    }
}


/* this function will also appear in the body of a program that uses */
/* install.c to load it's video parameter data from a file.  Usually */
/* the file is install.dat */
```

```c
int
load_video_data(filename)    /* load visible part of video data to global */
char *filename;              /* data defined in video.h */
{
    int temp;
    FILE *infile;

    infile = fopen(filename, "r");

    if (infile == NULL)
        return(0);

    get_from_file(&g_text_mode, 1  infile);
    get_from_file(&g_graph_mode, 1, infile);
    get_from_file(&g_dots_v, 1, infile);
    get_from_file(&g_dots_h, 1, infile);
    get_from_file(&g_norm_attrib, 1, infile);
    get_from_file(&g_cursor_attrib, 1, infile);
    get_from_file(&g_emph_attrib, 1, infile);
    get_from_file(&g_let_dots_v, 1, infile);
    get_from_file(&g_let_dots_h, 1, infile);
    get_from_file(&g_text_char_h, 1, infile);
    get_from_file(&g_text_char_v, 1, infile);
    get_from_file(&g_graph_char_h, 1, infile),
    get_from_file(&g_graph_char_v, 1, infile);
    get_from_file(&g_text_colors, 1, infile);
    get_from_file(&g_graph_colors, 1, infile);

    fclose(infile);
    return(1);
}



void
put_to_file(addr, size, stream)          /* put near int data to stream */
void *addr;
int size;
FILE *stream;
{
    int i, end;
    char *caddr;

    caddr = (char *)addr;
    end = size * sizeof(int);

    for(i = 0; i < end; i++){
        fputc(*caddr++, stream);
    }
}
```

```
void
get_from_file(addr, size, stream)   /* get int data from stream, put into */
void *addr;                         /* near memory */
int size;
FILE *stream;
{
    int i, end;
    char *caddr;

    caddr = (char *)addr;
    end = size * sizeof(int);

    for(i = 0; i < end; i++){
        *caddr++ = fgetc(stream);
    }
}
```

```
/* makesong.c   Simple example of creating a song file for MT */
/* writes random quarter notes to file "TESTSONG.SNG" */


#include <stdio.h>
#include <stdlib.h>

#include "standard.h"
#include "screenf.h"
#include "mpu401.h"
#include "filefunc.h"

#define NTRACK          8
#define NUM_EVENTS      50        /* must be even number */
#define HIGH_NOTE       72
#define LOW_NOTE        60
#define METER           4
#define TICKS_PER_BEAT  120

#define NOTE_ON         0x90

/* function prototypes */

void write_event(FILE *stream, int nbytes, int b0, int b1, int b2, int b3);
void putc_to_file(char *addr, int size, FILE *stream);
void puti_to_file(int *addr, int size, FILE *stream);
void putl_to_file(long *addr, int size, FILE *stream);

void
main()
{
    int metrate, meter, pitchbend, exclusive, channel, i, midivol,
        event_count, active, divisor, time, note;
    long numevents;
    char event_data[5];
    char *song_title = "Random notes test file.  From MAKESONG.C output.";
    char *track1_name = "TestTrak";
    char *empty_name = "<      >";
    FILE *stream;

    metrate = 100;
    meter = METER;
    pitchbend = FALSE;
    exclusive = FALSE;
    channel = 0;
    midivol = 100;
    numevents = NUM_EVENTS;
    active = FALSE;

    stream = fopen("TESTSONG.SNG", "wb");
    if (stream == NULL){
```

```
        fputs("\nCould not open file TESTSONG.SNG.", stdout);
        exit(0);
    }
    fputs("\nBuilding file TESTSONG.SNG...\n", stdout);

    putc_to_file(song_title, 51, stream);              /* store common data */
    puti_to_file(&metrate, 1, stream);
    puti_to_file(&meter, 1, stream);
    puti_to_file(&pitchbend, 1, stream);
    puti_to_file(&exclusive, 1, stream);

    putc_to_file(track1_name, 9, stream);              /* store track 1 header */
    puti_to_file(&channel, 1, stream);
    putl_to_file(&numevents, 1, stream);
    puti_to_file(&active, 1, stream);
    puti_to_file(&midivol, 1, stream);

    numevents = 1;
    for (i = 1; i < NTRACK; i++){              /* store other track's headers */
        putc_to_file(empty_name, 9, stream);
        puti_to_file(&channel, 1, stream);
        putl_to_file(&numevents, 1, stream);
        puti_to_file(&active, 1, stream);
        puti_to_file(&midivol, 1, stream);
    }

    /* rand() produces random digits between 0 and 32767 */

    divisor = 32767/(HIGH_NOTE - LOW_NOTE);
    time = 0;

    /* write track 1 midi data */

    write_event(stream, 2, 0, MES_END, 0, 0);    /* starting mes_end event */
    event_count = 1;

    while (event_count < NUM_EVENTS - 2){
        if (time >= meter * TICKS_PER_BEAT){      /* add mes_end if needed */
            write_event(stream, 2, 0, MES_END, 0, 0);
            time -= meter * TICKS_PER_BEAT;
            event_count += 1;
        }
        else {
            note = LOW_NOTE + ((HIGH_NOTE - LOW_NOTE) * rand()/divisor);
            write_event(stream, 4, 0, NOTE_ON + channel, note, 64);
            write_event(stream, 4, TICKS_PER_BEAT, NOTE_ON + channel,
                note, 0);
            event_count += 2;
            time += TICKS_PER_BEAT;
        }
    }
```

```
        write_event(stream, 2, 0, ALL_END, 0, 0); /* write track terminator */

        for (i = 1; i < NTRACK; i++)      /* rest of tracks have only one event */
            write_event(stream, 2, 0, MES_END, 0, 0);

        fclose(stream);
}


/* Writes the five data bytes in an event with one call to putc_to_file() */
void
write_event(stream, nbytes, b0, b1, b2, b3)
FILE *stream;
int nbytes, b0, b1, b2, b3;
{
    char data[5];

    data[0] = nbytes;
    data[1] = b0;
    data[2] = b1;
    data[3] = b2;
    data[4] = b3;
    putc_to_file(data, 5, stream);
}


void
putc_to_file(addr, size, stream)                /* put near char data to stream */
char *addr;
int size;
FILE *stream;
{
    int i;

    for(i = 0; i < size; i++){
        fputc(*addr++, stream);
    }
}


void
puti_to_file(addr, size, stream)                /* put near int data to stream */
int *addr;
int size;
FILE *stream;
{
    int i, end;
    char *caddr;

    caddr = (char *)addr;
```

```
    end = size * sizeof(int);

    for(i = 0; i < end; i++){
        fputc(*caddr++, stream);
    }
}


void
putl_to_file(addr, size, stream)          /* put near long int data to stream */
long *addr;
int size;
FILE *stream;
{
    int i, end;
    char *caddr;

    caddr = (char *)addr;
    end = size * sizeof(long);

    for(i = 0; i < end; i++){
        fputc(*caddr++, stream);
    }
}
```

```
/* mf_to_mt.c  converts Standard MIDI Files 1.0 format to MT song files */
/* `MIDI Sequencing In C', Jim Conger, M&T Books, 1989 */

/* #define TURBOC 1   Define if using TURBOC, leave out for Microsoft */

#include "standard.h"
#include <stdio.h>
#include <string.h>

#ifdef TURBOC
    #include <alloc.h>
#else
    #include <malloc.h>
#endif

#define NTRACK              8
#define TITLE_WIDE          51
#define TRACK_NAME_WIDE     9
#define MT_TICKS            120
#define NBYTES              60000   /* default track data buffer */
#define TIME_OUT            0xF8
#define MEAS_END            0xF9
#define ALL_END             0xFC

#define META                0xFF    /* meta event codes */
#define TEXTEVENT            0x01
#define SEQNAME             0x03
#define INSNAME             0x04
#define CHANPREF            0x20
#define ENDTRACK            0x2F
#define SETTEMPO            0x51
#define TIMESIG             0X58

/* function prototypes */

char *copy_event(unsigned char *buf, unsigned char nbyte, unsigned char b1,
    unsigned char b2, unsigned char b3, unsigned char b4);
void skip_byte(int n, FILE *infile);
long get_var_len(FILE *infile);
long get_long(FILE *infile);
int get_int(FILE *infile);
int get_tempo(FILE *infile);
void get_string(char *c, FILE *infile, int size);
void write_buf(char *sp, char *ep, FILE *outfile);
int find_str(FILE *infile, char *str);
long ratio_time(long input_time, int division);
FILE *open_file(char *filename, char *status);
void exit_program(void);

void
main(argc, argv)
```

```
int argc;
char *argv[];
{
    unsigned char *buf, *cp, nbyte, b0, b1, b2, b3, runstatus, chunk[5],
        fbyte, sbyte;
    unsigned char *title, *metrate, *meter, *pitchbend, *exclusive, *endp;
    unsigned char *trackname[NTRACK], *channel[NTRACK], *events[NTRACK],
        *status[NTRACK], *volume[NTRACK];
    int i, n, len, length, format, trk, tracks, end_track, meas_time,
        meas_ticks, add_data, division;
    long ln, time, eventcount;
    FILE *infile, *outfile;


    if (argc < 3){  /* did not specify infile and outfile on command line */
        exit_program();
    }
    infile = open_file(argv[1], "rb");
    outfile = open_file(argv[2], "wb");

    /* buf is a buffer that holds entire track until written to file */

    buf = (char *)malloc(NBYTES);
    if (buf == NULL){
        fputs("\nCould not allocate memory for track data.", stdout);
        exit(0);
    }

/* intialization portion of program */

    title = buf;                /* find pointers to all header items */
    metrate = title + TITLE_WIDE;
    meter = metrate + sizeof(int);
    pitchbend = meter + sizeof(int);
    exclusive = pitchbend + sizeof(int);
    endp = exclusive + sizeof(int);
    for (i = 0; i < NTRACK; i++){
        trackname[i] = endp;
        channel[i] = trackname[i] + TRACK_NAME_WIDE;
        events[i] = channel[i] + sizeof(int);
        status[i] = events[i] + sizeof(long);
        volume[i] = status[i] + sizeof(int);
        endp = volume[i] + sizeof(int);      /* endp points to start of */
    }                                        /* track data area */

    cp = buf;                          /* clear buffer area in header zone */
    while (cp != endp){
        *cp++ = '\0';
    }

    strcpy(title, "Not titled.");   /* put in default values */
```

```
    n = 100;
    memcpy(metrate, &n, sizeof(int));
    n = 4;
    memcpy(meter, &n, sizeof(int));
    meas_ticks = n * MT_TICKS;
    n = 0;
    memcpy(pitchbend, &n, sizeof(int));
    memcpy(exclusive, &n, sizeof(int));
    for (i = 0; i < NTRACK; i++){
        strcpy(trackname[i], "<     >");
        memcpy(channel[i], &i, sizeof(int));
        ln = 1;
        memcpy(events[i], &ln, sizeof(long));
        n = 0;
        memcpy(status[i], &n, sizeof(int));
        n = 100;
        memcpy(volume[i], &n, sizeof(int));
    }

/* end initialization */

    /* read by any junk in front of MThd chunk, such as 128 byte */
    /* header on files from a Mac. */

    if (find_str(infile, "MThd") == 0){
        fputs("\nInput file lacks header chunk, can't read it", stdout);
        exit(0);
    }
    length = get_long(infile);
    format = get_int(infile);
    if (format != 1){
        fputs("\nInput file does not use MIDI files format 1, can't read it.",
            stdout);
        exit(0);
    }
    tracks = get_int(infile);
    division = get_int(infile);

    fputs("\nConverting to MT .SNG file format (ESC to exit)...\n", stdout);

/* read each track's data in sequence and write to the buffer */

    for (trk = 0; trk < tracks && trk < NTRACK + 1; trk++){
        eventcount = runstatus = add_data = 0;
        get_string(chunk, infile, 4);
        length = get_long(infile);
        if (strcmp(chunk, "MTrk")){
            fputs("\nIgnored unrecognized chunk type ", stdout);
            fputs(chunk, stdout);
            fputc('\n', stdout);
            skip_byte(length, infile);
```

```
        }
        /* A track chunk, so reading data until end found */
else{
    meas_time = end_track = 0;
    while (!end_track){
        if (kbhit()){          /* allow keypress to stop program */
            if (ESC == getch()){
                fclose(infile);
                fclose(outfile);
                fputs("\nInterupted before conversion completed.\n",
                    stdout);
                exit(0);
            }
        }
        time = ratio_time(get_var_len(infile), division);
        fbyte = fgetc(infile);
        if (fbyte == META){      /* meta event ? */
            sbyte = fgetc(infile);
            len = (int)get_var_len(infile);
            if (len == -1){
                end_track = 1;
                fputs("\nRan off end of input file.\n", stdout);
            }
            switch (sbyte){
            case (1):            /* text meta event */
            case (3):            /* sequence/track name */
            case (4):            /* instrument name */
                if (trk == 0){
                    if (len < TITLE_WIDE - 1)
                        get_string(title, infile, len);
                    else{
                        get_string(title, infile, TITLE_WIDE - 1);
                        skip_byte(len - (TITLE_WIDE - 1), infile);
                    }
                }
                else {
                    if (len < TRACK_NAME_WIDE - 1)
                        get_string(trackname[trk - 1], infile, len);
                    else{
                        get_string(trackname[trk - 1], infile,
                            TRACK_NAME_WIDE - 1);
                        skip_byte(len - (TRACK_NAME_WIDE - 1),
                            infile);
                    }
                }
                break;
            case (0x20):         /* MIDI channel prefix */
                *channel[trk - 1] = (unsigned char)fgetc(infile);
                break;
            case (0x2F):         /* end of track */
                end_track = 1;
```

```
            break;
        case (0x51):         /* set tempo */
            n = get_tempo(infile);
            memcpy(metrate, &n, sizeof(int));
            break;
        case (0x58):         /* time signature */
            n = fgetc(infile);
            memcpy(meter, &n, sizeof(int));
            meas_ticks = *meter * MT_TICKS;
            skip_byte(3, infile);
            break;
        default:             /* ignore all other meta events */
            skip_byte(len, infile);
            break;
        }
    }
    else {                   /* if not a META event */
        if (!add_data){      /* if first event on track */
            add_data = 1;
            endp = copy_event(endp, 2, 0, MEAS_END, 0, 0);
            eventcount++;
        }
        /* if a four byte MIDI message */
        if (fbyte >= 0x80 && fbyte <= 0xBF ||
            fbyte >= 0xE0 && fbyte <= 0xEF){
            nbyte = 4;
            b1 = runstatus = fbyte;
            b2 = (char)fgetc(infile);
            b3 = (char)fgetc(infile);
            n = b1 & 0x0F;
            memcpy(channel[trk - 1], &n, sizeof(int));
        }
        /* if a three byte MIDI message */
        else if (fbyte >= 0xC0 && fbyte <= 0xDF){
            nbyte = 3;
            b1 = runstatus = fbyte;
            b2 = (char)fgetc(infile);
            b3 = 0;
        }
        else{   /* running status, so only two bytes fetched */
            b1 = runstatus;
            b2 = fbyte;
            if (nbyte > 3)
                b3 = (char)fgetc(infile);
            else
                b3 = 0;
        }

        while (time >= 0){    /* write event */
            if (meas_time + time < meas_ticks){
                if (time < 240){
```

```
                                b0 = (unsigned char)time;
                                endp = copy_event(endp, nbyte, b0, b1,
                                    b2, b3);
                                eventcount++;
                                meas_time += time;
                                time = -1;  /* wrote event, so quit loop */
                            }
                            else{      /* need to add a time out marker */
                                endp = copy_event(endp, 1, TIME_OUT, 0, 0, 0);
                                eventcount++;
                                time -= 240;
                                meas_time += 240;
                            }
                        }
                        else{      /* need measure end before event */
                            if (meas_ticks - meas_time < 240){
                                sbyte = meas_ticks - meas_time;
                                endp = copy_event(endp, 2, sbyte, MEAS_END,
                                    0, 0);
                                eventcount++;
                                time -= sbyte;
                                meas_time = 0;
                            }
                            else{      /* need to add a time out marker */
                                endp = copy_event(endp, 1, TIME_OUT, 0, 0, 0);
                                eventcount++;
                                time -= 240;
                                meas_time += 240;
                            }
                        }
                    }
                }
            } /* while (!end_track) */
            if (add_data){
                endp = copy_event(endp, 2, 0, ALL_END, 0, 0);
                eventcount++;
            }
            if (trk > 0){
                memcpy(events[trk - 1], &eventcount, sizeof(long));
            }
        } /* if track chunk */
    } /* for each track */

    /* add starting MEAS_END for any empty tracks */

    for (trk = tracks; trk < NTRACK + 1; trk++){
        endp = copy_event(endp, 2, 0, MEAS_END, 0, 0);
    }

    write_buf(buf, endp, outfile);      /* send all data to outfile */
    fclose(infile);                      /* close all files */
```

```
    fclose(outfile);
    fputs("\nCompleted data conversion.", stdout);
    exit(0);
}

/* copies five char values to one memory area in sequence */
char
*copy_event(buf, nbyte, b1, b2, b3, b4)
unsigned char *buf, nbyte, b1, b2, b3, b4;
{
    *buf++ = nbyte;
    *buf++ = b1;
    *buf++ = b2;
    *buf++ = b3;
    *buf++ = b4;
    return (buf);
}


/* skip over n bytes in infile */
void
skip_byte(n, infile)
int n;
FILE *infile;
{
    int i;

    for (i = 0; i < n; i++)
        fgetc(infile);
}

/* Get a variable length number from infile.  Variable length numbers are */
/* a part of the MIDI files specification.  Bit 7 in each byte is used to */
/* designate continuance of the number into the next byte.  The lower 7 */
/* bits hold the numeric information.  This allows numbers of different */
/* magnitudes to take up the minimum space on disk. */
long
get_var_len(infile)
FILE *infile;
{
    register long ln;
    unsigned char c;
    int i;

    i = ln = 0;
    do {
        c = fgetc(infile);
        ln = (ln << 7) + (c & 0x7F);
        i++;
    } while (c & 0x80 && i < 5);
    return (ln);
```

```
}


/* read and return long int value from file infile */
long
get_long(infile)
FILE *infile;
{
    int i;
    register long ln;

    ln = 0;
    for (i = 0; i < sizeof(long); i++){
        ln = (ln << 8) + fgetc(infile);
    }
    return (ln);
}

/* read and return int value from file infile */
int
get_int(infile)
FILE *infile;
{
    int i, n;

    n = 0;
    for (i = 0; i < sizeof(int); i++){
        n = (n << 8) + fgetc(infile);
    }
    return (n);
}

/* read string of size into memory pointed to by c */
void
get_string(c, infile, size)
char *c;
FILE *infile;
int size;
{
    int i;

    for (i = 0; i < size; i++){
        *c++ = (char)fgetc(infile);
    }
    *c = '\0';
}


/* read MIDI files tempo data in milliseconds/beat and return as MT tempo */
/* in beats per minute */
int
```

```
get_tempo(infile)
FILE *infile;
{
    long msec_beat;
    int i;

    msec_beat = 0;
    for (i = 0; i < 3; i++){
        msec_beat = (msec_beat << 8) + fgetc(infile);
    }
    i = (int)(60000000/msec_beat);
    return(i);
}

/* send bytes pointed to from s to e to outfile */
void
write_buf(s, e, outfile)
char *s, *e;
FILE *outfile;
{
    while (s != e)
        fputc(*s++, outfile);
}

/* find string in input stream, return 1 if found, 0 if not, leaves infile */
/* pointing to end of str, ready for next read */
int
find_str(infile, str)
FILE *infile;
char *str;
{
    char *s;
    int c;

    s = str;
    while (*s != '\0'){
        c = fgetc(infile);
        if (c == EOF)
            return(0);
        else if (c == *s)
            s++;
        else
            s = str;
    }
    return(1);
}

/* Round time to nearest MT clock tick.  Roundoff errors can accumulate if */
/* time values are truncated to match MT's clock. */
long
ratio_time(input_time, division)
```

```
long input_time;
int division;
{
    int time;
    float f, divf, intime;
    static int odd_even = 0;

    divf = division;
    intime = input_time;
    time = f = (intime * MT_TICKS) / divf;
    if (f - time == 0.5){              /* alternate distribution of even time */
        if (odd_even){                 /* splits to avoid one track gaining on */
            odd_even = 0;              /* another. */
            return(time);
        }
        else{
            odd_even = 1;
            return(time + 1);
        }
    }
    else if (f - time > 0.5){          /* otherwise, just round times */
        return(time + 1);
    }
    return(time);
}


/* Open a file.  status is "rb" for read binary, "wb" for write binary, etc */
FILE
*open_file(filename, status)
char *filename, *status;
{
    FILE *file;

    file = fopen(filename, status);
    if (file == NULL){
        fputs("\nCould not open file ", stdout);
        fputs(filename, stdout);
        fputc('\n', stdout);
        exit(0);
    }
    return(file);
}


void
exit_program()
{
    fputs("\nUsage:  mf_to_mt  infile  outfile", stdout);
    fputs("\nWhere infile is the Standard MIDI file file name;", stdout);
    fputs("\n outfile is the MT .SNG file name for output.\n", stdout);
    exit(0);
}
```

```
/* mt.c    root module for 8 track sequencer/editor */
/* `MIDI Sequencing In C', Jim Conger, M&T Books, 1989 */

#include <stdio.h>          /* compiler library files */
#include <conio.h>
#include <stdlib.h>

#include "standard.h"       /* header files */
#include "screenf.h"
#include "mpu401.h"

#define ALLOCATE            /* Because ALLOCATE is defined, all header data */
#include "mt.h"             /* is stored at the beginning of this module. */
#include "video.h"          /* See mt.h for example use of ALLOCATE. */
#include "filefunc.h"
#include "mtsc.h"
#include "mtdeclar.h"

/* main() controls MT's primary menu and directs execution to all other */
/* parts of the program */

void
main(void)
{
    int status, pick, lastpick, ans, i;
    char buf[17], nbuf[10];

    clearscreen(BWC);
    writeword("Loading M T  - Eight track MIDI Sequencer and Editor.",
        14, 3, BWC);
    writeword("Version 1.2.       Jim Conger 2/89", 25, 5, BWC);
        writeword("PLEASE do not distribute copies of this software.",
                  16, 8, BWC);
    writeword("Order `MIDI Sequencing In C' for program, source code, user's",
        10, 10, BWC);
     writeword("guide and documentation.   Contact M&T Books, 501 Galveston
Dr.",
        10, 11, BWC);
    writeword("Redwood City, Calif, 94063.  Phone 800-533-4372 to order.\n\n",
        10, 12, BWC);
        writeword("In California 800-356-2002.  8AM to 5PM Pacific Standard
Time.\n\n",
        10, 13, BWC);


    getcwd(g_prodir, 50);          /* put current directory name in dir */
    strcpy(g_songdir, g_prodir);   /* start with directory to program area */

    status = load_video_data("install.dat");
    if (!status){
        writeword("Video data file install.dat not found - run INSTALL.",
```

```
                5, 20, BWC);
            exit(0);
        }

        loadscrn(g_chain, NSCREEN, "mt");        /* load screens into memory */
        g_free_memory = free_memory();
        printf("\nFree memory = %d K bytes.", g_free_memory);

        init_edit_param();                        /* initialize data */
        init_tracks();

        writeword("Hit any key to start...", 28, 21, BWC);
        wait_for_key();


/* Put the primary menu on the screen, plus current settings */
/* Loop to and from dependent program segments based on selection */

        pick = 0;
        while(1){
            clearscreen(g_norm_attrib);       /* clear screen, display main menu */
            fdispchain(g_chain[1], 1, g_norm_attrib, g_text_mode);

                                      /* put directory and song name on screen */
            writeword(g_songdir, 47, 8, g_emph_attrib);
            writeword(g_filename, 47, 9, g_emph_attrib);
            writeword(g_songtitle, 26, 18, g_emph_attrib);

            lastpick = pick;         /* cursor selection of command */
            pick = movescrn(g_text_mode, mt1, pick, NPARAM1 - 1, g_norm_attrib,
                g_cursor_attrib);
            switch(pick){
            case(0):                          /* drive */
                getdrive(g_prodir, g_songdir);
                break;
            case(1):                          /* load */
                load_song();
                break;
            case(2):                          /* edit */
                edit_menu();
                break;
            case(3):                          /* record */
                record_menu();
                break;
            case(4):                          /* title */
                getstr(g_text_char_v - 1, "Enter title ->", g_songtitle,
                    TITLE_WIDE - 1, g_norm_attrib);
                break;
            case(5):                          /* save */
                save_song();
                break;
```

```
      case(6):                              /* clear */
          writeword("Are you sure you want to erase all track data in
memory? (Y/N)->",
              1, g_text_char_v - 1, g_norm_attrib);
          ans = getche();
          if (toupper(ans) == 'Y'){
              erase_all();
              strcpy(g_songtitle, " ");
              strcpy(g_filename, "NO_NAME.SNG");
              init_tracks();
          }
          break;
      case(7):                              /* import */
          import_menu();
          break;
      case(8):                              /* help */
          help_control();
          break;
      case(-2):                             /* esc key */
      case(NPARAM1 - 1):                    /* quit */
          writeword("Don't forget to SAVE data.  Quit? (Y/N) "
                  ,1 , g_text_char_v - 1, g_norm_attrib);
          ans = getche();
          if(toupper(ans) != 'Y'){
              pick = lastpick;
              break;
          }
          else{
              clearscreen(BWC);
              exit(0);
          }
      default:
          writerr("Use arrow keys to move cursor, ret to select.",
              g_text_char_v - 1, g_norm_attrib, g_emph_attrib);
          pick = lastpick;
      }
  }
}
```

```
/* mted1.c    editor central module for mt */
/* `MIDI Sequencing In C', Jim Conger, M&T Books, 1989 */

#include <stdio.h>   /* compiler library headers */
#include <conio.h>
#include <string.h>

#include "screenf.h"
#include "standard.h"
#include "mpu401.h"
#include "mt.h"
#include "video.h"
#include "mtdeclar.h"


/* Controls the Measure Level Edit menu. */
void
edit_menu(void)
{
    int i, ans, pick, lastpick, track, param, item_no, pick2, enter_int,
        edit_measure;
    struct item meas_item;
    char buf[80], nbuf[10];

    pick = 0;
    while (1){
        clearscreen(g_norm_attrib);      /* clear screen and display screen */
        fdispchain(g_chain[3], 1, g_norm_attrib, g_text_mode);

        /* initialize menu top for note symbols, track names; then display */
        init_meas_data();
        finitscrn(mt3, 0, NPARAM3 - 1, g_emph_attrib, g_text_mode);

        write_int(g_current_measure + 1, 64, 16, g_norm_attrib);
        calc_pct_free();                 /* update free memory value */
        write_int(g_pct_free_memory, 62, 20, g_norm_attrib);

        lastpick = pick;                 /* allow cursor selection of item */
        pick = movescrn(g_text_mode, mt3, pick, NPARAM3 - 1, g_emph_attrib,
            g_cursor_attrib);

        /* if in the top half of the screen, track # and position can be */
        /* calculated from the menu item number (pick) selected. */

        track = (pick - NMEASURE_DISP) / (NMEASURE_DISP + 2);
        item_no = (pick - NMEASURE_DISP) % (NMEASURE_DISP + 2);

        if (pick == -2)                  /* Quit if ESC key */
            return;
        else if (pick < 0){
            writerr("Use arrow keys to move cursor, ret to select.",
```

```
                g_text_char_v - 1, g_norm_attrib, g_emph_attrib);
        pick = lastpick;
    }
                                /* top line - select new start measure */
    else if (pick < NMEASURE_DISP){
        goto_measure(g_current_measure + pick);
        g_current_measure = g_current_measure + pick;
        pick = 0;
    }
                        /* see if the cursor is in the track data area */
    else if (pick < (NMEASURE_DISP * (NTRACK + 1)) + (2 * NTRACK)){

        if (item_no == 0){                    /* track name */
            ans = getstr(g_text_char_v - 1,"Enter track name (8 chars
max)->",
                buf, 8, g_norm_attrib);
            if (ans){
                strcpy(mt3[pick].content, buf);
                strcpy(g_trackarray[track].name, buf);
            }
        }
        else if (item_no == 1){          /* MIDI channel number */
            ans = getint(g_text_char_v - 1,
                "Enter the MIDI channel number for this track (1-16)->",
                    &enter_int, 1, 16, g_norm_attrib, g_emph_attrib);
            if (ans){
                itoa(enter_int, nbuf, 10);
                strcpy(mt3[pick].content, nbuf);
                g_trackarray[track].midichan = --enter_int;
                change_channel(track, enter_int);
            }
        }
        else{       /* selected a measure for Note Level Edit */
            edit_measure = scrn_edit_control(track,
                g_current_measure + item_no - 2);

            /* on return from NLE, update measure cursor is on */

            if (edit_measure >= g_current_measure && edit_measure
                < g_current_measure + NMEASURE_DISP){
                pick = NMEASURE_DISP + (track * (NMEASURE_DISP + 2)) +
                    edit_measure - g_current_measure + 2;
                goto_measure(g_current_measure);
            }
            else{
                g_current_measure = goto_measure(edit_measure);
                pick = NMEASURE_DISP + (track * (NMEASURE_DISP + 2)) + 2;
            }
        }
    }
    else{       /* must be bottom (command) area of MLE screen */
```

```
switch(pick){
case(151):                      /* block start */
    if (g_block_on){
        g_block_on = 0;         /* kill block if already on */
        g_block_start = g_block_end = -1;
    }
    else {
        writeword(
            "Move the cursor to the first measure of the block."
            , 1, g_text_char_v - 1, g_norm_attrib);
        ans = select_measure(&meas_item);
        if (ans){
            g_block_track = meas_item.track;
            g_block_start = meas_item.measure;
            g_block_on = 1;
            g_block_end = -1;

            /* add empty measures if needed to extend track */
            /* to measure selected for block start */
            advance_to_measure(g_block_track, g_block_start + 1);
        }
        else{
            g_block_on = 0;
            writerr("Measure not selected, so block cancelled.",
                g_text_char_v, g_norm_attrib, g_norm_attrib);
        }
    }
    break;
case(152):                      /* end tracks */
    g_current_measure = goto_measure(32000);
    g_current_measure -= 2;     /* display last two measures */
    goto_measure(g_current_measure);
    break;
case(153):                      /* measure no. */
    ans = getint(g_text_char_v - 1,
        "Enter the measure number to start on ->",
        &enter_int, 0, 32000, g_norm_attrib, g_emph_attrib);
    if (ans){
        g_current_measure = enter_int - 1;
        goto_measure(g_current_measure);
    }
    break;
case(154):                      /* Block End */
    writeword("Move the cursor to the last measure of the block."
        , 1, g_text_char_v - 1, g_norm_attrib);
    ans = select_measure(&meas_item);
    if (ans){
        if (meas_item.track == g_block_track){
            g_block_end = meas_item.measure;
            if (g_block_end < g_block_start){
                writerr("The block must end at or after start.",
```

```
                        g_text_char_v, g_norm_attrib, g_emph_attrib);
                    g_block_end = -1;
                }
                else{         /* add measure data if off end of track */
                    advance_to_measure(g_block_track,
                        g_block_end + 1);
                }
            }
            else{
                writerr("The block must start and end on one track.",
                    g_text_char_v, g_norm_attrib, g_emph_attrib);
                g_block_end = -1;
            }
        }
        break;
    case(155):                      /* Fast forward */
        g_current_measure += 10;
        goto_measure(g_current_measure);
        break;
    case(156):                      /* Erase Track */
        erase_track();
        goto_measure(g_current_measure);
        calc_pct_free();
        g_block_on = 0;
        break;
    case(157):                      /* Block Paste */
        block_paste();
        calc_pct_free();
        break;
    case(158):                      /* Forward */
        goto_measure(++g_current_measure);
        break;
    case(159):                      /* Erase Forward */
        clear_forward();
        g_block_on = 0;
        break;
    case(160):                      /* Block empty */
        if (!g_block_on || g_block_end == -1){
            writerr("First mark the START and END of the block",
                g_text_char_v - 1, g_norm_attrib, g_emph_attrib);
            break;
        }
        writeword(
            "Are you sure you want to empty the marked block? (Y/N)->"
            , 1, g_text_char_v - 1, g_norm_attrib);
        ans = getche();
        if (toupper(ans) == 'Y'){
            empty_block(g_block_track, g_block_start, g_block_end);
            calc_pct_free();
            g_block_on = 0;
            goto_measure(g_current_measure);
```

```
            }
            break;
        case(161):                      /* Rewind */
            g_current_measure = (g_current_measure - 1 < 0 ?
                0 : g_current_measure - 1);
            goto_measure(g_current_measure);
            break;
        case(162):                      /* Data Dump */
            data_dump();
            break;
        case(163):                      /* Block repeat */
            block_repeat();
            calc_pct_free();
            break;
        case(164):                      /* Fast Rewind */
            g_current_measure = (g_current_measure - 10 < 0 ?
                0 : g_current_measure - 10);
            goto_measure(g_current_measure);
            break;
        case(165):                      /* Block Transpose */
            if (!g_block_on || g_block_end == -1){
                writerr("First mark the START and END of the block",
                    g_text_char_v - 1, g_norm_attrib, g_emph_attrib);
            }
            else{
                transpose_block();
            }
            break;
        case(166):                      /* Begin Tracks */
            g_current_measure = goto_measure(0);
            break;
        case(167):                      /* Quit */
            return;
        }
    }
}
```

```
/* mted2.c   editor second module for mt */
/* `MIDI Sequencing In C', Jim Conger, M&T Books, 1989 */

#include <stdio.h>  /* compiler library headers */
#include <conio.h>
#include <string.h>

#include "screenf.h"
#include "standard.h"
#include "mpu401.h"
#include "mt.h"
#include "video.h"
#include "mtdeclar.h"

/* load the MLE screen data array (mt3[]) with current measure data */
void
init_meas_data(void)
{
    int i, j, k, status, end_track;
    char nbuf[10];
    struct event far *measurep;

    for (i = 0; i < NMEASURE_DISP; i++){     /* put measure #s at top */
        itoa(i + 1 + g_current_measure, nbuf, 10);
        strcpy(mt3[i].content, nbuf);
    }
    for (i = 0; i < NTRACK; i++){            /* add track names */
        k = NMEASURE_DISP + (i * (NMEASURE_DISP + 2));
        strcpy(mt3[k].content, g_trackarray[i].name);
    }
    for (i = 0; i < NTRACK; i++){            /* add midi channel numberr */
        k = NMEASURE_DISP + 1 + (i * (NMEASURE_DISP + 2));
        itoa(g_trackarray[i].midichan + 1, nbuf, 10);
        strcpy(mt3[k].content, nbuf);
    }
    for (i = 0; i < NTRACK; i++){            /* see if midi data in measure */
        measurep = g_trackarray[i].current;
        if (measurep == g_trackarray[i].last)
            end_track = 1;
        else
            end_track = 0;
        for (j = 0; j < NMEASURE_DISP; j++){
            k = j + 2 + NMEASURE_DISP + (i * (NMEASURE_DISP + 2));
            if (end_track){
                strcpy(mt3[k].content, " ");
            }
            else{     /* put in special chars for MIDI data, empty meas.. */
                if ((status = has_midi_data(measurep)) == 2)
                    strcpy(mt3[k].content, g_note_char);
                else if(status == 1)
                    strcpy(mt3[k].content, g_meas_char);
```

```
                else{
                    strcpy(mt3[k].content, " ");
                    end_track = 1;
                }
                measurep = increment_measure(measurep);
            }
        }
    }
    if (g_block_on){                                /* put block markers in */
        if (g_block_end >= g_current_measure && g_block_end <=
            g_current_measure + NMEASURE_DISP){
            k = NMEASURE_DISP + 2 + (g_block_track * (NMEASURE_DISP + 2)) +
                g_block_end - g_current_measure;
            strcpy(mt3[k].content, g_blocke_char);
        }
        if (g_block_start >= g_current_measure && g_block_start <=
            g_current_measure + NMEASURE_DISP){
            k = NMEASURE_DISP + 2 + (g_block_track * (NMEASURE_DISP + 2)) +
                g_block_start - g_current_measure;
            if (g_block_start == g_block_end)
                strcpy(mt3[k].content, g_smallb_char);
            else
                strcpy(mt3[k].content, g_blocks_char);
        }
    }
}

/* Checks if MIDI Note On within given measure.  Returns 0 if off end of */
/* data, 1 if measure is empty, and 2 if measure has midi data. */
int
has_midi_data(struct event far *measurep)
{
    int first;
    struct event far *eventp;
    eventp = measurep;
    first = 1;

    while (eventp != NULL){
        if (eventp->b[1] < 0xF0 && eventp->b[3] != 0)
            return(2);
        else if (eventp->b[1] == MES_END)
            if (!first)
                return(1);
            else{
                eventp = eventp->next;
                first = 0;
            }
        else if (eventp->b[1] == DATA_END)
            return(0);
        else{
            eventp = eventp->next;
```

```
                first = 0;
        }
    }
    return(0);
}


/* find next measure end, return pointer to it.  Return NULL if off end */
/* of the track's event list. */
struct event far
*increment_measure(struct event far *eventp)
{
    if (eventp == NULL || eventp->b[1] == ALL_END)
        return(NULL);
    else if (eventp->next != NULL){
        eventp = eventp->next;
        while (eventp != NULL){
            if (eventp->b[1] == MES_END)
                return(eventp);
            else if (eventp->b[1] == ALL_END)
                return(NULL);
            else
                eventp = eventp->next;
        }
    }
    return(NULL);
}

/* Allow cursor movement on top half of MLE screen to select a measure.  */
/* Returns 0 for abort, 1 if successful. */
int
select_measure(struct item *item)
{
    int pick, track, measure;
                        /* allow cursor movement - but only at screen top */
    pick = movescrn(g_text_mode, mt3, NMEASURE_DISP + 2, NMEASURE_DISP +
        (NTRACK * (NMEASURE_DISP + 2)), g_emph_attrib, g_cursor_attrib);

                                /* check if on left side or top */
    if (pick < NMEASURE_DISP || ((pick - NMEASURE_DISP) %
        (NMEASURE_DISP + 2) < 2))
        return(0);              /* note that ESC will return -2, quitting */
    else{
        track = (pick - NMEASURE_DISP)/(NMEASURE_DISP + 2);
        measure = (pick - NMEASURE_DISP - 2) - (track * (NMEASURE_DISP
            + 2)) + g_current_measure;
        item->track = track;
        item->measure = measure;
        return(1);
    }
}
```

```
/* Move to given measure, add empty measures at end of track as needed */
/* to extend track to measure number specified.  Returns pointer to first */
/* event of that measure. */
struct event far
*advance_to_measure(int track, int measure)
{
    int m, tot_ticks, first;
    struct event far *ep;
    struct event far *lp;

    m = 0;
    first = 1;
    ep = g_trackarray[track].first;
    lp = g_trackarray[track].last;

    while (ep != lp){            /* run through events counting measures */
        if (ep->b[1] == MES_END){
            if (!first)          /* ignore first event - always meas end */
                m++;
            first = 0;
        }
        if (m >= measure)
            return(ep);          /* found measure within existing data */
        else
            ep = ep->next;
    }
    while (m++ < measure){       /* if not, add empty measures as needed */
        ep = add_measure(ep);    /* overwrites existing ALL_END event */
    }
    ep->next = eventalloc();     /* put end of track marker at tail */
    if (ep->next == NULL)
        return(NULL);
    ep->next->next = NULL;
    ep->next->nbytes = 2;
    ep->next->b[0] = 0;
    ep->next->b[1] = ALL_END;
    ep->next->b[2] = ep->next->b[3] = 0;
    g_trackarray[track].last = ep->next;
    return(ep);                  /* returns pointer to right before ALL_END */

}

/* Add an empty measure at starting point.  Return pointer to end event. */
struct event far
*add_measure(struct event far *ep)
{
    int tot_ticks;

    if (ep->b[1] == MES_END)                /* don't overwrite last measure end */
        ep = ep->next = eventalloc();
```

```
        if (ep == NULL)
            return(NULL);

    tot_ticks = g_meter * g_tick;
    do {
        if (tot_ticks < MAX_CLOCK){      /* measure end within 240 ticks */
            ep->nbytes = 2;
            ep->b[0] = tot_ticks;
            ep->b[1] = MES_END;
            ep->b[2] = ep->b[3] = 0;
        }
        else{                            /* time out before measure end */
            ep->nbytes = 1;
            ep->b[0] = TIME_OUT;
            ep->b[1] = ep->b[2] = ep->b[3] = 0;
            ep = ep->next = eventalloc();
            if (ep == NULL)
                return(NULL);
        }
        tot_ticks -= MAX_CLOCK;
    } while (tot_ticks >= 0 );
    return(ep);
}

/* Add the MIDI data from the measure pointed to by source_p to the data */
/* in the measure pointed to by dest_p.  Correct timing bytes as needed. */
struct event far
*merge_measure(struct event far *dest_p, struct event far *source_p)
{
    int i, d_time, s_time, new_dest, new_source;
    struct event far *dp_next;
    struct event far *sp_next;
    struct event far *newp;

    dp_next = dest_p->next;
    sp_next = source_p->next;
    new_dest = new_source = 1;
    d_time = s_time = 0;
    init_note_array();

    do {
        if (new_dest){
            while (dp_next->b[0] == TIME_OUT){     /* add up TIME_OUTs */
                newp = dp_next->next;
#ifdef TURBOC
                farfree(dp_next);
#else
                _ffree(dp_next);                   /* free their space */
#endif
                dp_next = newp;
                d_time += MAX_CLOCK;
```

```
        }
    d_time += dp_next->b[0];
    new_dest = 0;
}
                            /* keep track of notes left on or off */
fill_note_array(dp_next, dp_next->next);

if (new_source){
    while (sp_next->b[0] == TIME_OUT){
        sp_next = sp_next->next;         /* don't free from source */
        s_time += MAX_CLOCK;
    }
    s_time += sp_next->b[0];
    new_source = 0;
}

if (d_time <= s_time){                   /* dest event is next one */
    if (d_time >= MAX_CLOCK){
        d_time -= MAX_CLOCK;             /* add TIME_OUT if needed */
        s_time -= MAX_CLOCK;
        dest_p->next = newp = eventalloc();
        if (newp == NULL)
            return(NULL);
        newp->next = dp_next;
        newp->nbytes = 1;
        newp->b[0] = TIME_OUT;
        for (i = 1; i < 4; i++){
            newp->b[i] = 0;
        }
        dest_p = newp;
    }
    else{
        s_time -= d_time;
        dp_next->b[0] = d_time;
        dest_p = dp_next;                /* no need to allocate - */
        dp_next = dest_p->next;          /* dest is already there */
        d_time = 0;
        new_dest = 1;
    }
}
else{                                    /* source event is next */
    if (s_time >= MAX_CLOCK){
        d_time -= MAX_CLOCK;             /* add TIME_OUT if needed */
        s_time -= MAX_CLOCK;
        dest_p->next = newp = eventalloc();
        if (newp == NULL)
            return(NULL);
        newp->next = dp_next;
        newp->nbytes = 1;
        newp->b[0] = TIME_OUT;
        for (i = 1; i < 4; i++){
```

```
                              newp->b[i] = 0;
                          }
                      dest_p = newp;
                  }
              else{                          /* add source event to dest - */
                  d_time -= s_time;          /* need to alocate a new event */
                  dest_p->next = newp = eventalloc();
                  if (newp == NULL)
                      return(NULL);
                  newp->next = dp_next;
                  newp->nbytes = sp_next->nbytes;
                  newp->b[0] = s_time;
                  for(i = 1; i < 4; i++){
                      newp->b[i] = sp_next->b[i];
                  }
                  dest_p = newp;
                  source_p = sp_next;
                  sp_next = sp_next->next;
                  s_time = 0;
                  new_source = 1;
              }
          }
      } while (dest_p->b[1] != MES_END && source_p->b[1] != ALL_END);
      return(dest_p);
}


/* Set all g_note_array[] values to 0 in preparation for using the array */
/* to keep track of which notes have been left on after an operation. */
void
init_note_array(void)
{
    int i;

    for (i = 0; i < NNOTES; i++){
        g_note_array[i] = 0;
    }
}


/* Keep track of notes on/off between start_event and end_event. Notes On */
/* add to the array, Notes Off subtract. */
void
fill_note_array(struct event far *start_event, struct event far *end_event)
{
    int b1, b2;
    struct event far *ep;

    ep = start_event;

    while (ep != end_event){
        b1 = ep->b[1];
        b2 = ep->b[2];
```

```
        if (b1 >= NOTE_ON && b1 < NOTE_ON + NCHANNEL){  /* if note on/off */
            if (ep->b[3])                /* if a note on */
                g_note_array[b2]++;
            else{                        /* if a note off */
                if (g_note_array[b2])    /* can't have negative note count */
                    g_note_array[b2]--;
            }
        }
        else if (b1 >= NOTE_OFF && b1 < NOTE_OFF + NCHANNEL){ /* note off */
            if (g_note_array[b2])
                g_note_array[b2]--;
        }
        ep = ep->next;
    }
}

/* Add note offs at end of block, based on g_note_array[] values for */
/* number of notes left on for each MIDI note number.  Returns pointer */
/* to last added event. */
struct event far
*add_note_offs(struct event far *dest_event, int channel)
{
    int i, j;
    struct event far *old_nextp;

    old_nextp = dest_event->next;

    for (i = 0; i < NNOTES; i++){   /* for every note in MIDI scale... */
        while (g_note_array[i]--){  /* for each of this note left on ... */
            dest_event = dest_event->next = eventalloc();
            if (dest_event == NULL){
                dest_event->next = old_nextp;
                return(NULL);
            }
            dest_event->nbytes = 4; /* add a note off with same note number */
            dest_event->b[0] = 0;
            dest_event->b[1] = NOTE_ON + channel;
            dest_event->b[2] = i;
            dest_event->b[3] = 0;
        }
    }
    dest_event->next = old_nextp;
    return(dest_event);
}
```

```
/* mted3.c    editor third module for multi */
/* `MIDI Sequencing In C', Jim Conger, M&T Books, 1989 */

#include <stdio.h>  /* compiler library headers */
#include <conio.h>

#include "screenf.h"
#include "standard.h"
#include "mpu401.h"
#include "mt.h"
#include "video.h"
#include "mtdeclar.h"

/* Convert measures from b_start to b_end to empty measures.  Shut down */
/* any notes playing at start of block to avoid hung notes. */
void
empty_block(int track, int b_start, int b_end)
{
    int i;
    struct event far *begin_block;
    struct event far *end_block;
    struct event far *ep1;
    struct event far *ep2;

    begin_block = advance_to_measure(track, b_start);
    init_note_array();
    fill_note_array(g_trackarray[track].first, begin_block);

    end_block = advance_to_measure(track, b_end + 1);
    end_block = end_block->next;    /* end is event after block's last m.e. */

    ep1 = begin_block->next;    /* free memory for all events in block */
    while (ep1 != end_block){
        ep2 = ep1;
        ep1 = ep1->next;
#ifdef TURBOC
        farfree(ep2);
#else
        _ffree(ep2);
#endif
    }
                    /* put in note offs for notes on at start */
    begin_block = add_note_offs(begin_block, g_trackarray[track].midichan);

                    /* put in sacraficial event to prepare for add_measure */
    begin_block = begin_block->next = eventalloc();
        begin_block->b[0] = begin_block->b[1] = 0;
    for (i = 0; i <= b_end - b_start; i++)    /* add back in empty meas's */
        begin_block = add_measure(begin_block);

    begin_block->next = end_block;
    clean_track(track);
}
```

```
/* Copy contents of marked block repeatedly starting at the measure */
/* selected.  Prompts for number of repetitions. */
void
block_repeat(void)
{
    int i, status, reps;
    struct item dest_item;

    if(g_block_on && g_block_end != -1){
        writeword("Move the cursor to the starting point of the repetitions.",
            1, g_text_char_v - 1, g_norm_attrib);
        status = select_measure(&dest_item);
        if (!status){
            writerr("Block repeat was cancelled.", g_text_char_v,
                g_norm_attrib, g_norm_attrib);
            return;
        }
        clearline(g_text_char_v - 1, g_norm_attrib);
        status = getint(g_text_char_v - 1,
            "Enter the number of times to repeat the marked block ->",
            &reps, 0, 32000, g_norm_attrib, g_emph_attrib);
        if (!status || !reps){
            writerr("Block repeat was cancelled.", g_text_char_v,
                g_norm_attrib, g_norm_attrib);
            return;
        }

        repeat_copy(g_block_start, g_block_track, dest_item.measure,
            dest_item.track, g_block_end - g_block_start + 1, reps);
        change_channel(dest_item.track,
            g_trackarray[dest_item.track].midichan);
    }
    else{
        writerr("Mark the start end end of the source block, then repeat.",
            g_text_char_v, g_norm_attrib, g_emph_attrib);
    }
}

/* Copy source block repeatedly to destination track starting at dest_meas */
/* Do this reps times. */
void
repeat_copy(int source_meas, int source_track, int dest_meas, int dest_track,
    int n_meas, int reps)
{
    int i, j, sm;
    struct event far *source_p;
    struct event far *dest_p;

    clearline(g_text_char_v - 1, g_norm_attrib);
    writeword("Copying.  Hit ESC to interupt.  Now on repetition:", 1,
        g_text_char_v - 1, g_norm_attrib);
```

```
        /* build empty measures for destination, then move pointer to start */
        advance_to_measure(dest_track, 1 + dest_meas + (n_meas * reps));
        dest_p = advance_to_measure(dest_track, dest_meas);

        for (i = 0; i < reps; i++){
            write_int(i + 1, 60, g_text_char_v - 1, g_norm_attrib);
            init_note_array();        /* prepart to track notes left on */
            sm = source_meas;
            for (j = 0; j < n_meas; j++){
                source_p = advance_to_measure(source_track, sm++);
                dest_p = merge_measure(dest_p, source_p);
                if (dest_p == NULL){
                    writerr("Out of memory.", g_text_char_v - 1, g_norm_attrib,
                        g_emph_attrib);
                    return;
                }
                if (kbhit()){
                    if (getch() == ESC){
                        add_note_offs(dest_p, g_trackarray[dest_track].midichan);
                        writerr("Copy process interrupted.", g_text_char_v,
                            g_norm_attrib, g_emph_attrib);
                        return;
                    }
                }
            }
            add_note_offs(dest_p, g_trackarray[dest_track].midichan);
        }
}

void
transpose_block(void)    /* move all midi data within block up/down n notes */
{
    int *offset, x, status, b1, b2, time;
    struct event far *ep;
    struct event far *start_p;
    struct event far *end_p;
    struct event far *before_end;
    offset = &x;

    status = getint(g_text_char_v - 1,
        "Enter the number of MIDI note numbers to add/subtract ->",
        offset, -1 * NNOTES, NNOTES, g_norm_attrib, g_emph_attrib);
    if (!status || !*offset){
        writerr("Block transpose was cancelled.", g_text_char_v,
            g_norm_attrib, g_norm_attrib);
        return;
    }
                /* shut all notes off at start of block */
    init_note_array();
    start_p = advance_to_measure(g_block_track, g_block_start);
    fill_note_array(g_trackarray[g_block_track].first, start_p);
    start_p = add_note_offs(start_p, g_trackarray[g_block_track].midichan);
```

```
                    /* shut all notes off at end of block */
    init_note_array();
    end_p = advance_to_measure(g_block_track, g_block_end + 1);
    before_end = find_event_before(g_block_track, end_p);
    fill_note_array(start_p, end_p);
    add_note_offs(before_end, g_trackarray[g_block_track].midichan);
                    /* adjust timing byte of note_offs to fall at measure end */
    time = end_p->b[0];
    end_p->b[0] = 0;
    before_end->next->b[0] = time;

    ep = start_p->next;
    while (ep != end_p){          /* transpose within block */
        b1 = ep->b[1];
        b2 = ep->b[2];
        if (b1 >= NOTE_ON && b1 < NOTE_ON + NCHANNEL ||
            b1 >= NOTE_OFF && b1 < NOTE_OFF + NCHANNEL){
            b2 += *offset;
            while (b2 >= NNOTES){      /* if transposition exceeds MIDI */
                b2 -= OCTIVE;         /* note range, adjust by octives */
            }
            while (b2 <= -1 * NNOTES){
                b2 += OCTIVE;
            }
        }
        ep->b[2] = b2;
        ep = ep->next;
    }
    clean_track(g_block_track);
}

struct event far                 /* find and return event right before ep */
*find_event_before(int track, struct event far *ep)
{
    struct event far *nextp;
    struct event far *lastp;

    nextp = g_trackarray[track].first;

    while (nextp != ep && nextp != NULL){
        lastp = nextp;
        nextp = nextp->next;
    }
    if (nextp != NULL)
        return (lastp);
    else
        return (NULL);
}
```

```
/* Purge any unnecessary events from track.  Takes care of special cases */
/* in merge process.  Converts explicit Note Off's to implied ones. */
void
clean_track(int track)
{
    int i, time, no_change;
    unsigned int b1, b2, b3;
    struct event far *ep;
    struct event far *np;
    struct event far *oldp;

    init_note_array();
    ep = g_trackarray[track].first;
    np = ep->next;

    while (1){
        no_change = 1;
        b1 = np->b[1];
        b2 = np->b[2];
        b3 = np->b[3];
        if (b1 >= NOTE_OFF && b1 < NOTE_OFF + NCHANNEL){
            b1 = (b1 & 0x0F) + NOTE_ON;
            b3 = 0;      /* convert explicity note_offs to note on, vel = 0 */
            np->b[1] = b1;
            np->b[3] = 0;
        }
        if (b1 == ALL_END)
            break;
        else if (b1 >= NOTE_ON && b1 < NOTE_ON + NCHANNEL){
            if (b3)                                    /* if a note on */
                g_note_array[b2]++;
            else{                                      /* a note off */
                if (g_note_array[b2])                  /* if already an on */
                    g_note_array[b2]--;
                else{                                  /* loose note off - */
                    time = np->b[0];                   /* so delete it */
                    oldp = np;
                    np = np->next;
                    ep->next = np;
#ifdef TURBOC
                    farfree(oldp);
#else
                    _ffree(oldp);
#endif
                    no_change = 0;
                    while (np->b[0] == TIME_OUT) {     /* find event after */
                        ep = ep->next;                 /* time_outs */
                        np = np->next;
                    }
                    if (np->b[0] + time < MAX_CLOCK)   /* adjust clock */
                        np->b[0] += time;              /* count */
```

```
                else{
                    ep = ep->next = eventalloc();
                    ep->next = np;
                    ep->b[0] = TIME_OUT;
                    for (i = 1; i < 4; i++){
                        ep->b[i] = 0;
                    }
                    np->b[0] = np->b[0] + time - MAX_CLOCK;
                }
            }
        }
    }
    if (no_change){
        ep = np;
        np = ep->next;
    }
}
add_note_offs(ep, g_trackarray[track].midichan);

ep = np->next;              /* points to event past ALL_END if any */
np->next = NULL;
g_trackarray[track].last = np;

while (ep != NULL){         /* delete any events past first ALL_END */
    np = ep->next;
#ifdef TURBOC
    farfree(oldp);
#else
    _ffree(ep);
#endif
    ep = np;
}
}

void
block_paste(void)                /* copies marked block to targeted spot */
{
    int i, ans, source_track, source_measure, dest_track, dest_measure;
    struct item meas_item;
    struct event far *source_event;
    struct event far *dest_event;

    if (!g_block_on || g_block_end == -1){
        writerr("First mark the START and END of the block",
            g_text_char_v, g_norm_attrib, g_emph_attrib);
        return;
    }
    writeword(
        "Move the cursor to the measure to start the pasted block"
        , 1, g_text_char_v - 1, g_norm_attrib);
    ans = select_measure(&meas_item);
```

```
    if (!ans)
        return;
    else{
        clearline(g_text_char_v - 1, g_norm_attrib);
        writeword("Copying.  Hit ESC to terminate.", 1, g_text_char_v - 1,
            g_norm_attrib);

        init_note_array();
        source_track = g_block_track;
        dest_track = meas_item.track;
        source_measure = g_block_start;
        dest_measure = meas_item.measure;

                        /* build empty measures as needed in dest track */
        advance_to_measure(dest_track, dest_measure +
            g_block_end - g_block_start + 1);
        dest_event = advance_to_measure(dest_track, dest_measure);

                        /* merge each measure successively from front */
        for (i = 0; i <= g_block_end - g_block_start; i++){
            source_event = advance_to_measure(source_track,
                source_measure++);
            if (source_event == dest_event){
                writerr("Source and destination measures cannot be the same.",
                    g_text_char_v, g_norm_attrib, g_norm_attrib);
                return;
            }
            dest_event = merge_measure(dest_event, source_event);
            if (dest_event == NULL){
                writerr("Out of memory.", g_text_char_v - 1, g_norm_attrib,
                    g_emph_attrib);
                return;
            }
            if (kbhit()){
                if (getch() == ESC){
                    writerr("Copy process interrupted.", g_text_char_v,
                        g_norm_attrib, g_emph_attrib);
                    break;
                }
            }
        }
        add_note_offs(dest_event, g_trackarray[dest_track].midichan);
        clean_track(dest_track);
        change_channel(dest_track, g_trackarray[dest_track].midichan);
        goto_measure(g_current_measure);
    }
}
```

```
/* mtrc1.c    recorder module for mt */
/* `MIDI Sequencing In C', Jim Conger, M&T Books, 1989 */

#include <stdio.h>  /* compiler library headers */
#include <conio.h>
#include <string.h>
#include <stdlib.h>

#include "screenf.h"
#include "standard.h"
#include "mpu401.h"
#include "mt.h"
#include "video.h"
#include "mtdeclar.h"


void
record_menu(void)              /* runs MT's record menu */
{
    int i, ans, pick, lastpick, track, param, x, nevent;
    int *enter_int;
    char buf[80], nbuf[10];

    calc_pct_free();           /* update amount of free memory available */
    enter_int = &x;
    pick = 0;

    while (1){
        init_track_str();                 /* put track names, etc in menu */
        clearscreen(g_norm_attrib);       /* clear screen and disp menu */
        fdispchain(g_chain[2], 1, g_norm_attrib, g_text_mode);

                                          /* put values at top */
        finitscrn(mt2, 0, NPARAM2 - 1, g_emph_attrib, g_text_mode);
        init_rec_val();                   /* put values at bottom */

        /* allow cursor movement to select a menu item, pick is item # */
        lastpick = pick;
        pick = movescrn(g_text_mode, mt2, pick, NPARAM2 - 1, g_emph_attrib,
            g_cursor_attrib);

                        /* if at the top part of the record screen... */
        if (pick >= 0 && pick < NTRACK * N_TRACK_PARAM){
            track = pick % NTRACK;
            param = (pick - track) / NTRACK;
            switch (param){
            case (0):          /* track name */
                ans = getstr(g_text_char_v - 1,"Enter track name (8 chars
max)->",
                    buf, 8, g_norm_attrib);
                if (ans){
```

```
                strcpy(mt2[pick].content, buf);
                strcpy(g_trackarray[track].name, buf);
            }
            break;
        case (1):                /* midi channel number */
            ans = getint(g_text_char_v - 1,
                "Enter the MIDI channel number for this track (1-16)->",
                    enter_int, 1, 16, g_norm_attrib, g_emph_attrib);
            if (ans){
                itoa(*enter_int, nbuf, 10);
                strcpy(mt2[pick].content, nbuf);
                g_trackarray[track].midichan = --*enter_int;
                change_channel(track, *enter_int);
            }
            break;
        case (2):                /* track select toggle */
            if (g_record_track == track)
                g_record_track = -1;
            else
                g_record_track = track;
            break;
        case (3):                /* play toggle */
            if (g_trackarray[track].active){
                g_trackarray[track].active = 0;
            }
            else{
                g_trackarray[track].active = 1;
                if (track == g_record_track)
                    g_record_track = -1;
            }
            break;
        case (4):                /* record toggle */
            if (g_record_track == track)
                g_record_track = -1;
            else
                g_record_track = track;
            break;
        case (5):                /* MIDI volume */
            ans = getint(g_text_char_v - 1, "Enter MIDI volume (1-100)->",
                enter_int, 1, 100, g_norm_attrib, g_emph_attrib);
            if (ans){
                itoa(*enter_int, nbuf, 10);
                strcpy(mt2[pick].content, nbuf);
                g_trackarray[track].midivol = *enter_int;
            }
            break;
        case (6):                /* bytes */
            writerr("You can not change this value - automatically set.",
                g_text_char_v - 1, g_norm_attrib, g_emph_attrib);
            break;
    }
```

```
    }
    else{       /* must be at the bottom, command part of record screen */
        switch (pick){
        case (56):      /* RECORD */
            record();
            break;
        case (57):      /* End Tracks */
            g_current_measure = goto_measure(32000);
            break;
        case (58):      /* Erase Track */
            erase_track();
            calc_pct_free();
            break;
        case (59):      /* MET ON/OFF */
            if (g_meton)
                g_meton = 0;
            else
                g_meton = 1;
            break;
        case (60):      /* Fast Forward */
            g_current_measure = goto_measure(g_current_measure + 10);
            break;
        case (61):      /* Clear Forward */
            clear_forward();
            g_block_on = 0;
            calc_pct_free();
            break;
        case (62):      /* Beats/Measure */
            if (count_events() > NTRACK)
                writerr("You can only change meter if tracks are empty.",
                    g_text_char_v - 1, g_norm_attrib, g_emph_attrib);
            else{
                ans = getint(g_text_char_v - 1,"Enter beats per measure -
>",
                    enter_int, 1, 20, g_norm_attrib, g_emph_attrib);
                if (ans == 1)
                    g_meter = *enter_int;
            }
            break;
        case (63):      /* PLAY */
            play();
            break;
        case (64):      /* Forward */
            g_current_measure = goto_measure(g_current_measure + 1);
            break;
        case (65):      /* Data Dump */
            data_dump();
            break;
        case (66):      /* BPM */
            ans = getint(g_text_char_v - 1,
                "Enter metronome rate in beeps/min ->",
```

```
                    enter_int ,8, 200, g_norm_attrib, g_emph_attrib);
              if (ans == 1)
                  g_metrate = *enter_int;
              break;
          case (67):      /* Rewind */
              g_current_measure = goto_measure(g_current_measure - 1 < 0 ?
                  0 : g_current_measure - 1);
              break;
          case (68):      /* pitch bend toggle */
              if (g_pitchbend)
                  g_pitchbend = 0;
              else
                  g_pitchbend = 1;
              break;
          case (69):      /* all notes off */
              if (g_trace_on)
                  trace_header();
              all_notes_off();
              if (g_trace_on)
                  wait_for_key();
              break;
          case (70):      /* Fast Rewind */
              g_current_measure = goto_measure(g_current_measure - 10 < 0 ?
                  0 : g_current_measure - 10);
              break;
          case (71):      /*  Exclusive pass through on/off */
              if (g_exclusive)
                  g_exclusive = 0;
              else
                  g_exclusive = 1;
              break;
          case (73):      /* Begin Tracks */
              g_current_measure = goto_measure(0);
              break;
          case (74):      /* Data Trace */
              if (g_trace_on)
                  g_trace_on = 0;
              else
                  g_trace_on = 1;
              break;
          case (-2):          /* ESC key */
          case (72):   /* QUIT */
              return;
          default:
              writerr("Use arrow keys to move cursor, ret to select.",
                  g_text_char_v - 1, g_norm_attrib, g_emph_attrib);
              pick = lastpick;
          }
      }
  }
}
```

```
/* mtrc2.c */
/* `MIDI Sequencing In C', Jim Conger, M&T Books, 1989 */

#include <stdio.h>
#include <conio.h>
#include <string.h>

#include "screenf.h"
#include "standard.h"
#include "mpu401.h"
#include "mt.h"
#include "video.h"
#include "mtdeclar.h"


/* play() is called from record_menu().  Controls playing up to eight */
/* tracks.  Calls play_event() to send event data.  Uses maybe_measure_ */
/* number() to update measure number during playback. */

void
play(void)
{
    int cmd, track, firstcmd, status, trackbits, stop_play, c;
    struct event far *ep[NTRACK];    /* temporary pointers to note data */

    writeword("Hit ESC or SPACEBAR to stop playback.", 1, g_text_char_v - 1,
        g_norm_attrib);
    if (g_trace_on){
        trace_header();
        fputs("Hit ESC key to stop playback.\n\n", stdout);
    }

    firstcmd = 1;
    trackbits = init_401(ep);        /* reset and intialize MPU-401 */
    if (trackbits == 0){
        writerr("No data-containing tracks have PLAY turned ON.",
            g_text_char_v - 1, g_norm_attrib, g_norm_attrib);
        return;
    }

    stop_play = 0;
    while (1){
        cmd = get401();              /* get next mpu-401 request */
        if (cmd == -1){              /* initiate exit of play mode on keypress */
            while (kbhit()){
                c = getch();
                if (c == ESC || c == ' '){
                    if (stop_play)
                        break;
                    else
                        stop_play = 1;
```

```
                    }
                }
            }
            else if (cmd >= REQ_T1 && cmd <= REQ_T8){        /* track req */
                firstcmd = 0;
                track = cmd - REQ_T1;

                if (ep[track]->b[1] == MES_END)              /* update measure # */
                    maybe_measure_number(track, trackbits);

                if (stop_play){                              /* shutdown track */
                    putdata401(0);                           /* wait for ALL_END */
                    putdata401(DATA_END);                    /* to stop play */
                }
                else{
                    play_event(track, ep[track]);            /* send data bytes */
                }

                /* advance track pointer to next event */

                if (ep[track]->next != NULL){
                    ep[track] = ep[track]->next;
                    if (ep[track]->b[1] == DATA_END)     /* track goes inactive */
                        trackbits &= ~(1 << track);      /* erase from trackbits */
                }
            }
            else if (cmd == ALL_END){
                if (firstcmd)              /* don't quit if received at start */
                    firstcmd = 0;
                else
                    break;                 /* must be at end of song data */
            }
            else{
                /* ignore anything else */
            }
        }
        repeat_cmd401(STOP_PLAY);          /* final MPU shutdown command sequence */
        repeat_cmd401(CLEAR_PMAP);
        repeat_cmd401(MET_OFF);

        if (g_trace_on)
            wait_for_key();
        goto_measure(g_current_measure);     /* end on even meas */
}


/* record() is the front end to record_track().  Checks if a track is */
/* active - then records one track.  */
void
record(void)
```

```
{
    if (g_record_track == -1){
        writerr("No track is active for recording.",
            g_text_char_v - 1, g_norm_attrib, g_emph_attrib);
    }
    else{                               /* start on even measure number */
        g_trackarray[g_record_track].current =
            advance_to_measure(g_record_track, g_current_measure);
        writeword("Hit ESC or SPACEBAR to stop recording.", 1,
            g_text_char_v - 1, g_norm_attrib);
        if (g_trace_on)
            trace_header();             /* if trace is on, put header on screen */

        /* go ahead and start record process */
        g_trackarray[g_record_track].last = record_track(g_record_track);

        clean_track(g_record_track);    /* set all recorded data to the */
        change_channel(g_record_track,  /* the track's MIDI channel */
            g_trackarray[g_record_track].midichan);
        goto_measure(g_current_measure);            /* end on even meas */
        if (g_trace_on){
            fputs("\nHit a key to return.", stdout);
            wait_for_key();
        }
    }
    calc_pct_free();                            /* update the free memory left */
}



/* record_track() is the function that controls the recording process */
/* Records a track while playing back any others set to PLAY.   Stops on */
/* ESC or spacebar keypress. */

struct event far
*record_track(int rec_track)    /* rec_track is the track # set to record */
{
    int first, second, third, fourth, mstatus, track, i, status, c, trackbits;
    struct event far *firstnode;
    struct event far *next_to_last_node;
    struct event far *nextnode;
    struct event far *ep[NTRACK];   /* temp pointers to note data */

    mstatus = 0;
    firstnode = g_trackarray[rec_track].current;
    nextnode = firstnode->next = eventalloc();  /* create first new event */

    trackbits = init_401(ep);               /* reset and initialize MPU-401 */
    repeat_cmd401(START_REC);               /* start record process */

    while (1){
```

353

```
    first = get401();                  /* get 1 byte of data from MPU-401 */
    if (first == -1){                   /* get401() returns -1 on keypress */
        c = getch();
        if (c == ESC || c == ' ')
            repeat_cmd401(STOP_REC); /* tell MPU to stop recording */
        first = get401();          /* cont. record until ALL_END rcvd */
    }
    next_to_last_node = nextnode;    /* keep current for returned value */

    if (first <= 0xEF){         /* timing byte */
        second = get401();         /* so get second byte from MPU */
        if (second <= 0x7F){       /* MIDI data, running status assumed */
            third = get401();    /* so get third byte from MPU */
            nextnode = store(nextnode, 4, first, mstatus, second, third);
        }
        else if (second <= 0xBF){    /* MIDI message, note on/off */
            mstatus = second;       /* after touch or control change */
            third = get401();       /* so get two more bytes */
            fourth = get401();
            nextnode = store(nextnode, 4, first, second, third, fourth);
        }
        else if (second <= 0xDF){    /* prog change or chan after touch */
            mstatus = second;       /* so get just one more byte */
            third = get401();
            nextnode = store(nextnode, 3, first, second, third, 0);
        }
        else if (second <= 0xEF){    /* pitch wheel */
            mstatus = second;       /* so get to more bytes */
            third = get401();
            fourth = get401();
            nextnode = store(nextnode, 4, first, second, third, fourth);
        }
        else if (second == 0xF9){    /* measure end - store it */
            if (!g_trace_on)        /* and update measure # on screen */
                write_int(++g_current_measure + 1, 53, 18, g_norm_attrib);
            nextnode = store(nextnode, 2, first, second, 0, 0);
        }
        else if (second == 0xFC){    /* data end - record process done */
            store(nextnode, 2, first, second, 0, 0);
            nextnode->next = NULL;  /* null markes end of track list */
            stop_401(trackbits);       /* allow all tracks to s/d */
            return(next_to_last_node); /* return pointer to end */
        }
        else{
            clearline(g_text_char_v, g_norm_attrib);    /* show ?? data */
            csrplot(g_text_char_v, 1);              /* but continue */
            printf("Unrecognized data %x %x", first, second);
        }
    }
    else if (first <= 0xF7){                       /* track data request */
        track = first - REQ_T1;                    /* track number */
```

```
        play_event(track, ep[track]);              /* send data bytes */

        if (ep[track]->next != NULL){
                              /* advance track pointer to next event */
            ep[track] = ep[track]->next;
        }
    }
    else {      /* first byte was not a timing byte - so decode */
        switch(first){
        case(TIME_OUT):
            nextnode = store(nextnode, 1, first, 0, 0, 0);
            break;
        case(CONDUCT):  /* conductor (tempo change) not implemented */
            clearline(g_text_char_v, g_norm_attrib);
            writeword("Unexpected conductor data request.", 1,
                g_text_char_v, g_norm_attrib);
            break;
        case(DATA_END):
            clearline(g_text_char_v, g_norm_attrib);
            writeword("All playback tracks are finished.", 1,
                g_text_char_v, g_norm_attrib);
            break;
        case(CLOCK_OUT):
            clearline(g_text_char_v, g_norm_attrib);
            writeword("Unexpected clock out signal ", 1,
                g_text_char_v, g_norm_attrib);
            break;
        }
    }

    if (nextnode == NULL){  /* ran out of memory for recording data */
        writeword(
            "Could not allocate more memory (full?), record stopped.", 1,
            g_text_char_v, g_emph_attrib);
        repeat_cmd401(STOP_REC);
        stop_401(trackbits);
        return(next_to_last_node);
    }
}
return(next_to_last_node);
}
```

```
/* mtrc3.c  -  record and play functions for recorder */
/* `MIDI Sequencing In C', Jim Conger, M&T Books, 1989 */

/* #define TURBOC 1   Define if using TURBOC, leave out for Microsoft */

#include <stdio.h>  /* compiler library headers */
#include <conio.h>
#include <string.h>
#include <stdlib.h>

#ifdef TURBOC
    #include <alloc.h>
#else
    #include <malloc.h>
#endif

#include "screenf.h"
#include "standard.h"
#include "mpu401.h"
#include "mt.h"
#include "video.h"
#include "mtdeclar.h"


/* Sends single event's data.  MIDI vol corrected if g_track_vel_used */
/* is set true, meaning that at least one track has vol set to < 100 */
void
play_event(int track, struct event far *ep) /* ep points to event data */
{
    int bytes, secbyte;

    bytes = ep->nbytes;      /* use int to avoid repeatedly doing -> calcs. */
    secbyte = ep->b[1];     /* ditto */
    putdata401(ep->b[0]);                       /* send first byte to MPU */
    if (bytes > 1){
        putdata401(secbyte);                /* send second byte */
        if (bytes > 2){
            putdata401(ep->b[2]);           /* send third byte */
                        /* if b2 = note on, adjust volume */
            if (bytes > 3){
                if (secbyte >= NOTE_ON && secbyte < NOTE_ON+NTRACK
                    && g_track_vel_used)    /* send fourth byte - adj. vel */
                    putdata401(ep->b[3] * g_track_vel[track] / 100);
                else
                    putdata401(ep->b[3]);   /* send fourth byte, no vel adj */
            }
        }
    }
}
```

```
/* issue MPU commands to shut down record process.  Shuts each track down */
/* individually to avoid hung notes */
void
stop_401(int tracks_on)
{
    int i, cmd;

    if (tracks_on){
        for (i = 0; i < NTRACK; i++){
            cmd = get401();                        /* get track request from MPU */
            if (cmd == ALL_END || cmd == -1)
                break;                             /* MPU sends ALL_END when done */
            else if (cmd >= REQ_T1 && cmd <= REQ_T8){
                putdata401(0);                     /* shut each play track */
                putdata401(DATA_END);              /* down individually */
            }
        }
    }
    repeat_cmd401(MET_OFF);         /* final MPU shutdown command sequence */
    repeat_cmd401(STOP_PLAY);       /* after all tracks are s/d */
    repeat_cmd401(CLEAR_PMAP);
}


/* Reset and initialize MPU-401.  Returns track bit map (trackbits) */
/* as an int.  Called before start of record and play process. */
/* Also sets temp array ep[] so that each element points to first event */
/* int the track to be played. */
int
init_401(struct event far *ep[])
{
    int i, status, trackbits;

    g_track_vel_used = trackbits = 0;
                                    /* build track bit map */
    for (i = NTRACK - 1; i >= 0; i--){
        trackbits <<= 1;
        if (g_trackarray[i].active && g_trackarray[i].numevents > 1)
            trackbits++;
        ep[i] = g_trackarray[i].current;
        if (ep[i]->b[1] == MES_END) /* skip first measure end mark */
            ep[i] = ep[i]->next;

        g_track_vel[i] = g_trackarray[i].midivol;   /* build velocity data */
        if (g_track_vel[i] != 100)
            g_track_vel_used = 1;   /* if any track vel != 0, vel correct */
    }

    status = repeat_cmd401(RESET);  /* send all initializing commands */
    if (status == -1){
        writerr("Unable to reset MPU-401 - play process aborted.",
```

```
                    g_text_char_v - 1, g_norm_attrib, g_emph_attrib);
          return(0);
     }
     if (g_pitchbend)                    /* send setup command sequence to MPU */
          repeat_cmd401(BEND_ON);
     if (g_exclusive)
          repeat_cmd401(EXCL_THRU);
     repeat_cmd401(SET_TEMPO);
          putdata401(g_metrate);
     repeat_cmd401(METRO_MEAS);
          putdata401(g_meter);
     repeat_cmd401(TB_120);         /* MT uses only 120 ticks/beat timebase */
     repeat_cmd401(MIDI_METRO);  /* metro always beets every quarter note */
          putdata401(24);
     if (g_meton)
          repeat_cmd401(MET_ON_WOUT);
     repeat_cmd401(ACT_TRACK);
          putdata401(trackbits);
     repeat_cmd401(CLEAR_PCOUNT);
     repeat_cmd401(START_PLAY);
     return(trackbits);            /* return bit map of tracks set to play */
}


/* Update measure number - only if highest active track.  Used in play */
/* process to avoid measure number advancing on very measure end sent */
/* when multiple tracks are playing. */
void
maybe_measure_number(int track, int trackbits)
{
    int hi_act_track, i;

    for (i = 0; i < NTRACK; i++){   /* find the track # of highest track */
        if (trackbits & (1 << i))   /* set to play.  Only this one trips */
            hi_act_track = i;        /* update of measure # on screen. */
    }

    if ((track == hi_act_track) && !g_trace_on)
        write_int(++g_current_measure + 1, 53, 18, g_norm_attrib);
}


/* prompt for track number, then erase all track data.  Called from both */
/* the Record and MLE screens.  Uses erase_one() to do erasing. */
void
erase_track(void)
{
    int track, ans;
    char nbuf[10], buf[SCRNWIDE];

    ans = getint(g_text_char_v - 1,
```

```
            "Which track number do you wish to erase? ->",
            &track, 1, NTRACK, g_norm_attrib, g_norm_attrib);

    if (ans){
        strcpy(buf, "Erase track number ");
        itoa(track, nbuf, 10);
        strcat(buf, nbuf);
        strcat(buf, " ? (Y/N)->");
        clearline(g_text_char_v - 1, g_norm_attrib);
        writeword(buf, 1, g_text_char_v - 1, g_norm_attrib);
        ans = getche();
        if (toupper(ans) == 'Y')
            erase_one(--track);
    }
}


/* workhorse track eraser.  Updates g_trackarray[], and calls clear_events */
/* to free all memory associated with track's event list */
void
erase_one(int track)
{
    clear_events(g_trackarray[track].first->next);
    g_trackarray[track].current = g_trackarray[track].first;
    g_trackarray[track].last = g_trackarray[track].first;
    g_trackarray[track].first->next = NULL;
    g_trackarray[track].current->nbytes = 2;
    g_trackarray[track].current->b[0] = 0;
    g_trackarray[track].current->b[1] = MES_END;
    g_trackarray[track].current->b[2] = 0;
    g_trackarray[track].current->b[3] = 0;
    if (track == g_block_track)
        g_block_on = 0;
}


/* erase all data on all tracks.  This is only called from the MT primary */
/* menu as the CLEAR command. */
void
erase_all(void)
{
    int i;

    for (i = 0; i < NTRACK; i++)
        erase_one(i);
    g_current_measure = 0;
}


/* updates the screen data for top of record screen.  These items are */
/* all elements of the mt2[] menu defined in MTSCREEN.H.   After the update */
```

```
/* the normal menu functions are used to control the screen display. */
void
init_track_str(void)
{
    int i;
    char buf[10];

    for (i = 0; i < NTRACK; i++){
        strcpy(mt2[i].content, g_trackarray[i].name);

        itoa(g_trackarray[i].midichan + 1, buf, 10);    /* channel number */
        strcpy(mt2[i + NTRACK].content, buf);

        itoa(g_trackarray[i].midivol, buf, 10);          /* MIDI volume */
        strcpy(mt2[i + (5 * NTRACK)].content, buf);

        ltoa(g_trackarray[i].numevents, buf, 10);        /* event count */
        strcpy(mt2[i + (6 * NTRACK)].content, buf);

        if (i != g_record_track){
            strcpy(mt2[i + (2 * NTRACK)].content, "      ");
            strcpy(mt2[i + (4 * NTRACK)].content, "OFF");
        }
        else{
            strcpy(mt2[i + (2 * NTRACK)].content, "*ACTIVE*");
            strcpy(mt2[i + (4 * NTRACK)].content, "ON ");
            g_trackarray[i].active = 0;     /* can't play & record at once */
        }

        if (g_trackarray[i].active){         /* update play status */
            strcpy(mt2[i + (3 * NTRACK)].content, "ON ");
        }
        else{
            strcpy(mt2[i + (3 * NTRACK)].content, "OFF");
        }
    }
}


/* update event count for each track, ret total number.  This is needed */
/* to keep the calculation of the amount of memory used up-to-date */
long
count_events(void)
{
    int i;
    long track_total, total;
    struct event far *tp;

    total = 0;

    for (i = 0; i < NTRACK; i++){
```

```
        tp = g_trackarray[i].first;
        track_total = 0;
        do {                            /* compute events stored in track */
            tp = tp->next;
            track_total++;
        } while (tp != NULL);
        g_trackarray[i].numevents = track_total;
        total += track_total;
    }
    return(total);
}


/* updates all values at bottom of the recorder screen */
void
init_rec_val(void)
{
    write_int(g_metrate, SCRNWIDE - 6, 16, g_norm_attrib);
    write_int(g_meter, SCRNWIDE - 6, 15, g_norm_attrib);
    write_int(g_current_measure + 1, 53, 18, g_norm_attrib);
    write_int(g_pct_free_memory, 53, 19, g_norm_attrib);
    write_on_off(g_meton, SCRNWIDE - 6, 14);
    write_on_off(g_pitchbend, SCRNWIDE - 6, 17);
    write_on_off(g_exclusive, SCRNWIDE - 6, 18);
    write_on_off(g_trace_on, SCRNWIDE - 6, 19);
}


void
calc_pct_free(void)                         /* calculate % free memory */
{
    int free;
    float f;

    count_events();
    f = g_free_memory - used_memory();
    g_pct_free_memory = 100 * f/g_free_memory;
}


void
write_on_off(int param, int column, int row)  /* put an ON or OFF on screen */
{
    if (param)
        writeword("ON ", column, row, g_emph_attrib);
    else
        writeword("OFF", column, row, g_norm_attrib);
}


/* Sends all notes off message on all channels.  This is a menu item on */
```

```
/* on the RECORD screen. */
void
all_notes_off(void)
{
    int i;

    repeat_cmd401(UART);
    for(i = 0; i < NCHANNEL; i++){
        putdata401(MODE_MESSAGE + i);
        putdata401(ALL_NOTES_OFF);
        putdata401(0);
    }
    sendcmd401(RESET);
}


/* Writes a message at the top of the screen prior to the data trace output */
void
trace_header(void)
{
    clearscreen(g_norm_attrib);
    writeword("Data Trace Option - all data in hex.", 1, 1, g_emph_attrib);
    writeword("rc=recieved, tc=trans command, td=trans data\n\n", 1, 2,
        g_emph_attrib);
}
```

```
/* mtrc4.c */
/* `MIDI Sequencing In C', Jim Conger, M&T Books, 1989 */

/* #define TURBOC 1   Define if using TURBOC, leave out for Microsoft */

#include <stdio.h>
#include <conio.h>
#include <string.h>

#ifdef TURBOC
    #include <alloc.h>
#else
    #include <malloc.h>
#endif

#include "screenf.h"
#include "standard.h"
#include "mpu401.h"
#include "mt.h"
#include "video.h"
#include "mtdeclar.h"


/* allocate a block of far memory big enough to hold one event. */
/* returns pointer to memory area. */
struct event far
*eventalloc(void)
{
#ifdef TURBOC
    return((struct event far *)farmalloc(sizeof(struct event)));
#else
    return((struct event far *)_fmalloc(sizeof(struct event)));
#endif
}


/* store an event in far memory , return pointer to next event. */
/* node is the last (empty) event created. */
struct event far
*store(struct event far *node, int nbytes, int b0, int b1, int b2, int b3)
{
    node->next = eventalloc();
    (node->next)->next = NULL;   /* null pointer in next node to mark end */
    node->nbytes = nbytes;
    node->b[0] = b0;
    node->b[1] = b1;
    node->b[2] = b2;
    node->b[3] = b3;
    return(node->next);
}
```

```
/* This block contains the communications functions to/from the MPU-401 */
/* At the lowest level these use the MIO401.ASM assembly language calls. */
/* Only get401(), sendcmd401(), repeat_cmd401() and putdata401() are used */
/* outside of this block.  The remainder handle data buffering. */

#define BUFSIZE     100
int cmdbuf[BUFSIZE];            /* global buffer for pending MPU commands */
int cmdbufp = 0;                /* next free position in cmdbuf */

 /* get a possibly pushed back command from MPU or cmdbuf */
int
getnext401(void)
{
    return((cmdbufp > 0) ? cmdbuf[--cmdbufp] : getdata());
}


void
ungetnext401(int n)                         /* push a command back on input */
{
    if (cmdbufp > BUFSIZE)
        printf("\nungetnext401 ran out of buffer space.");
    else
        cmdbuf[cmdbufp++] = n;
}


int
get401(void)            /* get next byte from mpu401 (or pending buffer) */
{                       /* try forever, stop on keypress */
    int i;

    while (1){
        if (kbhit())
            return(-1);
        i = getnext401();
        if (g_trace_on){
            if (i != -1)
                printf(" rc=%0x", i);
        }
        if (i != -1)
            return(i);
    }
    return(-1);
}


void
putdata401(int n)           /* send data byte to MPU, print it if trace is on */
{
```

```
    putdata(n);
    if (g_trace_on)
        printf(" td=%0x", n);
}


int                 /* send a command, check for ACK, if not save MPU data */
sendcmd401(int n)    /* until it stops sending */
{
    int ans;

    if (g_trace_on)
        printf(" tc=%0x", n);
    ans = putcmd(n);
    if (ans == ACK){
        if (g_trace_on)
            fputs("(ACK)", stdout);
        return(ans);
    }
    else if (ans != -1){
        if (g_trace_on)
            fputs("(No ACK)", stdout);
        ungetnext401(ans);        /* put pending data on stack */
        while (1){                /* check for more incoming data */
            ans = getdata();
            if (ans == ACK || ans == -1)
                return(ans);
            else
                ungetnext401(ans);
        }
    }
    return(ans);
}


int
repeat_cmd401(int n)     /* determined command send -  max tries = 10 */
{
    int i, j, m;
    char buf[SCRNWIDE], nbuf[10];

    for (i = 0; i < 10; i++){
        m = sendcmd401(n);
        if (m != -1)
            return(m);
        else{
            for (j = 0; j < 10; j++){
                getdata();      /* clear any stray data from input */
            }
        }
    }
```

```
        strcpy(buf, "Error in sending command ");
        itoa(n, nbuf, 16);
        strcat(buf, nbuf);
        strcat(buf, " hex. (repeat_cmd401)");
        writeword(buf, 1, g_text_char_v, g_emph_attrib);
        return(-1);
}

/* end of MPU communications function block */

/* Move all track counters to given measure.  Returns measure number of */
/* the highest measure reached before running off end of longest track. */
int
goto_measure(int meas)
{
    int end_meas, count, i;
    struct event far *ep;
    struct event far *lep;
    struct event far *startp;

    end_meas = 0;
    for (i = 0; i < NTRACK; i++){
        startp = ep = g_trackarray[i].first;
        lep = g_trackarray[i].last;
        count = 0;
        while (count != meas){
            if (ep == lep){                  /* if reached end of track */
                break;
            }
            if ((ep->b[1]) == MES_END){      /* found measure end mark */
                if (ep != startp){           /* don't count first event */
                    count++;
                }
            }
            ep = ep->next;
        }
        if (count > end_meas)
            end_meas = count;
        g_trackarray[i].current = ep;
    }
    return(end_meas);
}


/* adjust all MIDI data on track to channel specified */
void
change_channel(int track, int channel)
{
    unsigned int data, root;
    struct event far *ep;
```

```
    ep = g_trackarray[track].first;

    while (ep->next != NULL){
        data = ep->b[1];                        /* get second byte of data */
                                                /* check if it is a MIDI message */
        if (data >= 0x90 && data <= 0xEF){
            root = data - (data % 0x10);
            ep->b[1] = root + channel;
        }
        ep = ep->next;
    }
}


/* put default values in track data array.  Allocate first event for each */
/* track and set it to a MES_END.  Called on startup from main(). */
void
init_tracks(void)
{
    int i, j;
    struct event far *ep;

    for (i = 0; i < NTRACK; i++){
        strcpy(g_trackarray[i].name, "<       >");
        g_trackarray[i].midichan = i;
        g_trackarray[i].numevents = 1;
        g_trackarray[i].active = 0;
        g_trackarray[i].midivol = 100;
        ep = eventalloc();
        g_trackarray[i].first = ep;
        g_trackarray[i].current = ep;
        g_trackarray[i].last = ep;

        ep->next = NULL;               /* starting event is a mes_end */
        ep->nbytes = 2;
        ep->b[1] = MES_END;
        ep->b[0] = ep->b[2] = ep->b[3] = 0;
    }
    g_trackarray[0].active = 1;        /* start with track 1 active */
}


/* Find the number of K bytes free in memory on startup.  Allocates 10K */
/* blocks until not further space.  Can leave smaller space unnoticed. */
int
free_memory(void)
{
    void far *node[64];
    int i, j;

    i = 0;
```

```
    do{
#ifdef TURBOC
        node[i] = farmalloc(1024 * 10); /* allocate one 10 K byte */
#else
        node[i] = _fmalloc(1024 * 10);  /* allocate one 10 K byte */
#endif
    }while (node[i++] != NULL);

    for (j = 0; j < i; j++){              /* free memory for use */
#ifdef TURBOC
        farfree(node[j]);
#else
        _ffree(node[j]);
#endif
    }
    return(10 * i);
}


/* returns the number of K bytes used by all track data. */
int
used_memory(void)
{
    int i;
    long bytes, ln;

    bytes = 0;
    for (i = 0; i < NTRACK; i++){
        ln = g_trackarray[i].numevents;
        bytes += ln * (sizeof(struct event) + FMALLOC_BYTES);
    }
    i = bytes/1024;             /* convert to integer K bytes */
    return(i);
}


/* Display track data until esc key is pressed.  This is a menu item on */
/* both the Record and MLE screens. */
void
data_dump(void)
{
    int i, j, k;
    struct event far *ep[NTRACK];

    for (i = 0; i < NTRACK; i++){
        ep[i] = g_trackarray[i].current;
    }

    while (1){
        clearscreen(g_norm_attrib);
        fputs("MIDI data in hex for tracks 1-8:\n\n", stdout);
```

```
        for (i = 0; i < 20; i++){
            for (j = 0; j < NTRACK; j++){
                for (k = 0; k < 4; k++){
                    if (ep[j] != NULL)
                        printf("%02x", ep[j]->b[k]);
                    else
                        fputs("  ", stdout);
                }
                fputs("-", stdout);
                if (ep[j] != NULL)
                    ep[j] = ep[j]->next;
            }
            fputs("\n",stdout);
        }
        while(kbhit())
            getch();
        fputs("\nHit space to continue, ESC to quit.", stdout);
        while(!kbhit())
            ;
        if (getch() == ESC)
            return;
    }
}


/* Erases all track data forward of the current measure number.  Prompts */
/* for track number.  Sticks new track terminator event at end. */
void
clear_forward(void)
{
    int ans, track;
    char nbuf[10], buf[SCRNWIDE];
    struct event far *ep;
    struct event far *np;

    ans = getint(g_text_char_v - 1,
        "Enter the track number to clear forward ->",
        &track, 1, 8, g_norm_attrib, g_emph_attrib);
    if (ans){
        strcpy(buf, "Clear track number ");
        itoa(track, nbuf, 10);
        strcat(buf, nbuf);
        strcat(buf, " from current measure to end? (Y/N)->");
        writeword(buf, 1, g_text_char_v - 1, g_norm_attrib);
        ans = getche();
        if (toupper(ans) == 'Y'){
            track--;
            ep = advance_to_measure(track, g_current_measure);
            np = ep->next;                 /* point to event past meas end */
            clear_events(np);
            np = ep->next = eventalloc();
```

369

```
            np->next = NULL;                /* add track terminator to end */
            np->nbytes = 2;
            np->b[1] = ALL_END;
            np->b[0] = np->b[2] = np->b[3] = 0;
            clean_track(track);
            g_trackarray[track].current = advance_to_measure(track,
                g_current_measure);
        }
    }
}


/* Does the work of clearing all events from start to end of event list */
/* from memory.  */
void
clear_events(struct event far *start)
{
    struct event far *nextevent;

    while (start != NULL){
        nextevent = start->next;
#if TURBOC
        farfree(start);
#else
        _ffree(start);
#endif
        start = nextevent;
    }
}


void
wait_for_key(void)                      /* pause until a key is pressed */
{
    while (kbhit())    /* clear key buffer */
        getch();
    while (!kbhit())    /* wait for key */
        ;
    getch();
}
```

```
/* mtsc1.c  central module for screen editing functions of mt */
/* `MIDI Sequencing In C', Jim Conger, M&T Books, 1989 */

#include <stdio.h>
#include <conio.h>

#include "standard.h"
#include "screenf.h"
#include "mpu401.h"
#include "mt.h"
#include "video.h"
#include "mtsc.h"
#include "mtdeclar.h"


/* Central module for Note Level editor.  Returns measure number ended on */
int
scrn_edit_control(int track, int measure)
{
    int i, beat, pick;
    char buf[SCRNWIDE], nbuf[10];
    struct note_time far *note_list;
    beat = 0;

    setvideomode(g_graph_mode);

    strcpy(buf, "MIDI Note Editor  -   Track Number ");
    itoa(track + 1, nbuf, 10);
    strcat(buf, nbuf);
    strcat(buf, ".  [");
    strcat(buf, g_trackarray[track].name);
    strcat(buf, "]");
    writeword(buf, 20, 1, g_norm_attrib);

    display_keyboard();
    mark_middle_c(TRUE);

    initscrn(mt6, 0, NPARAM6 - 1, g_emph_attrib);    /* put menu at bottom */
    init_screen_box(beat, measure);                  /* draw in edit area */
    name_top_note(g_oct_shown);
    name_measure(measure);

    writeword("Compiling note data.  Hit ESC to terminate.",
        1, g_graph_char_v, g_norm_attrib);
    note_list = build_note_list(track);              /* build note list */
    if (note_list == NULL){
        writerr("ESC key hit (or not enough memory to compile note list.)",
            g_graph_char_v, g_norm_attrib, g_emph_attrib);
        setvideomode(g_text_mode);
        return(measure);
    }
```

```
disp_notes(note_list, measure, beat);              /* draw note lines */
clearline(g_graph_char_v, g_norm_attrib);          /* clear bottom line */

pick = 0;
while(1){                          /* cursor selection of a command */
    pick = movescrn(g_graph_mode, mt6, pick, NPARAM6 - 1,
        g_line_color, g_line_color);
    switch(pick){
        case(0):          /* Up Octive */
            if (g_top_note < NNOTES - 12){
                g_top_note += 12;
                g_bot_note += 12;
                name_top_note(g_oct_shown);
                mark_middle_c(FALSE);
                init_screen_box(beat, measure);
                disp_notes(note_list, measure, beat);
            }
            else
                writerr("You are at the top of the MIDI scale already.",
                    g_graph_char_v, g_norm_attrib, g_norm_attrib);
            break;
        case(1):          /* Next Measure */
            measure++;
            name_measure(measure);
            init_screen_box(beat, measure);
            disp_notes(note_list, measure, beat);
            break;
        case(2):          /* Note Delete */
            note_list = delete_note(note_list, measure, track);
            break;
        case(3):          /* tick */
            break;
        case(4):          /* Down Octive */
            if (g_top_note - ((g_oct_shown + 1) * 12) + 1 >= 0){
                g_top_note -= 12;
                g_bot_note -= 12;
                name_top_note(g_oct_shown);
                mark_middle_c(FALSE);
                init_screen_box(beat, measure);
                disp_notes(note_list, measure, beat);
            }
            else
                writerr("You are already at the bottom of the MIDI scale.",
                    g_graph_char_v, g_norm_attrib, g_norm_attrib);
            break;
        case(5):          /* Next Beat */
            if (beat < g_meter - 1)
                beat++;
            else{
```

```
            beat = 0;
            measure++;
        }
        name_measure(measure);
        init_screen_box(beat, measure);
        disp_notes(note_list, measure, beat);
        break;
    case(6):        /* Note Add */
        add_note(note_list, measure, track);
        break;
    case(7):        /* Note = */
        break;
    case(8):        /* Expand Scale */
        if (g_scale > 1){
            g_scale /= 2;
            init_screen_box(beat, measure);
            disp_notes(note_list, measure, beat);
        }
        else
            writerr("Already at most expanded scale possible, 1/1.",
                g_graph_char_v, g_norm_attrib, g_norm_attrib);
        break;
    case(9):        /* Prev. Beat */
        if (beat > 0)
            beat--;
        else{
            if (measure > 0){
                measure--;
                beat = g_meter - 1;
            }
        }
        name_measure(measure);
        init_screen_box(beat, measure);
        disp_notes(note_list, measure, beat);
        break;
    case(10):       /* Velocity Change */
        change_vel(note_list, measure);
        break;
    case(11):       /* Key Velocity (not an command) */
        break;
    case(12):       /* Shrink Scale */
        if (g_scale < 8){
            g_scale *= 2;
            init_screen_box(beat, measure);
            disp_notes(note_list, measure, beat);
        }
        else{
            writerr("Scale already shrunk to maximum possible.",
                g_graph_char_v, g_norm_attrib, g_norm_attrib);
        }
        break;
```

```
            case(13):        /* Prev Measure */
                if (measure){
                    measure--;
                    name_measure(measure);
                    init_screen_box(beat, measure);
                    disp_notes(note_list, measure, beat);
                }
                else{
                    writerr("Already at beginning of track.", g_graph_char_v,
                        g_norm_attrib, g_norm_attrib);
                }
                break;
            case(14):        /* Quit */
            case(-2):        /* ESC */
                            setvideomode(6);            /* kludge to get vga
back to 25 line */
                setvideomode(g_text_mode);
                free_note_list(note_list);
                return(measure);
            default:
                writerr("Use arrow keys to make selection, then hit return.",
                    g_graph_char_v, g_norm_attrib, g_norm_attrib);
                break;
        }
    }
    return(measure);
}


/* Initialize global variables used in NLE graphics display based on */
/* video data read in on startup of MT. */
void
init_edit_param(void)
{
    int i, text_lines;

    text_lines = SC_TOP_LINES + SC_MENU_LINES + SC_BOT_LINES;
    g_oct_shown = (g_dots_v - (text_lines * g_let_dots_v)) / OCTIVE_HIGH;
    g_top_note_line = (SC_TOP_LINES * g_let_dots_v) + HALF_NOTE_DOTS;
    g_bot_note_line = g_top_note_line + (g_oct_shown * OCTIVE_HIGH) -
        (2 * HALF_NOTE_DOTS);
    g_top_note = 71 + (6 * (g_oct_shown - 2));
    g_bot_note = g_top_note - (g_oct_shown * 12) + 1;


    /* if in mode with more than 25 lines of text on screen */
    /* adjust the graphics menu to be at the bottom of screen. */

    if (g_graph_char_v > SCRNTALL){
        for (i = 0; i < NPARAM6; i++){
            mt6[i].ypos += g_graph_char_v - SCRNTALL;
```

```
        }
    }
}


void
display_keyboard(void)              /* put a keyboard image on left of screen */
{
    int m, n, y;

    y = g_top_note_line - HALF_NOTE_DOTS;
    for (m = 0; m < g_oct_shown; m++){
        for (n = 0; n < 7; n++){
            draw_rectangle(FALSE, 1, y, LEFT_BORDER - 2, y + 8,
                g_line_color);
            if (n != 0 && n != 4 && n != 7){
                draw_rectangle(TRUE, 1, y - 2, (LEFT_BORDER - 2)/2,
                    y + 2, g_line_color);
            }
            y += 2 * HALF_NOTE_DOTS;
        }
    }
}
```

```
/* mtsc2.c */
/* `MIDI Sequencing In C', Jim Conger, M&T Books, 1989 */

/* #define TURBOC 1    Define if using TURBOC, leave out for Microsoft */

#include <stdio.h>
#include <conio.h>
#include <stdlib.h>

#ifdef TURBOC
    #include <alloc.h>
#else
    #include <malloc.h>
#endif

#include "standard.h"
#include "screenf.h"
#include "mpu401.h"
#include "mt.h"
#include "video.h"
#include "mtsc.h"
#include "mtdeclar.h"


/* Draw the note edit area box on the graphics screen. */
void
init_screen_box(int beat, int measure)
{
    int x1, x2, y1, y2;

    x1 = LEFT_BORDER;
    y1 = g_top_note_line - HALF_NOTE_DOTS;
    x2 = g_dots_h - 1;
    y2 = g_bot_note_line + HALF_NOTE_DOTS;

    draw_rectangle(FALSE, x1, y1, x2, y2, g_line_color);
    draw_rectangle(TRUE, x1 + 1, y1 + 1, x2 - 1, y2 - 1, g_back_color);
    top_scale(beat, x1, y1, x2, y2, measure);
    dotted_lines(x1, y1, x2, y2, 8, 20, g_line_color);
    g_sc_refresh = 1;
}


/* put top scale on screen, initialize globals for side boundaries */
void
top_scale(int beat, int leftside, int topline, int rightside, int botline,
    int measure)
{
    int i, tick, xpos;
    char nbuf[10];
```

```
    g_first_measure = measure;
    tick = 0;
    xpos = leftside;

    clearline(2, g_norm_attrib);
    writeword("Beat:", 1, 2, g_norm_attrib);

    /* put in tick marks at the top of the NLE edit box */
    for (i = leftside; i < rightside; i += MIN_SPACE){
        if (tick % TICK_PER_BEAT == 0){
            drawline(xpos, topline, xpos, botline, g_line_color);
            write_int(beat + 1, 1 + (xpos/g_let_dots_h), 2, g_emph_attrib);
            if (beat < g_meter - 1)
                beat++;
            else{
                beat = 0;
                tick = 0;
                measure++;
            }
        }
        else if (tick % (TICK_PER_BEAT/2) == 0)
            drawline(xpos, topline - 6, xpos, topline, g_line_color);
        else if (tick % (TICK_PER_BEAT/4) == 0)
            drawline(xpos, topline - 4, xpos, topline, g_line_color);
        else if (tick % (TICK_PER_BEAT/8) == 0)
            drawline(xpos, topline - 2, xpos, topline, g_line_color);
        else
            drawline(xpos, topline - 1, xpos, topline, g_line_color);
        tick += g_scale;
        xpos += MIN_SPACE;
    }
}


/* Write top note name on screen and initialize global for bottom note */
void
name_top_note(int oct_shown)
{
    int ypos;
    char buf[10];

    g_bot_note = g_top_note - (oct_shown * 12) + 1;

    writeword("        ", 72, g_graph_char_v - 2, g_norm_attrib);
    writeword(g_notes[g_top_note].name, 72, g_graph_char_v - 2,
        g_norm_attrib);
}


void
name_measure(int measure)          /* put measure number at top left corner */
```

```
{
    char buf[20], nbuf[10];

    strcpy(buf, "Meas:    ");
    itoa(measure + 1, nbuf, 10);
    strcat(buf, nbuf);
    strcat(buf, "    ");
    writeword(buf, 1, 1, g_norm_attrib);
}




/* puts dotted lines in rectangular region */
void
dotted_lines(int topx, int topy, int botx, int boty, int vspace, int hspace,
    int color)
{
    int x, y;


    for (y = topy + (vspace/2) ; y < boty; y += vspace){
        for (x = topx; x < botx; x += hspace){
            dotplot(x, y, color);
        }
    }
}


/* Convert track data from event list to temporary form used for editing. */
/* The note_time structure makes it easier to locate and draw single notes. */
struct note_time far
*build_note_list(int track)
{
    int measure, tick, i, b0, b1, b2, b3;
    struct event far *ep;
    struct note_time far *notep;
    struct note_time far *first_notep;
    struct on_event on_array[NNOTES];

    for (i = 0; i < NNOTES; i++){    /* keeps track of pending note_ons */
        on_array[i].event = NULL;
    }

    ep = g_trackarray[track].first;
    if (ep->b[1] == MES_END)          /* skip start of track marker */
        ep = ep->next;

    notep = first_notep =
#ifdef TURBOC
        (struct note_time far *)farmalloc(sizeof(struct note_time));
#else
```

```
                (struct note_time far *)_fmalloc(sizeof(struct note_time));
#endif
    notep->on_event = NULL;
    notep->off_event = NULL;
    notep->on_measure = notep->off_measure = 0;
    notep->on_tick = notep->off_tick = 0;
    notep->note_number = 0;
    notep->next = NULL;

    measure = tick = 0;
    while (ep != NULL){
        b0 = ep->b[0];
        b1 = ep->b[1];
        b2 = ep->b[2];
        b3 = ep->b[3];
        if (b1 == MES_END){
            measure++;
            tick = 0;
        }
        else if (b1 == ALL_END)
            break;
        else if (b1 >= NOTE_ON && b1 < NOTE_ON + NCHANNEL ||
            b1 >= NOTE_OFF && b1 < NOTE_OFF + NCHANNEL){
            tick += b0;
                        /* if already have note on, and this is note off */
            if (on_array[b2].event != NULL &&
                (b3 == 0 || (b1 >= NOTE_OFF && b1 < NOTE_OFF + NCHANNEL))){
                notep->on_event = on_array[b2].event;
                notep->on_measure = on_array[b2].measure;
                notep->on_tick = on_array[b2].tick;
                notep->note_number = b2;
                notep->off_event = ep;
                notep->off_measure = measure;
                notep->off_tick = tick;
                notep = notep->next = (struct note_time far *)
#ifdef TURBOC
                    farmalloc(sizeof(struct note_time));
#else
                    _fmalloc(sizeof(struct note_time));
#endif
                if (notep == NULL){
                    free_note_list(first_notep);
                    return(NULL);
                }
                notep->next = NULL;
                on_array[b2].event = NULL;
            }
            else if (b3 != 0){                  /* if not a loose note off */
                on_array[b2].event = ep;
                on_array[b2].measure = measure;
                on_array[b2].tick = tick;
```

```
                on_array[b2].vel = b3;
            }
        }
        else if (b0 == TIME_OUT){
            tick += MAX_CLOCK;
        }
        else{
            tick += b0;      /* all data except note on/off ignored */
        }                    /* but timing value added to running count. */

        if (kbhit()){        /* quit if ESC key hit */
            if (getch() == ESC){
                free_note_list(first_notep);
                return(NULL);
            }
        }
        ep = ep->next;
    }
    return(first_notep);
}


/* Free memory used for temporary note list.  Used on exit from NLE. */
void
free_note_list(struct note_time far *np)
{
    struct note_time far *nextp;

    while (np != NULL){
        nextp = np->next;
#if TURBOC
        farfree(np);
#else
        _ffree(np);
#endif
        np = nextp;
    }
}


/* Display all notes within screen boundaries as horiz. lines */
void
disp_notes(struct note_time far *first_notep, int first_measure, int beat)
{
    int start_x, end_x;
    struct note_time far *np;

    g_first_tick = beat * TICK_PER_BEAT;

    np = first_notep;
    do {                    /* check if within 10 measures to avoid overflow */
```

```
        if (abs(np->on_measure - first_measure) < 10 &&
            abs(np->off_measure - first_measure) < 10){
                draw_note(np, g_emph_color);
        }
        np = np->next;
    } while (np != NULL);
}



/* put line on screen for note duration */
void
draw_note(struct note_time far *np, int color)
{
    int ypos, start_x, end_x;

    start_x = LEFT_BORDER + ((((np->on_measure - g_first_measure) *
        TICK_PER_BEAT * g_meter) + np->on_tick - g_first_tick) *
        MIN_SPACE)/g_scale;

    end_x = LEFT_BORDER + ((((np->off_measure - g_first_measure) *
        TICK_PER_BEAT * g_meter) + np->off_tick - g_first_tick) *
        MIN_SPACE)/g_scale;

    if ((start_x >= LEFT_BORDER + MIN_SPACE) &&
        (start_x < g_dots_h) ||
        (end_x >= LEFT_BORDER + MIN_SPACE) &&
        (end_x < g_dots_h)){

        if (np->note_number > g_top_note || np->note_number < g_bot_note)
            return;

        if (start_x < LEFT_BORDER + MIN_SPACE)
            start_x = LEFT_BORDER + MIN_SPACE;
        if (end_x > g_dots_h - 1)
            end_x = g_dots_h - 1;

        ypos = find_note_line(np->note_number);
        drawline(start_x, ypos, end_x, ypos, color);
    }
}


void
mark_middle_c(int first)  /* put little m on middle C key on keyboard image */
{
    static int ypos = 0;    /* static to save last value of ypos */

    if (ypos && !first)     /* erase old m, unless first time or off scale */
        xsprite(little_m, 40, ypos - 3, g_line_color);
```

```
    ypos = find_note_line(60);                    /* Middle C is note 60 */

    if (ypos)
        xsprite(little_m, 40, ypos - 3, g_line_color);
}


/* Returns the screen line number for note.  Returns 0 if note is outside */
/* of range displayed on screen. */
int
find_note_line(int note_no)
{
    int ypos, note;

    if (note_no > g_top_note || note_no < g_bot_note)
        return(0);

    ypos = g_top_note_line;
    note = g_top_note;

    while (note > note_no)
        ypos += g_notes[note--].down_dots;

    return(ypos);
}
```

```
/* mtsc3.c */
/* `MIDI Sequencing In C', Jim Conger, M&T Books, 1989 */

/* #define TURBOC 1   Define if using TURBOC, leave out for Microsoft */

#include <stdio.h>
#include <conio.h>
#include <stdlib.h>

#ifdef TURBOC
    #include <alloc.h>
#else
    #include <malloc.h>
#endif

#include "standard.h"
#include "screenf.h"
#include "mpu401.h"
#include "mt.h"
#include "video.h"
#include "mtsc.h"
#include "mtdeclar.h"

/* Erase one note in both note and event lists */
struct note_time far
*delete_note(struct note_time far *first_notep, int measure, int track)
{
    struct note_time far *np;
    struct note_pos *notepos;
    int status;

    writeword(
        "To Delete: Move cross hair to a note, then hit return (ESC to
exit).",
            1, g_graph_char_v, g_norm_attrib);
    notepos = select_note(measure, FALSE);
    if (notepos == NULL){
        clearline(g_graph_char_v, g_norm_attrib);
        return(NULL);
    }
    else{
        np = find_note(first_notep, notepos->note, notepos->measure,
            notepos->tick);
        if (np != NULL){
            status = remove_event(np->on_event, track);
            if (!status)
                writerr("Memory pointer error in deleting note-on event.",
                    g_graph_char_v, g_norm_attrib, g_norm_attrib);
            status = remove_event(np->off_event, track);
            if (!status)
                writerr("Memory pointer error in deleting note-off event.",
```

```
                         g_graph_char_v, g_norm_attrib, g_norm_attrib);

              draw_note(np, g_back_color);    /* erase note on screen */
              clearline(g_graph_char_v, g_norm_attrib);
              return(remove_note(first_notep, np));
          }
          else{
              clearline(g_graph_char_v, g_norm_attrib);
              writerr("You did not select an existing note.", g_graph_char_v,
                  g_norm_attrib, g_norm_attrib);
              clearline(g_graph_char_v, g_norm_attrib);
              return(first_notep);
          }
      }
  }
}


/* Cursor movement to select note, option to leave cross hair at point */
struct note_pos
*select_note(int measure, int option)
{
    int c, i, vert_sum, horz_sum;
    static int oldx, oldy, newx, newy, note, tick, csr_measure;
    char nbuf[10];
    static struct note_pos on_ev;
    struct note_pos *notepos;

    notepos = &on_ev;

    if (g_sc_refresh == 1){ /* fix cursor pos. unless screen is refreshed */
                            /* find measure, tick for center of screen */
        csr_measure = measure;
        newx = LEFT_BORDER - CROSS_HALF;
        tick = g_first_tick;
        for (i = LEFT_BORDER; i <= g_dots_h; i += MIN_SPACE * 2){
            tick += g_scale;
            newx += MIN_SPACE;
            if (tick >= TICK_PER_BEAT * g_meter){
                csr_measure++;
                tick = 0;
            }
        }
        note = (g_top_note + g_bot_note)/2;
    }
    else if (g_sc_refresh == 2){    /* only used for add_note, 2nd pass */
        tick += g_scale;
        newx += MIN_SPACE;
        if (tick >= TICK_PER_BEAT * g_meter){
            csr_measure++;
            tick = 0;
        }
    }
```

```
oldx = newx;

g_sc_refresh = 0;
oldy = newy = find_note_line(note) - CROSS_HALF;

xsprite(cross, newx, newy, g_emph_color);
clear_select_lines();
write_int(tick, g_graph_char_h - 9, g_graph_char_v - 5, g_norm_attrib);
writeword(g_notes[note].name, g_graph_char_h - 9, g_graph_char_v - 4,
    g_norm_attrib);
write_int(csr_measure + 1, g_graph_char_h - 9, g_graph_char_v - 3,
    g_norm_attrib);

while(1){
    vert_sum = horz_sum = 0;

    while(!kbhit())
        ;                          /* wait for keypress */

    while(kbhit()){                /* sum all pending cursor keystrokes */
        c = getch();
        while (!c)
            c = getch();           /* pass over null chars */
        switch (c){
        case ESC:             /* quit on ESC */
            xsprite(cross, oldx, oldy, g_emph_color);
            clear_select_lines();
            return(NULL);
        case BACKSP:
        case KLEFT:
            horz_sum--;
            break;
        case KUP:
            vert_sum++;
            break;
        case KDOWN:
            vert_sum--;
            break;
        case KRIGHT:
        case ' ':
            horz_sum++;
            break;
        case TAB:
        case SKRIGHT:
            horz_sum += 10;
            break;
        case BTAB:
        case SKLEFT:
            horz_sum -= 10;
            break;
        case KPGUP:
```

```
                vert_sum += 12;
                break;
           case KPGDN:
                vert_sum -= 12;
                break;
           case KHOME:
                vert_sum += 48;
                break;
           case KEND:
                vert_sum -= 48;
                break;
           default:     /* hitting key/return to select a marked note */
                if (!option)     /* clear cross hairs if option == 0 */
                     xsprite(cross, oldx, oldy, g_emph_color);
                clear_select_lines();
                notepos->measure = csr_measure;
                notepos->tick = tick;
                notepos->note = note;
                notepos->sprite_x = oldx;
                notepos->sprite_y = oldy;
                return(notepos);
           }
      }

      if (abs(horz_sum) > 2)              /* increase horz speedup */
           horz_sum *= 2;

      while (horz_sum < 0){              /* compute new cursor location */
           if (newx > LEFT_BORDER - CROSS_HALF){
                newx -= MIN_SPACE;
                tick -= g_scale;
                if (tick < 0){
                     tick = (TICK_PER_BEAT * g_meter) - g_scale;
                     csr_measure--;
                }
           }
           horz_sum++;
      }
      while (horz_sum > 0){
           if (newx < g_dots_h - 2 * CROSS_HALF){
                newx += MIN_SPACE;
                tick += g_scale;
                if (tick > (TICK_PER_BEAT * g_meter) - 1){
                     tick = 0;
                     csr_measure++;
                }
           }
           horz_sum--;
      }
      while (vert_sum > 0){
           if (newy >= g_top_note_line - CROSS_HALF + HALF_NOTE_DOTS)
```

```
                newy -= g_notes[note++].up_dots;
            vert_sum--;
        }
        while (vert_sum < 0){
            if (newy <= g_bot_note_line - HALF_NOTE_DOTS - CROSS_HALF)
                newy += g_notes[note--].down_dots;
            vert_sum++;
        }
        xsprite(cross, oldx, oldy, g_emph_color);
        xsprite(cross, newx, newy, g_emph_color);
        clear_select_lines();
            write_int(tick, g_graph_char_h - 9,   g_graph_char_v  -   5,
g_norm_attrib);
        writeword(g_notes[note].name, g_graph_char_h - 9, g_graph_char_v - 4,
            g_norm_attrib);
         write_int(csr_measure + 1, g_graph_char_h - 9, g_graph_char_v - 3,
g_norm_attrib);
        oldx = newx;
        oldy = newy;
    }
    return(NULL);
}


void
clear_select_lines(void)        /* blank out the note name and tick areas */
{
    writeword("             ", g_graph_char_h - 9, g_graph_char_v - 5,
g_norm_attrib);
    writeword("             ", g_graph_char_h - 9, g_graph_char_v - 4,
g_norm_attrib);
    writeword("             ", g_graph_char_h - 9, g_graph_char_v - 3,
g_norm_attrib);
}


/* Locate a note within the note list, given that the cursor is on the */
/* specified measure and tick.  Return pointer to it, or NULL if not found. */
struct note_time far
*find_note(struct note_time far *first_notep, int note, int measure, int tick)
{
    float startn, endn, noten;  /* decimal measure.xx fraction of measure */

    noten = note_to_float(measure, tick);
    while (first_notep->next != NULL){
        if (first_notep->note_number == note){         /* if same note */
            startn = note_to_float(first_notep->on_measure,
                first_notep->on_tick);
            endn = note_to_float(first_notep->off_measure,
                first_notep->off_tick);
            if (noten >= startn && noten <= endn)
```

```
                    return(first_notep);
        }
        first_notep = first_notep->next;   /* no match, so try next note */
    }
    return(NULL);
}

/* Convert note timing as measure, tick to floating point value */
float
note_to_float(int measure, int tick)
{
    float fm, ft, fn;

    fm = measure;
    ft = tick;
    ft = ft/(TICK_PER_BEAT * g_meter);
    fn = fm + ft;
    return(fn);
}


/* Removes one event from the event list.  Corrects timing bytes as needed */
int
remove_event(struct event far *eventp, int track)
{
    int ticks;

    struct event far *ep;
    struct event far *lastep;
    struct event far *nextep;

    lastep = ep = g_trackarray[track].first;

    while (ep != eventp && ep != NULL){
        lastep = ep;
        ep = ep->next;
    }

    if (ep == NULL)
        return(0);

    nextep = ep->next;
    while (nextep->b[0] == TIME_OUT){    /* go past any linked TIME_OUT's */
        nextep = nextep->next;           /* nextep is first event with a */
    }                                    /* timing byte. */

    ticks = ep->b[0] + nextep->b[0];
    if (ticks < MAX_CLOCK){              /* adjust next clock byte, then */
        nextep->b[0] = ticks;            /* delete the marked event. */
        lastep->next = ep->next;
#ifdef TURBOC
```

```
        farfree(ep);
#else
        _ffree(ep);
#endif
    }
    else{
        nextep->b[0] -= MAX_CLOCK - ep->b[0];   /* if clock is too large, */
        ep->nbytes = 1;                         /* use (not) deleted event */
        ep->b[0] = TIME_OUT;                    /* to hold a new TIME_OUT. */
        ep->b[1] = ep->b[2] = ep->b[3] = 0;
    }
    return(1);
}

/* Remove one note's data from note list. */
struct note_time far
*remove_note(struct note_time far *first_notep, struct note_time far *notep)
{
    struct note_time far *np;
    struct note_time far *lastnp;

    if (notep == first_notep){      /* if deleting first note */
        lastnp = notep;
        first_notep = first_notep->next;
#ifdef TURBOC
        farfree(lastnp);
#else
        _ffree(lastnp);
#endif
        return(first_notep);
    }
    else{
        lastnp = np = first_notep;

        while (np != notep && np != NULL){
            lastnp = np;
            np = np->next;
        }

        if (np == NULL)
            return(0);

        lastnp->next = np->next;
#ifdef TURBOC
        farfree(np);
#else
        _ffree(np);
#endif
        return(first_notep);
    }
}
```

```
/* mtsc4.c */
/* `MIDI Sequencing In C', Jim Conger, M&T Books, 1989 */

/* #define TURBOC 1    Define if using TURBOC, leave out for Microsoft */

#include <stdio.h>
#include <conio.h>
#include <stdlib.h>

#ifdef TURBOC
    #include <alloc.h>
#else
    #include <malloc.h>
#endif

#include "standard.h"
#include "screenf.h"
#include "mpu401.h"
#include "mt.h"
#include "video.h"
#include "mtsc.h"
#include "mtdeclar.h"


/* Adds note to track event list and not_time note list. Returns 1 if */
/* added, 0 if aborted */
void
add_note(struct note_time far *first_notep, int measure, int track)
{
    int on_meas, on_tick, on_note, off_meas, off_tick, vel, *velp, status,
        on_x, on_y, off_x, off_y;
    float time_on, time_off;
    struct note_time far *notetime;
    struct note_pos *notepos;
    struct event far *on_event;
    struct event far *off_event;

    velp = &vel;
    writeword("Move cross hair to NOTE START, then hit return (ESC to exit)",
        1, g_graph_char_v - 1, g_norm_attrib);
    notepos = select_note(measure, FALSE);
    if (notepos == NULL){
        clearline(g_graph_char_v - 1, g_norm_attrib);
        return;
    }
    else{
        on_meas = notepos->measure;
        on_tick = notepos->tick;
        on_note = notepos->note;
        on_x = notepos->sprite_x;
        on_y = notepos->sprite_y;
```

```
        xsprite(cross, on_x, on_y, g_emph_color);
    }

    g_sc_refresh = 2;
    clearline(g_graph_char_v - 1, g_norm_attrib);
    writeword("Move cross hair to NOTE END, then hit return (ESC to exit)",
        1, g_graph_char_v - 1, g_norm_attrib);
    notepos = select_note(measure, FALSE);
    if (notepos == NULL){
        clearline(g_graph_char_v - 1, g_norm_attrib);
        xsprite(cross, on_x, on_y, g_emph_color);
        return;
    }
    else{
        off_meas = notepos->measure;
        off_tick = notepos->tick;
        off_x = notepos->sprite_x;
        off_y = notepos->sprite_y;
        xsprite(cross, off_x, off_y, g_emph_color);
    }
    clearline(g_graph_char_v - 1, g_norm_attrib);

    time_on = note_to_float(on_meas, on_tick);
    time_off = note_to_float(off_meas, off_tick);
    if (time_off < time_on){
        clearline(g_graph_char_v - 1, g_norm_attrib);
        writerr("Note OFF must be after note ON - No note added.",
            g_graph_char_v, g_norm_attrib, g_norm_attrib);
        xsprite(cross, on_x, on_y, g_emph_color);    /* erase cross hairs */
        xsprite(cross, off_x, off_y, g_emph_color);
        return;
    }

    status = getint(g_graph_char_v - 1, "Enter note VELOCITY (volume) (0 -
127)->",
        velp, 0, 127, g_norm_attrib, g_norm_attrib);
    if (!status)
        vel = 64;

    advance_to_measure(track, off_meas + 1);    /* make sure measures exist */

    on_event = add_event(track, on_meas, on_tick, 4, NOTE_ON +
        g_trackarray[track].midichan, on_note, vel);
    off_event = add_event(track, off_meas, off_tick, 4, NOTE_ON +
        g_trackarray[track].midichan, on_note, 0);
    notetime = add_note_time(first_notep, on_event, on_meas, on_tick,
        off_event, off_meas, off_tick);

    xsprite(cross, on_x, on_y, g_emph_color);    /* erase cross hairs */
    xsprite(cross, off_x, off_y, g_emph_color);
    draw_note(notetime, g_emph_color);                 /* show new note on screen */
```

```
        clearline(g_graph_char_v - 1, g_norm_attrib);
}


/* add an event to track data.  Measure must exist - no check for off end */
struct event far
*add_event(int track, int measure, int tick, int event_bytes, int b1, int b2,
    int b3)
{
    int time, lastime, addtime, b0;
    struct event far *ep;
    struct event far *lastep;
    struct event far *newep;
    struct event far *nextep;

    ep = advance_to_measure(track, measure + 1);    /* make sure measure */
    ep = advance_to_measure(track, measure);        /* exists, then find */

    time = 0;
    while (time <= tick){    /* find event just past tick */
        lastep = ep;
        ep = ep->next;
        b0 = ep->b[0];
        if (b0 < MAX_CLOCK){         /* if a timing byte */
            time += b0;
            lastime = b0;
        }
        else if (b0 == TIME_OUT){
            time += MAX_CLOCK;
            lastime = MAX_CLOCK;
        }
    }
    time -= lastime;    /* time now equals ticks for lastep, before ep */
    addtime = tick - time;

    nextep = ep;
    while (nextep->b[0] == TIME_OUT){    /* go past any linked TIME_OUT's */
        nextep = nextep->next;               /* nextep is first event with a */
    }                                        /* timing byte, (not a TIME_OUT). */

    if (ep->b[0] != TIME_OUT){                 /* normal case - just add event */
        lastep->next = newep = eventalloc();
        newep->next = ep;
        newep->nbytes = event_bytes;
        newep->b[0] = addtime;
        newep->b[1] = b1;
        newep->b[2] = b2;
        newep->b[3] = b3;
        ep->b[0] -= addtime;
    }                        /* next event is time_out, convert it to new event */
    else if (nextep->b[0] < addtime){
```

```
            newep = ep;
            ep->b[0] = addtime;
            ep->b[1] = b1;
            ep->b[2] = b2;
            ep->b[3] = b3;
            ep->nbytes = event_bytes;
            nextep->b[0] += MAX_CLOCK - addtime;
        }
        else{              /* next event is time_out, but still need a time_out */
            lastep->next = newep = eventalloc();
            newep->next = ep;
            newep->nbytes = event_bytes;
            newep->b[0] = addtime;
            newep->b[1] = b1;
            newep->b[2] = b2;
            newep->b[3] = b3;
            nextep->b[0] -= addtime;
        }
    return(newep);
}


/* put a new note into the note_time linked list */
struct note_time far
*add_note_time(struct note_time far *first_np, struct event far *on_event,
    int on_meas, int on_tick, struct event far *off_event, int off_meas,
    int off_tick)
{
    int first;
    struct note_time far *lastnt;
    struct note_time far *nextnt;
    struct note_time far *newnt;

    first = 1;
    lastnt = nextnt = first_np;

    while (nextnt->next != NULL && (nextnt->on_measure < on_meas ||
        nextnt->on_tick <= on_tick)){
        lastnt = nextnt;
        nextnt = nextnt->next;
        first = 0;
    }
#ifdef TURBOC
    newnt = (struct note_time far *)farmalloc(sizeof(struct note_time));
#else
    newnt = (struct note_time far *)_fmalloc(sizeof(struct note_time));
#endif
    if (newnt == NULL){
        writerr("Unable to allocate memory for note, full?", g_graph_char_v,
            g_emph_attrib, g_norm_attrib);
        return(NULL);
```

```
        }

                    /* if newnt becomes new first note_list item */
                    /* then put new data in old first item. */
    if (first){
        newnt->on_event = first_np->on_event;
        newnt->on_measure = first_np->on_measure;
        newnt->on_tick = first_np->on_tick;
        newnt->note_number = first_np->on_event->b[2];
        newnt->off_event = first_np->off_event;
        newnt->off_measure = first_np->off_measure;
        newnt->off_tick = first_np->off_tick;
        newnt->next = first_np->next;

        first_np->on_event = on_event;
        first_np->on_measure = on_meas;
        first_np->on_tick = on_tick;
        first_np->note_number = on_event->b[2];
        first_np->off_event = off_event;
        first_np->off_measure = off_meas;
        first_np->off_tick = off_tick;
        first_np->next = newnt;
        return(first_np);
    }
    else{
        newnt->on_event = on_event;
        newnt->on_measure = on_meas;
        newnt->on_tick = on_tick;
        newnt->note_number = on_event->b[2];
        newnt->off_event = off_event;
        newnt->off_measure = off_meas;
        newnt->off_tick = off_tick;
        lastnt->next = newnt;
        newnt->next = nextnt;
        return(newnt);
    }
}


/* Allow the key velocity (volume) of a note to be changed */
void
change_vel(struct note_time far *first_notep, int measure)
{
    int vel, *velp, status;
    char buf[SCRNWIDE], nbuf[10];
    struct event far *ep;
    struct note_pos *notepos;
    struct note_time far *note_t;

    velp = &vel;
```

```
    writeword("Move the cross hair to a NOTE, then hit return (ESC to exit)",
        1, g_graph_char_v - 1, g_norm_attrib);
    notepos = select_note(measure, FALSE);
    clearline(g_graph_char_v - 1, g_norm_attrib);
    if (notepos == NULL)
        return;
    else
        note_t = find_note(first_notep, notepos->note, notepos->measure,
            notepos->tick);

    ep = note_t->on_event;
    vel = ep->b[3];
    itoa(vel, nbuf, 10);
    strcpy(buf, "Note vel = ");
    strcat(buf, nbuf);
    strcat(buf, "  Enter new value (1 - 127), RET to exit.->");
    status = getint(g_graph_char_v - 1, buf, velp, 0, 127, g_norm_attrib,
        g_norm_attrib);
    clearline(g_graph_char_v - 1, g_norm_attrib);
    if (!status)
        return;
    else
        ep->b[3] = vel;
}
```

```
/* mtut1.c save and load functions */
/* `MIDI Sequencing In C', Jim Conger, M&T Books, 1989 */

#include <stdio.h>
#include <conio.h>
#include <string.h>

#include "screenf.h"
#include "standard.h"
#include "mpu401.h"
#include "mt.h"
#include "video.h"
#include "filefunc.h"
#include "mtdeclar.h"


/* Write track data to a selected file. */
void
save_song(void)
{
    int ans;
    char tempfile[14], buf[SCRNWIDE];
    FILE *stream;

    clearscreen(g_norm_attrib);
    disp_files(g_songdir, "*.sng");      /* put all song file names up */

    if (strcmpi(g_filename, DEFAULT_FILE_NAME) != 0){
        strcpy(buf, "The current song file name is: ");
        strcat(buf, g_filename);
        writeword(buf, 1, g_text_char_v - 4, g_norm_attrib);

        while(kbhit())
            getch();                /* clear input buffer */

        writeword("Keep this song file name?  (ESC to exit) (y/n):",
            1, g_text_char_v - 3, g_norm_attrib);
        ans = getche();
    }
    else{
        ans = 'N';
    }

    if(ans == ESC){
        return;
    }
    else if(toupper(ans) != 'Y'){
        while(1){
            clearline(g_text_char_v - 2, g_norm_attrib);
            getstr(g_text_char_v - 2,
                "Enter song file name for disk storage (no .SNG):",
```

```
                        tempfile, 12, g_norm_attrib);

            if(*tempfile == '\0' || *tempfile == '\n')
                return;
            if(!strchr(tempfile, '.'))/* add file extension if not present */
                strcat(tempfile, ".SNG");

            chdir(g_songdir);        /* change directory to song file area */
            stream = fopen(tempfile, "wb");     /* open file */

            if(stream == NULL){
                strcpy(buf, "Could not open library file ");
                strcat(buf, tempfile);
                writerr(buf, g_text_char_v, g_norm_attrib, g_norm_attrib);
            }
            else{
                strcpy(g_filename, tempfile);
                break;
            }
        }
    }
    else{
        chdir(g_songdir);        /* change directory to song file area */
        stream = fopen(g_filename, "wb");        /* open file */
        if(stream == NULL){
            writerr("Failed to open data file, disk problem?", g_text_char_v,
                g_norm_attrib, g_norm_attrib);
            return;
        }
    }

    save_tracks(stream);    /* write track data to file */

    fclose(stream);
    chdir(g_prodir);            /* change directory back to MT program area */
    return;
}


void
save_tracks(FILE *stream) /* workhorse function to write track data to file */
{
    int i, j, events;
    struct event far *ep;

    count_events();
    put_to_file(g_songtitle, TITLE_WIDE, stream);
    put_to_file(&g_metrate, sizeof(int), stream);
    put_to_file(&g_meter, sizeof(int), stream);
    put_to_file(&g_pitchbend, sizeof(int), stream);
    put_to_file(&g_exclusive, sizeof(int), stream);
```

```
    for (i = 0; i < NTRACK; i++){
        put_to_file(g_trackarray[i].name, TRACK_NAME_WIDE, stream);
        put_to_file(&g_trackarray[i].midichan, sizeof(int), stream);
        put_to_file(&g_trackarray[i].numevents, sizeof(long), stream);
        put_to_file(&g_trackarray[i].active, sizeof(int), stream);
        put_to_file(&g_trackarray[i].midivol, sizeof(int), stream);
    }

    for (i = 0; i < NTRACK; i++){
        events = g_trackarray[i].numevents;
        ep = g_trackarray[i].first;
        for (j = 0; j < events; j++){   /* write all five data bytes at once */
            fput_to_file(&ep->nbytes, 5, stream);
            ep = ep->next;
        }
    }
}


void
load_song(void)                     /* load a disk file into track memory */
{
    int pick, i, ans;
    long count;
    char tempfile[14], buf[SCRNWIDE], *s;
    FILE *stream;

    count = 0;      /* check if data in any track, if so warn user */
    for (i = 0; i < NTRACK; i++){
        count += g_trackarray[i].numevents;
    }
    if (count > NTRACK){
        writeword(
            "Loading a file will erase all track data in memory; OK? (y/N)->",
            1, g_text_char_v - 1, g_norm_attrib);
        ans = getche();
        if (toupper(ans) != 'Y')
            return;
        else
            erase_all();    /* user says OK, so erase all data */
    }

    pick = pick_file(g_songdir, "*.sng",
        "Select a song file to load.  ESC to escape without loading.");

    if (pick < 0){
        return;
    }

    strcpy(tempfile, g_file_disp[pick].content);
    chdir(g_songdir);                   /* change directory to song file area */
```

```
        stream = fopen(tempfile, "rb");      /* open file */
        if(stream == NULL){
            strcpy(buf, "Could not open song file ");
            strcat(buf, g_songdir);
            s = strchr(g_songdir, '\0');
            if(*--s != '\\'){
                strcat(buf, "\\");
            }
            strcat(buf, tempfile);
            writerr(buf, g_text_char_v, g_norm_attrib, g_norm_attrib);
            return;
        }

        recal_song(stream);      /* read data into memory */
        fclose(stream);          /* close file */
        chdir(g_prodir);             /* change directory back to MT program area */
        strcpy(g_filename, tempfile);   /* save file name for display */
        g_current_measure = 0;
    }


    void
    recal_song(FILE *stream)              /* do work of reading in file from disk */
    {
        int i, j, events;
        struct event far *ep;
        struct event far *lp;

        get_from_file(g_songtitle, TITLE_WIDE, stream);
        get_from_file(&g_metrate, sizeof(int), stream);
        get_from_file(&g_meter, sizeof(int), stream);
        get_from_file(&g_pitchbend, sizeof(int), stream);
        get_from_file(&g_exclusive, sizeof(int), stream);
        for (i = 0; i < NTRACK; i++){
            get_from_file(g_trackarray[i].name, TRACK_NAME_WIDE, stream);
            get_from_file(&g_trackarray[i].midichan, sizeof(int), stream);
            get_from_file(&g_trackarray[i].numevents, sizeof(long), stream);
            get_from_file(&g_trackarray[i].active, sizeof(int), stream);
            get_from_file(&g_trackarray[i].midivol, sizeof(int), stream);
        }

        /* The event lists are built for each track as the data is read off of */
        /* the disk file.  All 5 bytes for each event's data read in one shot. */
        for (i = 0; i < NTRACK; i++){
            events = g_trackarray[i].numevents;
            ep = g_trackarray[i].first = g_trackarray[i].current = eventalloc();
            for (j = 0; j < events; j++){
                fget_from_file(&ep->nbytes, 5, stream); /* read 5 bytes at once */
                lp = ep;
                ep = ep->next = eventalloc();  /* allocate space for next event */
            }
```

```
#ifdef TURBOC
        farfree(ep);
#else
        _ffree(ep);
#endif
        lp->next = NULL;
        g_trackarray[i].last = lp;
    }
}


/* Runs the help screen menu.  Selection of a topic causes another screen */
/* file to be temporarly loaded into memory and displayed. */
void
help_control(void)
{
    int pick, lastpick;

    pick = 0;
    while(1){
        clearscreen(g_norm_attrib);
        fdispchain(g_chain[4], 1, g_norm_attrib, g_text_mode);

        lastpick = pick;
        while(kbhit())
            getch();

        pick = movescrn(g_text_mode, mt4, pick, NPARAM4 - 1, g_norm_attrib,
            g_cursor_attrib);
        switch(pick){
        case(0):            /* general */
            helpdisp("mthelp1.scr");
            break;
        case(1):            /* mouse */
            helpdisp("mthelp2.scr");
            break;
        case(2):            /* file functions */
            helpdisp("mthelp3.scr");
            break;
        case(3):            /* edit */
            helpdisp("mthelp4.scr");
            break;
        case(4):            /* record */
            helpdisp("mthelp5.scr");
            break;
        case(5):            /* title */
            helpdisp("mthelp6.scr");
            break;
        case(6):            /* clear */
            helpdisp("mthelp7.scr");
            break;
```

```
        case(7):                /* import */
            helpdisp("mthelp8.scr");
            break;
        case(-2):               /* esc */
        case(8):                /* quit */
            return;
        default:
            writerr("Use arrow keys to move cursor, ret to select.",
                g_text_char_v, g_norm_attrib, g_norm_attrib);
            pick = lastpick;
        }
    }
}


/* Load and display one help screen.  Purge from memory after keypress. */
void
helpdisp(char *filename)
{
    struct strchain *chain;

    chain = inpchain(filename, SCRNWIDE);   /* read the screen */
    if(chain == NULL){
        chain = (struct strchain *) malloc(1);
        writerr("Could not open help file - probably not on disk.",
            g_text_char_v, g_emph_attrib, g_norm_attrib);
        return;
    }
    clearscreen(g_norm_attrib);
    fdispchain(chain, 1, g_norm_attrib, g_text_mode);   /* display screen */
    while(!kbhit())                         /* wait for keypress */
        ;
    dechain(chain);                         /* purge screen file from memory */
    getch();
}
```

```
/* mtut2.c save and load functions */
/* `MIDI Sequencing In C', Jim Conger, M&T Books, 1989 */

#include <stdio.h>
#include <conio.h>
#include <string.h>

#include "screenf.h"
#include "standard.h"
#include "mpu401.h"
#include "mt.h"
#include "video.h"
#include "filefunc.h"
#include "mtdeclar.h"


/* Runs the import menu for loading one track off of a disk file. */
void
import_menu(void)
{
    int source_track, dest_track, i, pick, temp_metrate, temp_meter,
        temp_pitchbend, temp_exclusive, ans;
    char tempfile[14], buf[SCRNWIDE], nbuf[10], *s,
        temp_songtitle[TITLE_WIDE];
    FILE *stream;
    struct trackdata temp_trackarray[NTRACK];

    while (1){
        pick = pick_file(g_songdir, "*.sng",
            "Select a file to use for loading track data.  ESC to quit.");
        if (pick < 0){
            return;
        }

        strcpy(tempfile, g_file_disp[pick].content);
        chdir(g_songdir);                   /* change directory to song area */
        stream = fopen(tempfile, "rb");
        if(stream == NULL){
            strcpy(buf, "Could not open song file ");
            strcat(buf, g_songdir);
            s = strchr(g_songdir, '\0');
            if(*--s != '\\'){
                strcat(buf, "\\");
            }
            strcat(buf, tempfile);
            writerr(buf, g_text_char_v, g_norm_attrib, g_norm_attrib);
                    chdir(g_prodir);
            return;
        }
        else{
            break;
```

```
        }
    }

    /* Read import file header, but not the track data (yet). */

    get_from_file(temp_songtitle, TITLE_WIDE, stream);
    get_from_file(&temp_metrate, sizeof(int), stream);
    get_from_file(&temp_meter, sizeof(int), stream);
    get_from_file(&temp_pitchbend, sizeof(int), stream);
    get_from_file(&temp_exclusive, sizeof(int), stream);
    for (i = 0; i < NTRACK; i++){
        get_from_file(temp_trackarray[i].name, TRACK_NAME_WIDE, stream);
        get_from_file(&temp_trackarray[i].midichan, sizeof(int), stream);
        get_from_file(&temp_trackarray[i].numevents, sizeof(long), stream);
        get_from_file(&temp_trackarray[i].active, sizeof(int), stream);
        get_from_file(&temp_trackarray[i].midivol, sizeof(int), stream);
    }

    /* clear screen and put import menu up */
    clearscreen(g_norm_attrib);
    fdispchain(g_chain[5], 1, g_norm_attrib, g_text_mode);

    /* put each track's name, channel and number of events on screen */

    fwriteword(temp_songtitle, 26, 5, g_emph_attrib, g_text_mode);
    for (i = 0; i < NTRACK; i++){
        fwriteword(temp_trackarray[i].name, 8 + (i * 9), 7, g_emph_attrib,
            g_text_mode);
        write_int(temp_trackarray[i].midichan + 1, 10 + (i * 9), 8,
            g_emph_attrib);
        write_int(temp_trackarray[i].numevents, 10 + (i * 9), 9,
            g_emph_attrib);
    }

    fwriteword(g_songtitle, 26, 13, g_emph_attrib, g_text_mode);
    for (i = 0; i < NTRACK; i++){
        fwriteword(g_trackarray[i].name, 8 + (i * 9), 15, g_emph_attrib,
            g_text_mode);
        write_int(g_trackarray[i].midichan + 1, 10 + (i * 9), 16,
            g_emph_attrib);
        write_int(g_trackarray[i].numevents, 10 + (i * 9), 17, g_emph_attrib);
    }

    if (temp_meter != g_meter){      /* warn if the meters do not match */
        strcpy(buf, "Note: Song in memory has meter = ");
        itoa(g_meter, nbuf, 10);
        strcat(buf, nbuf);
        strcat(buf, ", Source meter = ");
        itoa(temp_meter, nbuf, 10);
        strcat(buf, nbuf);
        writerr(buf, g_text_char_v, g_norm_attrib, g_norm_attrib);
```

```
        }


    pick = source_track = dest_track = 0;
    show_source(source_track);        /* highlight the default source and */
    show_dest(dest_track);            /* destination tracks on menu */

    /* Source and destination track selection rows on the import screen */
    /* are elements of the mt51[] and mt52 menus.  finitscrn() is used to */
    /* display the items.  Changed selections are made by updating the */
    /* menu's "content" fields in show_source() and show_dest(). */

    while (1){
        finitscrn(mt51, 0, NTRACK - 1, g_emph_attrib, g_text_mode);
        finitscrn(mt52, 0, NTRACK - 1, g_emph_attrib, g_text_mode);
        finitscrn(mt5, 0, NPARAM5 - 1, g_emph_attrib, g_text_mode);

        pick = movescrn(g_text_mode, mt5, pick, NPARAM5 - 1,
            g_emph_attrib, g_cursor_attrib);
        switch(pick){
        case(0):         /* pick source track */
            source_track = movescrn(g_text_mode, mt51, dest_track,
                NTRACK - 1, g_emph_attrib, g_cursor_attrib);
            if (source_track >= 0)
                show_source(source_track);
            break;
        case(1):         /* pick dest track */
            dest_track = movescrn(g_text_mode, mt52, source_track,
                NTRACK - 1, g_emph_attrib, g_cursor_attrib);
            if (dest_track >= 0)
                show_dest(dest_track);
            break;
        case(2):         /* import selected track */
            while(kbhit())
                getch();
            if (g_trackarray[dest_track].numevents > 1){
                writeword(
                    "Existing data in Dest track will be written over. OK?",
                    1, g_text_char_v - 1, g_norm_attrib);
                ans = getche();
                clearline(g_text_char_v - 1, g_norm_attrib);
                if (toupper(ans) != 'Y'){
                    break;
                }
            }
            clearline(g_text_char_v - 1, g_norm_attrib);
            writeword("Importing track data...", 1, g_text_char_v - 1,
                g_norm_attrib);
            import_track(stream, source_track, dest_track,
                temp_trackarray);
            fclose(stream);
```

```
                            chdir(g_prodir);
                g_current_measure = 0;
                change_channel(dest_track, g_trackarray[dest_track].midichan);
                return;
            case(3):          /* quit */
            case(-2):         /* ESC key */
                fclose(stream);
                            chdir(g_prodir);
                return;
        }
    }
}


/* Reads in one track's data by skipping over track data on disk for prior */
/* tracks, then building a new event list for the selected track as the */
/* data is being read off of the disk.   Old data on dest. track is purged. */
void
import_track(FILE *stream, int source_track, int dest_track,
    struct trackdata temp_trackarray[])
{
    int i, j, events;
    struct event far *ep;
    struct event far *lp;

    lp = eventalloc();                  /* lp points to a safe place */
    ep = g_trackarray[dest_track].first;
    clear_events(ep->next);             /* erase existing data in track */
    g_trackarray[dest_track].current = ep;

    for (i = 0; i < source_track; i++){    /* run though data ahead of */
        events = temp_trackarray[i].numevents;  /* source track */
        for (j = 0; j < events; j++){
            fget_from_file(&lp->nbytes, 5, stream);
        }
    }                   /* each event is copied to over the lp memory area */

#ifdef TURBOC
    farfree(lp);    /* no longer need dummy lp event to write over */
#else
    _ffree(lp);
#endif
                                        /* read source track into memory */
    events = temp_trackarray[source_track].numevents;
    for (j = 0; j < events; j++){
        fget_from_file(&ep->nbytes, 5, stream);
        lp = ep;
        ep = ep->next = eventalloc();    /* add new events to list for data */
    }
#ifdef TURBOC
    farfree(ep);
```

```
#else
    _ffree(ep);
#endif
    lp->next = NULL;
    g_trackarray[dest_track].last = lp;
    g_trackarray[dest_track].numevents = events;
    g_trackarray[dest_track].midivol = 100;
}


void
show_source(int track)              /* update import menu for selected track */
{
    int i;

    for (i = 0; i < NTRACK; i++){
        if (i == track)
            strcpy(mt51[i].content, "*Source*");
        else
            strcpy(mt51[i].content, "        ");
    }
}


void
show_dest(int track)                /* update import menu for destination track */
{
    int i;

    for (i = 0; i < NTRACK; i++){
        if (i == track)
            strcpy(mt52[i].content, "**Dest**");
        else
            strcpy(mt52[i].content, "        ");
    }
}
```

```
/* mt_to_mf.c  converts MT song files to Standard MIDI Files 1.0 format */
/* `MIDI Sequencing In C', Jim Conger, M&T Books, 1989 */

/* #define TURBOC  1   Define if using Turbo C, leave out for Microsoft C */

#include <stdio.h>
#include <string.h>

#ifdef TURBOC
    #include <alloc.h>
#else
    #include <malloc.h>
#endif

#define NTRACK            8
#define TITLE_WIDE        51
#define TRACK_NAME_WIDE   9
#define NBYTES            30000    /* default track data buffer */
#define TIME_OUT          0xF8
#define ALL_END           0xFC

#define META              0xFF     /* meta event codes */
#define TEXTEVENT         01
#define SEQNAME           03
#define INSNAME           04
#define CHANPREF          0x20
#define ENDTRACK          0x2F
#define SETTEMPO          0x51
#define TIMESIG           0X58

/* function prototypes */

void write_buf(char *sp, char *ep, FILE *outfile);  /* function prototypes */
char *copy_var_len(long n, char *cp);
void put_to_file(void *addr, int size, FILE *stream);
void put_len(long n, FILE *stream);
void write_mthd(int ntrack, FILE *outfile);
void get_from_file(void *addr, int size, FILE *stream);
FILE *open_file(char *filename, char *status);

void
main(argc, argv)
int argc;
char *argv[];
{
    char title[TITLE_WIDE], trackname[NTRACK][TRACK_NAME_WIDE];
    unsigned char *buf, *cp, *cp1, b[4], runstatus;
    int metrate, meter, ntrack, trk, midichan[NTRACK], i, n, at_end;
    long eventcount[NTRACK], event, ticks, msec_qnote;
    FILE *infile, *outfile;

    if (argc < 3){
        fputs("\nUsage:  mt_to_mf  infile  outfile", stdout);
        fputs("\nWhere infile is the MT .SNG file name;", stdout);
```

```
        fputs("\n outfile is the Standard MIDI file name for output.",
stdout);
      exit(0);
   }

  infile = open_file(argv[1], "rb");      /* open the files specified on */
  outfile = open_file(argv[2], "wb");     /* the command line. */

  /* All of the data is first written to a memory buffer called buf. */
  /* When conversion is complete, the buffer is written to disk. */
  /* This allows the length of the buffer to be know prior to writing. */

  buf = (char *)malloc(NBYTES);
  if (buf == NULL){
     fputs("\nCould not allocate memory for track data.", stdout);
     exit(0);
  }

  get_from_file(title, TITLE_WIDE, infile);   /* read infile header data */
  get_from_file(&metrate, sizeof(int), infile);
  get_from_file(&meter, sizeof(int), infile);
  get_from_file(&n, sizeof(int), infile);      /* ignore pitchbend flag */
  get_from_file(&n, sizeof(int), infile);      /* ignore exclusive flag */

  for (i = 0; i < NTRACK; i++){
     get_from_file(trackname[i], TRACK_NAME_WIDE, infile);
     get_from_file(&midichan[i], sizeof(int), infile);
     get_from_file(&eventcount[i], sizeof(long), infile);
     get_from_file(&n, sizeof(int), infile); /* ignore play status */
     get_from_file(&n, sizeof(int), infile); /* ignore midi volume */
  }

  fputs("\nConverting to MIDI Files Format...\n", stdout);

  ntrack = 0;
  for (i = 0; i < NTRACK; i++){   /* find number of tracks with data */
     if (eventcount[i] > 1)
        ntrack++;
  }
  write_mthd(ntrack + 1, outfile);     /* put header chunck to outfile */

  cp = buf;            /* cp points to start of allocated memory area */

  *cp++ = 0;           /* time sig., tempo and title track added first */
  *cp++ = META;        /* note that data is written to buffer. */
  *cp++ = TIMESIG;
  *cp++ = 4;
  *cp++ = (char)meter;
  *cp++ = 2;           /* MT always uses quarter note for beat, etc. */
  *cp++ = 24;
  *cp++ = 8;
```

```
*cp++ = 0;
*cp++ = META;          /* tempo, most significant bytes first */
*cp++ = SETTEMPO;
msec_qnote = 60000000/metrate;     /* a long data type (4 bytes) */
cp1 = (char *)&msec_qnote;         /* cp1 points to long's memory area */
*cp++ = 3;                         /* 3 is fixed value for this META */
*cp++ = *(cp1 + 2);                /* write value in correct order */
*cp++ = *(cp1 + 1);                /* opposite to the 80x86 convention */
*cp++ = *cp1;

*cp++ = 0;                         /* song name as meta text event */
*cp++ = META;
*cp++ = TEXTEVENT;
*cp++ = TITLE_WIDE;
strcpy(cp, title);                 /* title copied in one shot */
cp += TITLE_WIDE;                  /* update pointer */

*cp++ = 0;                         /* end of title meta event */
*cp++ = META;
*cp++ = ENDTRACK;
*cp++ = 0;

put_to_file("MTrk", 4, outfile);      /* write first track chunk */
put_len((long)(cp - buf), outfile);   /* write computed buffer length */
write_buf(buf, cp, outfile);          /* write whole buffer at once */

for (trk = 0; trk < NTRACK; trk++){
    if (eventcount[trk] > 1){
        cp = buf;              /* cp points back to start of memory buffer */
        *cp++ = 0;             /* track name as meta instrument name event */
        *cp++ = META;
        *cp++ = INSNAME;
        *cp++ = TRACK_NAME_WIDE;
        strcpy(cp, trackname[trk]);
        cp += TRACK_NAME_WIDE;

        *cp++ = 0;             /* track channel as MIDI channel prefix */
        *cp++ = META;
        *cp++ = CHANPREF;
        *cp++ = 1;
        *cp++ = midichan[trk];

        at_end = ticks = event = 0;
        runstatus = 0;
        while (event++ < eventcount[trk] && !at_end){
            fgetc(infile);
            for (i = 0; i < 4; i++){
                b[i] = (char) fgetc(infile);
            }
            if (b[1] == ALL_END)
                at_end = 1;
            else if (b[0] == TIME_OUT)
```

```
                                ticks += 240;
                        else{                    /* convert event data to files format */
                                ticks += b[0];
                                if (b[1] >= 0x80 && b[1] <= 0xEF){   /* if MIDI channel */
                                        cp = copy_var_len(ticks, cp);   /* voice message */
                                        if (b[1] == runstatus)        /* check running status */
                                                ;
                                        else
                                                *cp++ = b[1];
                                        *cp++ = b[2];
                                        if (b[1] < 0xC0 || b[1] >= 0xE0)
                                                *cp++ = b[3];              /* if four byte message */
                                        ticks = 0;
                                        runstatus = b[1];
                                }
                        }
                        if (cp - buf + 3 >= NBYTES){
                                fputs("\nTrack shortened, out of buffer space.", stdout);
                                break;
                        }
                }
                *cp++ = 0;
                *cp++ = META;
                *cp++ = ENDTRACK;
                *cp++ = 0;

                put_to_file("MTrk", 4, outfile);    /* write track chunk */
                put_len((long)(cp - buf), outfile); /* write data length */
                write_buf(buf, cp, outfile);        /* write all data at once */
        }
    } /* for (trk... */
    fclose(infile);                               /* close files and exit to dos */
    fclose(outfile);
    fputs("\nData conversion completed.", stdout);
    exit(0);
}

void
write_buf(sp, ep, outfile)
char *sp, *ep;
FILE *outfile;
{
    while (sp != ep)
        fputc(*sp++, outfile);
}

char
*copy_var_len(n, cp)
long n;
char *cp;
{
    register long buffer;
```

```
    buffer = n & 0x7F;
    while ((n >>= 7) > 0){
        buffer <<= 8;
        buffer |= 0x80;
        buffer += (n & 0x7F);
    }

    while (buffer & 0x80){
        *cp++ = (char) buffer;
        buffer >>= 8;
    }
    *cp++ = (char) buffer;
    return(cp);
}


void
put_len(n, stream)        /* chunk lengths are always 4 bytes long */
long n;
FILE *stream;
{
    char *cp;

    cp = (char *)&n;
    fputc(*(cp + 3), stream);
    fputc(*(cp + 2), stream);
    fputc(*(cp + 1), stream);
    fputc(*cp, stream);
}



void
write_mthd(ntrack, outfile)      /* write header chunk to output file */
int ntrack;
FILE *outfile;
{
    int i, n;

    put_to_file("MThd", 4, outfile);            /* MThd = chunk type */
    n = 0;
    for (i = 0; i < 3; i++)
        put_to_file(&n, 1, outfile);
    n = 6;
    put_to_file(&n, 1, outfile);                /* 00 00 00 06 = lenght*/
    n = 0;
    put_to_file(&n, 1, outfile);
    n = 1;
    put_to_file(&n, 1, outfile);                /* 00 01 = format */
    n = 0;
    put_to_file(&n, 1, outfile);
```

411

```
    put_to_file(&ntrack, 1, outfile);          /* 00 0n = number of tracks */
    put_to_file(&n, 1, outfile);
    n = 120;
    put_to_file(&n, 1, outfile);               /* 00 78 = 120 ticks/Q note */
}


void
get_from_file(addr, size, stream)    /* get data from stream, put into near */
void *addr;                          /* memory */
int size;
FILE *stream;
{
    int i;
    char *addr2;

    addr2 = (char *)addr;
    for(i = 0; i < size; i++){
        *addr2++ = fgetc(stream);
    }
}


void
put_to_file(addr, size, stream)      /* put near data to stream */
void *addr;
int size;
FILE *stream;
{
    int i;
    char *addr2;

    addr2 = (char *)addr;
    for(i = 0; i < size; i++){
        fputc(*addr2++, stream);
    }
}


FILE
*open_file(filename, status)
char *filename, *status;
{
    FILE *file;

    file = fopen(filename, status);
    if (file == NULL){
        fputs("\nCould not open file ", stdout);
        fputs(filename, stdout);
        fputc('\n', stdout);
        exit(0);
    }
    return(file);
}
```

```
/* videofnc.c   compiler graphics library dependent functions */
/* `MIDI Sequencing In C', Jim Conger, M&T Books, 1989 */

/* #define TURBOC 1    Define if using TURBOC, leave out for Microsoft */

#include <stdio.h>
#include <conio.h>

#ifdef TURBOC
    #include <graphics.h>
#else
    #include <graph.h>
#endif

#include "standard.h"
#include "screenf.h"
#include "video.h"

/* write string to x,y on screen.  Colors determinded by attrib. */
/* slow version using library functions */
void
writeword(char *string, int x, int y, int attrib)
{
#ifdef TURBOC
    textattr(attrib);
    gotoxy(x, y);
    cputs(string);
#else
    _setbkcolor((long)(attrib & 0x00F0) >> 4);
    _settextcolor(attrib & 0x000F);
    _settextposition(y, x);
    _outtext(string);
#endif
}


void
clearscreen(int attrib)        /* clears screen and homes cursor */
{
#ifdef TURBOC
    textattr(attrib);
    clrscr();
#else
    _setbkcolor((long)(attrib & 0xF0) >> 4);
    _settextcolor(attrib & 0x000F);
    _clearscreen(_GCLEARSCREEN);
    _settextposition(1, 1);
#endif
}

void
clearline(int lineno, int attrib)                /* blank out a line */
```

```
{
    static char buf[] = "
";

#ifdef TURBOC
    textattr(attrib);
    gotoxy(1, lineno);
    cputs(buf);
#else
    _setbkcolor((long)(attrib & 0x00F0) >> 4);
    _settextcolor(attrib & 0x000F);
    _settextposition(lineno, 0);
    _outtext(buf);
#endif
}

void
csrplot(int x, int y)       /* moves text cursor to x, y on screen */
{
#ifdef TURBOC
    gotoxy(x, y);
#else
    _settextposition(x, y);
#endif
}

void
setvideomode(int mode)      /* sets the video mode for screen output */
{
#ifdef TURBOC
    int gdriver, gmode, gerror;

    if (mode <= 3 || mode == 7){
        closegraph();
        textmode(mode);
        directvideo = 1;    /* use direct video RAM output */
    }
    else{   /* use Turbo C's ability to find highest res. graph mode */
        detectgraph(&gdriver, &gmode);
        if (gdriver < 0){
            writerr("Did not detect graphics hardware.", g_text_char_v,
                g_norm_attrib, g_emph_attrib);
            return;
        }
        switch (gdriver){   /* translate BIOS mode #'s to Turbo C codes */
        case (EGA):
        case (EGA64):
            if (mode == 15)
                gmode = 1;
            else
                gmode = 0;
```

```
                break;
        case (EGAMONO):
            gmode = 3;
            break;
        case (HERCMONO):
            gmode = 0;
            break;
        case (VGA):
            if (mode == 14)
                gmode = 0;
            else if (mode == 18)
                gmode = 2;
            else
                gmode = 1;
            break;
        case (CGA):
        case (MCGA):
            gmode = 4;
            break;
        default:
            gmode = 0;
        }
        initgraph(&gdriver, &gmode, "");
        gerror = graphresult();
        if (gerror < 0){
            writerr("Could not enter default graphics mode.", g_text_char_v,
                g_norm_attrib, g_emph_attrib);
            return;
        }
        directvideo = 0;     /* use BIOS calls during graphics output*/
    }
#else
        _setvideomode(mode);
#endif
}


void
dotplot(int x, int y, int color) /* sets one pixel color on screen at x, y */
{
#ifdef TURBOC
    putpixel(x, y, color);
#else
    _setcolor(color);
    _setpixel(x, y);
#endif
}

/* draws a rectangle on screen from top left x1,y1 to bot right x2,y2 */
/* if fill != 0, retangle area is filled in; else just border drawn */
void
draw_rectangle(int fill, int x1, int y1, int x2, int y2, int color)
```

```
{
#ifdef TURBOC
    if (fill){
        setfillstyle(SOLID_FILL, color);
        bar(x1, y1, x2, y2);
    }
    else{
        setcolor(color);
        setlinestyle(SOLID_LINE, 0xFFFF, NORM_WIDTH);
        rectangle(x1, y1, x2, y2);
    }
#else
    _setcolor(color);
    if (fill)
        _rectangle(_GFILLINTERIOR, x1, y1, x2, y2);
    else
        _rectangle(_GBORDER, x1, y1, x2, y2);
#endif
}


/* draws a line between x1,y1 and x2,y2 with given color */
void
drawline(int x1, int y1, int x2, int y2, int color)
{
#ifdef TURBOC
    setcolor(color);
    moveto(x1, y1);
    lineto(x2, y2);
#else
    _setcolor(color);
    _moveto(x1, y1);
    _lineto(x2, y2);
#endif
}


/* underline a string at character location x,y (not pixel x,y) */
/* mode is video mode - used to determine charater heights in pixels */
void
wordul(int mode, char *string, int x, int y, int color)
{
    int chary, charx, ypos, xpos, xorcolor, nchar, dotnow;

    switch(mode){
    case(7):
        chary = 16;
        charx = 9;
        break;
    case(15):
    case(16):
        chary = 14;
        charx = 8;
```

```
            break;
    case(17):
    case(18):
        chary = 16;
        charx = 8;
        break;
    default:
        chary = 8;
        charx = 8;
    }
    ypos = (y * chary) - 1;
    xpos = (x - 1) * charx;

#ifdef TURBOC
    dotnow = getpixel(xpos, ypos);
#else
    dotnow = _getpixel(xpos, ypos);
#endif
    xorcolor = dotnow ^ color;
    nchar = 0;
    while (*string++)
        nchar++;

    drawline(xpos, ypos, xpos + (nchar * charx), ypos, xorcolor);
}


/* draw sprite on screen at xpos,ypos */
void
draw_sprite(struct sprite spr, int xpos, int ypos, int line_color,
    int back_color)
{
    int i, j, k, x, y;
    char *sp;
    unsigned int drawbyte, dotput;

    y = ypos;
    sp = spr.sdata;

    for(i = 0; i < spr.stall; i++){
        x = xpos;
        for(j = 0; j < spr.swide; j++){
            drawbyte = *sp++;
            for(k = 0; k < 8; k++){
                dotput = (drawbyte & 0x80);
#ifdef TURBOC
                if (dotput)
                    putpixel(x++, y, line_color);
                else
                    putpixel(x++, y, back_color);
#else
```

```
                    if(dotput)
                        _setcolor(line_color);
                    else
                        _setcolor(back_color);
                    _setpixel(x++, y);
#endif
                    drawbyte <<= 1;
            }
        }
        y++;
    }
}


/* XOR sprite on screen at xpos,ypos */
/* color is color spite is to have over a black background */
void
xsprite(struct sprite spr, int xpos, int ypos, int color)
{
    int i, j, k, x, y;
    unsigned int drawbyte, dotnow;
    char *sp;

    y = ypos;
    sp = spr.sdata;

    for(i = 0; i < spr.stall; i++){
        x = xpos;
        for(j = 0; j < spr.swide; j++){
            drawbyte = *sp++;
            for(k = 0; k < 8; k++){
                if(drawbyte & 0x80){
#ifdef TURBOC
                    dotnow = getpixel(x, y);
                    putpixel(x, y, dotnow ^ color);  /* XOR color */
#else
                    dotnow = _getpixel(x, y);
                    _setcolor(dotnow ^ color);
                    _setpixel(x, y);
#endif
                }
                x++;
                drawbyte <<= 1;
            }
        }
        y++;
    }
}
```

```
/* writscrn.c  utilities to write chars to any position on screen */
/* uses hi res cursor functions in linedraw.c */
/* `MIDI Sequencing In C', Jim Conger, M&T Books, 1989 */

#include <stdio.h>
#include <conio.h>
#include <string.h>

#include "screenf.h"
#include "standard.h"


/* Moves highlighted cursor block based on arrow key input.  first is the */
/* menu array element to start on, last is the last (usually the number of */
/* array elements in the the menu deffinition - 1). */
/* Menu definition is in scrnarray[] (see MTSCREEN.H) */
/* Returns element no selected, -2 for ESC, -3 for help (?), -1 on error. */
int
movescrn(int vidmode, struct selement scrnarray[], int first, int last,
    int normal, int hilit)
{
    int c, k, i, oldk, curskey;

    if (first < 0)
        first = 0;
    i = k = first;
    to_new_csr(vidmode, scrnarray, k, -1, normal, hilit);

    while(1){
        oldk = k;
        while(kbhit())                /* clear keyboard buffer */
            getch();
        while(!kbhit())               /* wait for new keypress */
            ;

        if(c = getch()){              /* check for cursor keypress code 0 */
            curskey = 0;
        }
        else{
            curskey = 1;
            c = getch();      /* note null char and get next */
        }

        if(!curskey){         /* advance to first matching char */
            switch(c){
            case BACKSP:
                k = scrnarray[k].nleft;
                break;
            case TAB:
                k = scrnarray[k].nright;
                break;
```

```
                    case ESC:
                        return(-2);
                    case CR:
                    case '+':
                        to_new_csr(vidmode, scrnarray, k, -1, normal, hilit);
                        return(k);
                    }
                    if (i >= last || i <= 0)
                        i = 0;
                    else
                        i++;
                    for(; i <= last; i++){        /* see if letter matches command */
                        if(toupper(c) == toupper(*(scrnarray[i].content))){
                            k = i;
                            break;
                        }
                    }
                    if (k != i && oldk != 0){   /* if no match, but started after */
                        for(i = 0; i <= last; i++){   /* first element - try again */
                            if(toupper(c) == toupper(*(scrnarray[i].content))){
                                k = i;
                                break;
                            }
                        }
                    }
                }
            else{            /* must be cursor key */
                switch(c){
                case KUP:
                    k = scrnarray[k].nup;
                    break;
                case KDOWN:
                    k = scrnarray[k].ndown;
                    break;
                case KLEFT:
                    k = scrnarray[k].nleft;
                    break;
                case KRIGHT:
                    k = scrnarray[k].nright;
                    break;
                case KHOME:
                case KPGUP:
                    k = 0;
                    break;
                case KEND:
                case KPGDN:
                    k = last;
                    break;
                }
            }
            to_new_csr(vidmode, scrnarray, k, oldk, normal, hilit);
```

```
        }
    return(k);
}




/* Move highlight to new active menu item.  Uses vimode (video mode) to */
/* determine if in graphics or character mode.  In graphics modes the */
/* string is underlined.  In char. modes the string is switched from */
/* normal to hilit video attribute.  k is scrnarray[] element number. */
/* oldk is last item highlighted - now needs to be unhighlighted.  A -1 */
/* value for oldk skips the unhighlighting step (first time on menu). */
void
to_new_csr(int vidmode, struct selement scrnarray[], int k, int oldk,
    int normal, int hilit)
{
    if(vidmode < 4 || vidmode == 7){      /* char mode */
        if (oldk != -1){                  /* if not first time initialization */
            writeword(scrnarray[oldk].content, scrnarray[oldk].xpos,
                scrnarray[oldk].ypos, normal);
        }
        writeword(scrnarray[k].content, scrnarray[k].xpos,
            scrnarray[k].ypos, hilit);
    }
    else{                              /* graphics mode */
        if (oldk != -1){                  /* if not first time initialization */
            wordul(vidmode, scrnarray[oldk].content, scrnarray[oldk].xpos,
                scrnarray[oldk].ypos, hilit & 0x000F);
        }
        wordul(vidmode, scrnarray[k].content, scrnarray[k].xpos,
            scrnarray[k].ypos, hilit & 0x000F);
    }
}


/* Put an error message on screen, wait for keypress, then clear line. */
/* String s is written on line lineno with hilit attribute.  After the */
/* user hits a key the line is cleared using normal attribute. */
void
writerr(char *s, int lineno, int normal, int hilit)
{
    char c, str[SCRNWIDE + 1];

    while(kbhit())
        getch();

    clearline(lineno, normal);
    strcpy(str, s);
    strcat(str, " [Hit a key]");
    writeword(str, 1, lineno, hilit);
```

```
    while(!kbhit())                      /* wait for keypress */
            ;

    clearline(lineno, normal);
}


/* Writes the menu item strings on the screen in color attrib.  Starts */
/* on scrnarray[] element first, goes to last. */
/* bios screen write (slow) version - works in all video modes. */
void
initscrn(struct selement scrnarray[], int first, int last, int attrib)
{
    int k;

    for(k = first; k <= last; k++){
        writeword(scrnarray[k].content, scrnarray[k].xpos, scrnarray[k].ypos,
            attrib);
    }
}


/* direct video (fast) version of initscrn - only for char modes. */
void
finitscrn(struct selement scrnarray[], int first, int last, int attrib,
    int mode)
{
    int k;

    for(k = first; k <= last; k++){
        fwriteword(scrnarray[k].content, scrnarray[k].xpos, scrnarray[k].ypos,
            attrib, mode);
    }
}


/* Write string to x,y on screen, writes to screen memory directly */
/* String is written with color attrib. */
void
fwriteword(char *string, int x, int y, int attrib, int mode)
{
    unsigned int offset;

    x--;           /* To conform with library convention of having */
    y--;           /* the first row and column position be 1,1 not 0,0. */

    offset = (x * 2) + (y * SCRNWIDE * 2);

    while(*string != '\n' && *string){
        if (mode <= 6){
            *(char far *)(CVIDMEM + (offset++)) = *string++;
```

```
            *(char far *)(CVIDMEM + (offset++)) = attrib;
        }
        else if (mode == 7){
            *(char far *)(HVIDMEM + (offset++)) = *string++;
            *(char far *)(HVIDMEM + (offset++)) = attrib;
        }
        else {
            *(char far *)(EVIDMEM + (offset++)) = *string++;
            *(char far *)(EVIDMEM + (offset++)) = attrib;
        }
    }
}


void                        /* put an integer value on screen at x,y */
write_int(int value, int x, int y, int attrib)
{
    char buf[10];

    itoa(value, buf, 10);
    writeword(buf, x, y, attrib);
}
```

```
; MIO401.ASM   c calls for mpu-401 input/output. Medium memory model version.

DATAPORT   EQU      330H      ;MPU401 DATA PORT
STATPORT   EQU      331H      ;MPU401 STATUS PORT
DRR        EQU      040H
MPUACK     EQU      0FEH      ;MPU401 CODES: ACKNOWLEGE

TRIES      EQU      0FFH      ;MAXIMUM TRIES ON GETTING RESPONSE FROM 401
;-------------------------------------------------------------------
PUBLIC _getdata, _putdata, _putcmd
;-------------------------------------------------------------------

SAVSTK  MACRO                 ;MACRO TO SAVE REGS FOR C FUNCTION
        PUSH     BP
        MOV      BP,SP
        PUSH     DI
        PUSH     SI
        ENDM

RCLSTK  MACRO                 ;MACRO TO RECALL SAVED REGS FOR C
        POP      SI
        POP      DI
        MOV      SP,BP
        POP      BP
        ENDM


;-------------------------------------------------------------------

DOSSEG
.MODEL medium

.DATA
; no near data

.FARDATA
; no far data

.CODE
;-------------------------------------------------------------------
;       putcmd(n)
;       output a byte of data to MPU401, check for acknowledge

_putcmd PROC far
        SAVSTK
        MOV      DX,STATPORT
        MOV      CX,TRIES       ;RETRY COUNTER IN CL
LBL1:   IN       AL,DX          ;READ STATUS
        TEST     AL,DRR         ;FIND IF BIT 6 = 1
        JZ       LBL2           ;OK SO CONTINUE
        DEC      CX
        CMP      CX,1           ;USED UP ALL TRIES?
```

```
        JGE     LBL1            ;RETRY
        MOV     AX,-1
        JMP     LBL5            ;QUIT RETURNING -1

LBL2:
        MOV     AX,[BP+6]       ;PUT CHAR (AS INT) IN AX (AL)
        OUT     DX,AL           ;OUTPUT CHAR

        MOV     CX,TRIES
LBL3:   IN      AL,DX           ;READ STATUS
        ROL     AL,1            ;PUT BIT 7 TO CARRY
        JNB     LBL4            ;IF CARRY <> 1, NOT READY
        DEC     CX
        CMP     CX,1            ;USED UP ALL TRIES?
        JGE     LBL3            ;RETRY
        MOV     AX,-1
        JMP     LBL5            ;QUIT RETURNING -1

LBL4:   MOV     DX,DATAPORT     ;ELSE READ DATA
        IN      AL,DX
        CMP     AL,MPUACK
        JZ      LBL5            ;GOT ACK SO RETURN
        MOV     AX,-1           ;IF NOT, RETURN -1
LBL5:
        RCLSTK
        RET
_putcmd ENDP


;---------------------------------------------------------------
;       getdata()
;       get a byte of data from MPU401

_getdata PROC far
        SAVSTK
        MOV     DX,STATPORT
        MOV     CX,TRIES        ;RETRY COUNTER IN CL
LBL6:   IN      AL,DX           ;READ STATUS
        ROL     AL,1            ;PUT BIT 7 TO CARRY
        JNB     LBL7            ;IF CARRY <> 1, NOT READY
        DEC     CX
        CMP     CX,1            ;USED UP ALL TRIES?
        JGE     LBL6            ;RETRY
        MOV     AX,-1
        JMP     GEND            ;QUIT RETURNING -1

LBL7:   MOV     DX,DATAPORT     ;ELSE READ DATA
        MOV     AH,0            ;CLEAR AH FOR C RETURN
        IN      AL,DX
GEND:   RCLSTK
        RET
_getdata ENDP
```

```
;-----------------------------------------------------------------
;       putdata()
;       send a byte of data to MPU401

_putdata PROC far
        SAVSTK
        MOV     DX,STATPORT
        MOV     CX,TRIES        ;RETRY COUNTER IN CL
LBL8:   IN      AL,DX           ;READ STATUS
        TEST    AL,DRR          ;TEST BIT 6
        JZ      LBL9            ;OK SO CONTINUE
        DEC     CX
        CMP     CX,1            ;USED UP ALL TRIES?
        JGE     LBL8            ;RETRY
        MOV     AX,-1
        JMP     LBL10           ;QUIT RETURNING -1

LBL9:   MOV     DX,DATAPORT
        MOV     AX,[BP+6]       ;PUT DATA IN AX (AL)
        OUT     DX,AL
LBL10:  RCLSTK
        RET
_putdata ENDP

        END
```

Appendix 1

MIDI Note Numbers and Percussion Sound Assignments for the MT-32

Decimal	Hex	Note Name	
0	0	C - 5	**Lowest Note** – 5 octaves below Middle C
1	1	C#/Db - 5	
2	2	D - 5	
3	3	D#/Eb - 5	
4	4	E - 5	
5	5	F - 5	
6	6	F#/Gb - 5	
7	7	G - 5	
8	8	G#/Ab - 5	
9	9	A - 5	
10	A	A#/Bb - 5	
11	B	B - 5	
12C	C	- 4	
13	D	C#/Db - 4	
14	E	D - 4	
15	F	D#/Eb - 4	
16	10	E - 4	
17	11	F - 4	
18	12	F#/Gb - 4	
19	13	G - 4	
20	14	G#/Ab - 4	
21	15	A - 4	
22	16	A#/Bb - 4	
23	17	B - 4	

Decimal	Hex	Note Name	
24	18	C - 3	
25	19	C#/Db - 3	
26	1A	D - 3	
27	1B	D#/Eb - 3	
28	1C	E - 3	
29	1D	F - 3	
30	1E	F#/Gb - 3	
31	1F	G - 3	
32	20	G#/Ab - 3	
33	21	A - 3	
34	22	A#/Bb - 3	— Percussion Assignments —
35	23	B - 3	
36	24	C - 2	Acoustic Bass Drum
37	25	C#/Db - 2	Rim Shot
38	26	D - 2	Acoustic Snare Drum
39	27	D#/Eb - 2	Hand Clap
40	28	E - 2	Electric Snare Drum
41	29	F - 2	Acoustic Low Tom
42	2A	F#/Gb - 2	Closed High Hat
43	2B	G - 2	Acoustic Low Tom
44	2C	G#/Ab - 2	Open High Hat 2
45	2D	A - 2	Acoustic Mid Tom
46	2E	A#/Bb - 2	Open High Hat 1
47	2F	B - 2	Acoustic Mid Tom
48	30	C - 1	Acoustic High Tom
49	31	C#/Db - 1	Crash Cymbal
50	32	D - 1	Acoustic High Tom
51	33	D#/Eb - 1	Ride Cymbal
52	34	E - 1	
53	35	F - 1	
54	36	F#/Gb - 1	Tambourine
55	37	G - 1	
56	38	G#/Ab - 1	Cowbell
57	39	A - 1	
58	3A	A#/Bb - 1	

428

Decimal	Hex	Note Name	
59	3B	B - 1	
60	3C	**C Middle**	High Bongo
61	3D	C#/Db 1	Low Bongo
62	3E	D 1	Muted High Congo
63	3F	D#/Eb 1	High Congo
64	40	E 1	Low Conga
65	41	F 1	High Timbale
66	42	F#/Gb 1	Low Timbale
67	43	G 1	High Agogo
68	44	G#/Ab 1	Low Agogo
69	45	A 1	Cabasa
70	46	A#/Bb 1	Maracas
71	47	B 1	Samba Whistle High
72	48	C 2	Samba Whistle Low
73	49	C#/Db 2	Quijada
74	4A	D 2	Claves
75	4B	D#/Eb 2	
76	4C	E 2	
77	4D	F 2	
78	4E	F#/Gb 2	
79	4F	G 2	
80	50	G#/Ab 2	
81	51	A 2	
82	52	A#/Bb 2	
83	53	B 2	
84	54	C 3	
85	55	C#/Db 3	
86	56	D 3	
87	57	D#/Eb 3	
88	58	E 3	
89	59	F 3	
90	5A	F#/Gb 3	
91	5B	G 3	

Decimal	Hex	Note Name
92	5C	G#/Ab 3
93	5D	A 3
94	5E	A#/Bb 3
95	5F	B 3
96	60	C 4
97	61	C#/Db 4
98	62	D 4
99	63	D#/Eb 4
100	64	E 4
101	65	F 4
102	66	F#/Gb 4
103	67	G 4
104	68	G#/Ab 4
105	69	A 4
106	6A	A#/Bb 4
107	6B	B 4
108	6C	C 5
109	6D	C#/Db 5
110	6E	D 5
111	6F	D#/Eb 5
112	70	E 5
113	71	F 5
114	72	F#/Gb 5
115	73	G 5
116	74	G#/Ab 5
117	75	A 5
118	76	A#/Bb 5
119	77	B 5
120	78	C 6
121	79	C#/Db 6
122	7A	D 6
123	7B	D#/Eb 6
124	7C	E 6
125	7D	F 6

Decimal	Hex	Note Name	
126	7E	F#/Gb 6	
127	7F	G 6	**Highest Note**

MIDI Note Timing   120 Ticks Per Quarter Note

Quarter Note	8th Note	16th Note	32nd Note	64th Note	Triplets

Beat   **Ticks From Measure Start**

Beat	Quarter Note	8th Note	16th Note	32nd Note	64th Note	Triplets
1.0	0.0	0.0	0.0	0.0	0.0	0.0
					7.5	
			15.0	15.0		
				22.5		
			30.0	30.0	30.0	
					37.5	40.0
				45.0	45.0	
					52.5	
		60.0	60.0	60.0	60.0	
					67.5	
				75.0	75.0	80.0
					82.5	
			90.0	90.0	90.0	
					97.5	
				105.0	105.0	
					112.5	
2.0	120.0	120.0	120.0	120.0	120.0	120.0
					127.5	
				135.0	135.0	
					142.5	
			150.0	150.0	150.0	
					157.5	160.0
				165.0	165.0	

Beat	Quarter Note	8th Note	16th Note	32nd Note	64th Note	Triplets
				Ticks From Measure Start		
					172.5	
		180.0	180.0	180.0	180.0	
					187.5	
				195.0	195.0	200.0
					202.5	
			210.0	210.0	210.0	
					217.5	
				225.0	225.0	
					232.5	
3.0	240.0	240.0	240.0	240.0	240.0	240.0
					247.5	
				255.0	255.0	
					262.5	
			270.0	270.0	270.0	
					277.5	280.0
				285.0	285.0	
					292.5	
		300.0	300.0	300.0	300.0	
					307.5	
				315.0	315.0	320.0
					322.5	
			330.0	330.0	330.0	
					337.5	
				345.0	345.0	
					352.5	
4.0	360.0	360.0	360.0	360.0	360.0	360.0
					367.5	
				375.0	375.0	
					382.5	
			390.0	390.0	390.0	
					397.5	400.0
				405.0	405.0	